Asian American Education— Identities, Racial Issues, and Languages

A Volume In
Research on the Education of Asian and Pacific Americans

Series Editors:
Xue Lan Rong, *University of North Carolina*
Russell Endo, *University of Colorado*

Research on the Education of Asian and Pacific Americans

Xue Lan Rong and Russell Endo, Series Editors

Research on the Education of Asian and Pacific Americans (2002)
edited by Clara C. Park, A. Lin Goodwin, and Stacey J. Lee

Asian American Identities, Families, & Schooling (2003)
edited by Clara C. Park, A. Lin Goodwin, and Stacey J. Lee

Asian and Pacific American Education:
Learning, Socialization, and Identity (2005)
edited by Clara C. Park, Russell Endo, and A. Lin Goodwin

Asian American Education:
Acculturation, Literacy Development, and Learning (2007)
edited by Clara C. Park, Russell Endo, Stacey J. Lee, and Xue Lan Rong

New Perspectives on
Asian American Parents, Students and Teacher Recruitment (2009)
edited by Clara C. Park, Russell Endo, and Xue Lan Rong

Asian American Education— Identities, Racial Issues, and Languages

edited by

Xue Lan Rong
University of North Carolina

and

Russell Endo
University of Colorado

Information Age Publishing, Inc.
Charlotte, North Carolina • www.infoagepub.com

Library of Congress Cataloging-in-Publication Data

Asian American education : Asian American identities, racial issues, and languages / [edited by] Xue Lan Rong, Russell Endo.
p. cm. -- (Research on the education of Asian Pacific Americans)
Includes bibliographical references.
ISBN 978-1-61735-461-8 (pbk.) -- ISBN 978-1-61735-462-5 (hardcover) --
ISBN 978-1-61735-463-2 (e-book)
1. Asian Americans--Education. 2. Asian Americans--Ethnic identity. =
3.Asian Americans--Social conditions. 4. Asian Americans--Languages.
I. Rong, Xue Lan. II. Endo, Russell.=20
LC2632.A845 2011
371.829'95073--dc23
                                    2011016525

CONTENTS

PREFACE

Asian American Education—Identities, Racial Issues, and Languages contains nine chapters with narratives, quantitative data, and interpretive analyses that attempt to capture the essence and the uniqueness of Asian Americans' experiences with educational institutions. This is the sixth volume in the series on Research on the Education of Asian and Pacific Americans. The first was published a decade ago. When thinking about overarching research themes in this field over the past 10 years, there clearly has been much discourse on the model minority stereotype. This discourse is continued in the current book. The chapters in this anthology provide rich and detailed evidence of Asian Americans' struggles with racism and xenophobia in education and draw attention to the cultural and especially structural challenges they face when trying to make institutional changes. As a whole, this volume contributes to the deconstruction of the image of Asian Americans as a model minority and at the same time reconstructs theories to explain their diverse educational experiences.

The first three chapters offer views of K-12 Asian American students that complicate the model minority image. In the first chapter, "Tenth Grade Math Achievement of Asian Students: Are Asian Students Still the 'Model Minority'?—A Comparison of Two Educational Cohorts," Claudia Galindo and Suet-ling Pong compare data on 10th graders in 1990 and 2002 from the National Educational Longitudinal Study and the Educational Longitudinal Study respectively. Asian American students are often seen as excelling academically, especially in mathematics. However from 1990 to 2002, the Asian-White achievement gap in math disappears for reasons that are analyzed by the authors.

In Chapter 2, Liv Dávila shows how a group of refugee students from Vietnam's Central Highlands are "trapped" in the model minority stereotype and why "being good kids but poor students" unintentionally conveniences educational institutions. Urban schools are facing multiple competing priorities with fewer resources. They are able to ignore the needs of refugee students if they and their supporters do not complain loudly. As a result, many of these students will not be able to graduate from high school.

Yang Sao Xiong and Min Zhou, in the third chapter, use academic test scores and tracking data from the California Department of Education to identify three structural processes that segregate and trap Hmong students: state-mandated classification, selective testing, and tracking. Their findings reveal that these processes jointly limit students' educational choices, access to quality curricula, and opportunities to educationally advance beyond high school.

Chapters 4 through 7 in this volume investigate Asian Americans in higher education, focusing on the effects that racial context has on professional and personal life and on campus climate. This focus enables readers to be aware of and understand the multiple forms of discrimination, prejudice, and bias as well as overt, covert, and unconscious racially-related issues that Asian American faculty and students encounter. Terms such as alienation, marginalization, isolation, and invisibility are used in these chapters to describe the personal experiences of Asian American students and faculty and the campus climate.

In Chapter 4, "Racial Transformations in Higher Education: Emergent Meanings of Asian American Racial Identities," Michelle Samura uses narratives to show the complexity of Asian American students' perceived choices, opportunities, and challenges during their negotiation of their identities. The fifth chapter by Oiyan Poon examines how Asian American students are marginalized at the University of California at Los Angeles, a university where they have a critical mass in undergraduate enrollments. Her discussion of racial microaggressions calls into question the assumption that merely having a large number of Asian American students will alleviate their campus racial problems.

Chapter 6, "Teaching on the Edge: The Life Story of an Asian American Woman Literacy Professor in a Rural, Predominantly White University," and Chapter 7, "What Accounts for Tenure of Asian American Faculty? Findings from NSOPF:04" both deal with Asian American faculty in higher education, although these two studies differ in scope and methodology. In Chapter 6, Keonghee Tao Han describes her own experiences in an autobiographical narrative while in Chapter 7, Wenfan Yan and Qiuyun Lin report on research using a national sample and inferential statistics. Han's narrative can serve as a window into Yan and Lin's work, providing enrichment and interpretations; similarly, Yan and Lin's chapter reinforces Han's arguments that it is important to recognize the subtle and not so subtle racism on campus and that it is essential to create policies at the institutional level that support faculty of color.

The last two chapters of the book are about the teaching of the Chinese language. Yanan Fan, in Chapter 8, uses a single case study approach to address issues involved in training a preservice classroom teacher to teach Chinese as a foreign language. The concluding chapter by Maria Torres-Guzmán, Christy Lao, and Yi Han is titled "Hidden Jewels: San Francisco Chinese Language Immersion Programs" and is a multicase comparative description of Chinese immersion programs in the San Francisco Unified School District. Its purpose is to present the history and characteristics of these programs and to examine factors necessary for successful Chinese bilingual education efforts. While these two chapters are about teaching Chinese in public schools, from a broader perspective, both also speak to how the current context—including issues of globalization, immigration, diversity, and educational policies at national and local levels—influences Chinese language education and the future work educators need to do with practicing classroom teachers.

The main critiques in *Asian American Education—Identities, Racial Issues, and Languages* deal with cultural and structural barriers and reveal the interactions and intersections between these two dimensions. Cultural issues include factors such as ideologies, beliefs, values, and traditions while structural issues have to do with such things as power, policies and laws, and organization and operations. All of the studies in this volume are critical because they confront the invisibility and stereotyping of Asian Americans and the misunderstandings of their educational issues by disrupting "customary" discourse and disputing "familiar" knowledge. Findings and interpretations from these chapters will certainly complement and add to other recent work in Asian American education. Hopefully this will help efforts to move one more step toward an ultimate goal: transforming individuals, institutions, and society.

The editors would like to express their gratitude to the authors who have contributed to this book; readers, who may also share the information with friends, students, and colleagues; Information Age Publishing for its vital role in disseminating research; and the two sponsors of the series on Research on the Education of Asian and Pacific Americans, the Special Interest Group-Research on the Education of Asian and Pacific Americans (SIG-REAPA) of the American Educational Research Association and the National Association for Asian and Pacific American Education (NAAPAE).

CHAPTER 1

TENTH GRADE MATH ACHIEVEMENT OF ASIAN STUDENTS

Are Asian Students Still the "Model Minority"?— A Comparison of Two Educational Cohorts

Cohorts Claudia Galindo and Suet-ling Pong

Our study compares data twelve years apart to examine whether recent Asian American students' academic achievement can uphold over time the model minority label commonly associated with this group, since past research mostly conducted in the 1980s and 1990s has shown their academic success. We draw on data from the National Educational Longitudinal Study (NELS: 88) and the Educational Longitudinal Study (ELS: 02) to study two educational cohorts of Asian adolescents who were 10th graders in 1990 and 2002, respectively. We find that Asian students' math achievement significantly decreased between 1990 and 2001 and that the initial math advantage of Asian students over White students observed in 1990 disappeared in 2002, particularly for students with foreign-born parents. Although English proficiency and the school environment account for

Asian American Education—Identities, Racial Issues, and Languages, pp. 1–29

cohort differences in the Asian-White achievement gaps, family socioeconomic status and parental educational expectations are the strongest predictors. We discuss the implications of these findings for educators.

Asian students have been promoted by the mass media as the "model minority" for about 5 decades, triggering much debate in academia (Chou & Feagin, 2008; Hurh & Kim, 1989; Kao, 1995; Kitano & Sue, 1973; Li & Wang, 2008). This controversial label is most often used by public commentators to describe a high degree of academic achievement of Asian American students, which serves to prove correct the meritocratic view that hard work and talent are rewarded in the United States. Among academics, this label has been debunked as a "myth" (Chou & Feagin, 2008; Li & Wang, 2008). Researchers have documented wide variations in school performance by the country of origin (Rong & Preissle, 2009) as well as serious academic and school adjustment problems among some Asian subgroups (Lee, 2001; Ngo & Lee, 2007; Thao, 1999; Walker-Moffat, 1995). Scholars also warned that the label can divide minority groups or pit them against each other, instead of helping unite minority groups to work together.

Despite rejection of this broad-brush label, Asian American students as a group tend to exhibit a high degree of educational success that feeds the model minority image. Previous scholarly studies have found that Asian American students out-perform all other racial/ethnic minority students, and sometimes even non-Hispanic White students (Kao, 1995; Pong, Hao, & Gardner, 2005; Steinberg, Dornbusch, & Brown, 1992). However, the results of the Asian-White achievement gaps are mostly based on data collected in the 1980s and 1990s. Currently, it is not clear whether more recent data can uphold the model minority image in academic achievement.

One demographic characteristic unique to Asian Americans is the large percentage of foreign-born individuals in the Asian population. Among school-age children, almost 90% of Asian Americans were foreign-born or children of immigrants in the year 2000. This school-age figure is well above the national average of 20%, and it is also higher than the comparable figure of 70% among Hispanics (Rong & Preissle, 2009). Immigrant status is thus an important trait of Asian American students. Furthermore, previous studies suggest that the Asian effect on academic achievement is actually the immigrant effect (Kao, 2004; Kao & Tienda, 1995).

Immigrants arrive in the United States at different periods of time and with different resources. Earlier waves of Asian immigrant parents are likely to differ from Asian immigrant parents arriving in recent years, especially in terms of their education and job skills (Borjas, 1985). Changes in immigrant selectivity would have implications for children from immigrant families because the resources available to children for their education depend on the resources possessed by parents. Thus far, we know little about cohort differences in Asian students' academic achievement (Glick & White, 2003 is a rare exception).

Using two educational cohorts of Asian adolescents who were born about a decade apart and were 10th graders in 1990 and 2002 ("cohort" hereafter), our study addresses the question of cohort differences in the Asian-White achievement gap. Specifically, we ask three major questions: (1) Did the Asian math achievement change over the two cohorts of adolescents in 1990 and 2002, relative to academic achievement of non-Hispanic White adolescents? (2) Did family characteristics, English proficiency, and school characteristics of Asian students also change across cohorts? (3) If so, did family characteristics, English proficiency, and the school environment account for cohort differences in the Asian-White math achievement gap?

These questions aim to examine whether the Asian students' academic success that earned them the model minority image was a unique historical occurrence, or something that has happened in the past. We focus on math achievement test scores because math represents in-school learning more so than other content areas and math scores data are comparable across cohorts between NELS and ELS. Additionally, some may also argue that test scores are a more objective measure than one's GPA. In this chapter, we first review Asian American students' academic achievement, with special attention to generational differences. Then, we present several important demographic characteristics of Asian American children in the 2000 Census and discuss how changes in demographics over time may have implications for the Asian-White achievement gap.

ASIAN AMERICAN STUDENTS' ACHIEVEMENT
A REVIEW OF THE LITERATURE

Today, one out of five students in K-12 school is an immigrant child or child of immigrants (Zhou, 1997). The influx of immigrant children into the U.S. public school system has generated a great deal of concern about their school success and adaptation. This concern is particularly relevant to Asian Americans because of the high percentage of Asian school children living in immigrant families.

Previous studies on Asian American students' math test scores did not differentiate these students by their immigrant status. These studies showed that the math achievement scores of Asian American students exceeded those of non-Hispanic White American students (Stevenson et al., 1990), given similar socioeconomic status (Chen & Stevenson, 1995; Kao, 2004; Pong & Hao, 2007). The Asian-White achievement gap is even larger for students with the lowest level of parental education. Whereas non-Hispanic White students whose father did not finish high school had much lower math test scores than did their counterparts whose father had a high school education, Asian students' math test scores do not differ by whether their fathers complete high school (Chen & Stevenson, 1995). As mentioned above, a large percentage of Asian-American students have immigrant parents, the Asian students' math advantage is likely an immigrant advantage.

Other large-scale quantitative research has compared school performance or attainment of immigrants of different countries of origin, or the 1st-, 2nd-, and 3rd-plus generations of Asian students (e.g., Kao & Tienda, 1995; Pong et al., 2005; Rong & Grant, 1992), comparing 1st generation, foreign-born children to the U.S.-born, 2nd- and 3rd-plus children (Vernez & Abrahamse, 1996), or comparing immigrants' children of the 1st and 2nd generation to the U.S.-born children with native parents (3rd generation, Hao & Bonstead-Bruns, 1998). Some authors even differentiate the immigrant groups further into 1.5 or the preschool generation (Glick & White, 2003), while others use the length of residence in the United States as a proxy for generations (Hirschman, 2001). Regardless of the definition of what constitutes the comparison groups, a basic question common to these studies is: how well do Asian American children, especially immigrant children, perform in school? Because education provides immigrants the major channel of socioeconomic mobility, the question of the educational progress of immigrant children helps to answer a more fundamental question of how immigrant groups assimilate into American society.

With regard to their countries of origin, Asian students' achievement differs significantly, with Chinese, Korean, and Japanese students outperform Hmong, Cambodian, and Laotian students in GPA (Rumbaut, 1995) and standardized test scores (Harris, Jamison, & Trujillo., 2008). When Asian American students are divided into different generations for comparisons, the results supported unequivocally the "immigrant paradox" in education, that is, earlier generations perform better than later generations. It is paradoxical because low performance of earlier generations would be predicted given their lower socioeconomic status and lack of English language skills. On the contrary, a number of studies on immigrants' children have found first-generation students to perform academically as well as or better than their U.S.-born counterparts (Rumbaut, 1995; Schwartz & Stiefel, 2006; Vernez & Abrahamse, 1996). When the

U.S.-born children are divided into second and higher generations, the second generation has outperformed both first and third generations in unadjusted math, reading, and science tests (National Center for Education Statistics, 1999). This immigrant paradox appears to be the strongest and most consistent among Asian students (Harris et al., 2008; Kao, 2004; Pong, 2003).

The immigrant paradox continues to exist after adjustment for socioeconomic status and other family or parental factors. Second-generation Asian students outperform their third generation co-ethnic or White peers in GPA and math grades, and perform just as well in socioeconomic status—adjusted reading grades (Pong et al., 2005). Socioeconomic status—adjusted achievement is not different between the first and second generations (Bankston & Zhou, 2002; Fuligni, 1997; Kao & Tienda, 1995), and both of these earlier generations outperform the later generations in virtually all subjects except reading (Hao & Bonstead-Bruns, 1998; Kao, 2004).

Zhou and Bankston's (1998) study of Vietnamese children provides the most well-known example of the immigrant paradox. First-generation Vietnamese students have low socioeconomic status and attend poor inner-city schools. However, Vietnamese youngsters who adhere to traditional ethnic culture, such as respect for parents and elders, are more likely to excel in school. Controlling for their unfavorable background factors has revealed even higher achievement among these Vietnamese students, increasing their academic distance from their third-generation peers and third-generation White students.

Many explanations have been given for Asian American students' achievement, including their cultural traits, Confucian ideology, their dual frame of reference, support from co-ethnic communities, and the structure of opportunity in the United States (see reviews in Kao & Thompson, 2003; Rong & Preissle, 2009; Zhou & Kim, 2006). From our review above, it is clear that the extraordinary Asian academic achievement is concentrated mainly in the 1st and 2nd generations. The *immigrant optimism* hypothesis, proposed by Kao and Tienda (1995), is particularly relevant here. Parental immigrant status is the driving force for Asian children's school success. Immigrant parents have high hopes for their children's future, which is a source of support for their children's higher school achievement. Regardless of the youth's place of birth and ethnicity, having immigrant parents is associated with higher academic achievement. In the next section, we examine the demographic characteristics of Asian Americans, especially their salient feature of being a primarily immigrant population.

CONTEMPORARY DEMOGRAPHICS OF ASIAN STUDENTS

Since the passing of the Hart Celler Act in 1965, Asian immigrants have arrived in the United States in large numbers, and are now the second largest source of immigration following Latino immigrants. As shown in Table 1.1, the Asian population is heterogeneous; it is made up of people from more than 18 countries of origin. The Chinese and Filipinos are the largest groups, followed by the Japanese, Asian Indian, Korean, and the Vietnamese. However, age distribution differs across origin groups. Among children aged 5-18, the largest groups are the Chinese and Korean with each group making up 17% of the Asian child population. The next largest groups are Filipinos and Asian Indians, each occupying 15%. These four groups alone make up about 64% of the total Asian child population. It is important to bear in mind that the characteristics of the "average" Asian child likely reflect characteristics of these four groups.

Table 1.1.   The Asian Population Composition in 1990 and 2002 (in Percentages)

Country of Origin	1990	2000
Chinese	23.8	[a]23.0
Filipinos	20.4	19.9
Japanese	12.3	9.7
Asian Indian	11.8	16.0
Korean	11.6	10.3
Vietnamese	8.9	10.3
Laotian	2.2	1.7
Cambodian	2.1	1.7
Thai	1.3	1.3
Hmong	1.3	1.6
Burmese	0.1	0.1
Sri Lankan	0.2	0.2
Bangladeshi	0.2	0.5
Malayan/Malaysian	0.2	0.2
Indonesian	0.4	0.5
Pakistani	1.2	1.7
Nepalese	–	0.1
Okinawan	–	0.1
Taiwanese	–	1.2
Other (not specified)	2.1	3.1

[a] Not including Taiwanese.

Note: Data from the Census 1990 and 2000; adapted from Barnes and Bennett (2002, p. 9), and U.S. Department of Commerce (1993, p. 4.).

Based on the 2000 Census data compiled by Rong and Preissle (2009), we highlight below a few important demographic features of school-age Asian children aged 5-18. First, the majority of Asian school-age children are 2nd generation (62%), that is, U.S.-born children with foreign-born parents. The foreign-born children (1st and 1.5 generations included) make up about 28% and only 10% of Asian children are U.S.-born with native parents (3rd-plus generation). However, the likelihood of being foreign born is higher in Asian children from particular countries or cultures with over 95% of children of Korean, Asian Indians, Hmong, and Vietnamese descent being more recent arrivals who are either immigrant children or children of immigrants.

Additionally, the 2000 Census indicates that Asian children have diverse socioeconomic statuses and parental education levels based upon their country or their parent's country of origin. In general, the four largest Asian groups of children fare quite well socioeconomically, but some smaller groups of Asian children do not. Compared to the national average, poverty rates among the four largest Asian groups of children, especially Filipino and Asian Indian, are much lower, and family incomes among three of the four largest groups (Chinese, Korean, and Asian Indian) are higher. Asian Indian, Filipino, and Korean children also have parents whose education level is higher than the national average. However, three small Asian groups of Hmong, Cambodian, and Laotian children, each of which makes up 2 to 3% of the total Asian child population, are not as fortunate. These groups are more likely to have low levels of both family income and parental education. Over 40% of the Hmong or Cambodian population lives in poverty. The condition for foreign-born Hmong children is particularly disconcerting. About 59% of these children have fallen under the poverty line, compared to 15% of the national average. However, the one area where all Asian children are similar is their desirable family situation in terms of living with two parents. The 2000 Census shows that all Asian children, regardless of their socioeconomic status and nativity are uniformly more likely to live in two-parent households than U.S. children as a whole.

With regard to language, Asian children are much more likely than U.S. children as a whole to speak a home language other than English. The percentage of children using non-English at home is about 75% and 65% for the two largest groups of Chinese and Korean children, respectively. Despite that fact, self-reported English proficiency of these two groups of children is about the same as or slightly higher than the national average, suggesting that many of them are bilingual. The other two large Asian groups of children, the Asian Indians and Filipinos, are more likely to rate themselves higher than the national average in their English proficiency. Even Cambodian and Laotian children reported English proficiency that is similar to the national average (Rong & Preissle, 2009). This is not to say that Asian children experience no English difficulty. For example, only 4% of Hmong children use English at home and their self-reported English proficiency is lower than the national average (Rong & Preissle, 2009). Also, research showed that the limited English skills of some Korean or Chinese children was an important factor, among other variables, associated with their difficulties in school (Fung-Arto, 2007; Lew, 2006).

The above demographic portrait suggests that, on average, Asian children have family characteristics signifying higher socioeconomic status and better education than the average U.S. child. Although the majority of Asian children have immigrant parents, their English proficiency may not be compromised. In fact, some of these children have the benefits of being bilingual. Here we do not intend to ignore the disadvantaged groups of Cambodian, Laotian, and particularly Hmong children, but it is important to acknowledge that, as a group, Asian children are *on average* more advantageous socioeconomically and linguistically than U.S. children as a whole. High socioeconomic status, residence in two-parent families, bilingualism, and English proficiency are found to be positively associated with student achievement (Blau & Duncan, 1967; Coleman, 1990; Galindo, 2010; McLanahan & Sandefur, 1994; Pong, 1997; Portes & Hao, 1998; Wang & Goldschmidt, 1999; White, 1982). Also, Asian immigrant parents are a selective group because of their ambitions to take advantage of opportunities in the United States, including schooling for their children (Lew, 2006; Park, 2003). Many Asian immigrant parents may rely on their children to do well in school and obtain good jobs as part of a family economic survival strategy (Kibria, 1993). Thus, we would expect Asian children, on average, to achieve quite well in school. That said, we must also acknowledge that we have been comparing Asian children to U.S. children as a whole. The latter is an ambiguous reference category that includes a great deal of diversity. In our analysis below, we will use the non-Hispanic White children as the reference group and examine the Asian-White achievement gap over time.

IMMIGRANT SELECTIVITY

We suspect that the socioeconomic and linguistic advantage of Asian children may change more quickly over time than in any other ethnic group. Because Asian children are overwhelmingly 1st and 2nd generations, their family characteristics are very much tied to the nature of Asian migration and the characteristics of Asian immigrants, which are vulnerable to immigration policies and the context of reception. Migration scholars have long been interested in the overtime change in socioeconomic status of migrants from the same country of origin. The migration theory proposed by Douglas Massey and his colleagues (1993) argued that immigrants are more likely to be positively selected in terms of socioeconomic status during the initial stage of migration to a host country. To be a pioneer one needs not only resolve but resources to start a new life in a new land. Once these pioneers settle, they set up a network of support for newcomers, especially for family members and other relatives. Subsequent migrants do not have to incur as much psychological or financial costs as earlier migrants. Therefore, subsequent migration streams are likely to be less positively or even negatively selected along the socioeconomic dimension. This prediction has received support in studies of Mexican (Feliciano, 2005) and Chinese immigrants (Liang & Morooka, 2004).

Liang and Morooka's (2004) research on emigration from China is worth noting. They examine emigration from the Fujian province which has been sending many immigrants to the United States. Comparing the emigrants' social characteristics in the Chinese 1990 and 1995 censuses, they found that emigration became less selective along socioeconomic status over time. Recent emigrants in 1995 were more likely to have a rural background and less education than were emigrants in 1990. This research is relevant to Asian Americans in the U.S. since the Chinese population is the largest Asian subgroup. It is therefore reasonable to predict that selectivity by socioeconomic status among Asian students in the U.S. will reduce over cohorts.

Additionally, some theorists argued that current U.S. immigration policies contribute to the increase of Asian immigrants from lower socioeconomic backgrounds (Liu & Cheng, 1994; Martin & Midgley, 2006). The earlier waves of post-1965 Asian immigrants came to the U.S. primarily under the economic provisions of immigration policies, which tended to favor those who were better-educated and had good job skills. However, later waves of immigrants were able to use family reunification provisions of immigration policies to come to the United States. Therefore, later waves of immigrants tend to be more diverse in terms of their socioeconomic backgrounds (Borjas, 1985).

An alternative explanation is related to the refugee status of some Asians (especially Southeast Asians) coming to the United States. The first wave of Asian refugees, around 1975, often came with skills and education that aided their economic assimilation and social mobility; later waves however were more diverse, often lacking education and job skills (Lew, 2006; Park, 2003). This immigration pattern may be another contributing factor to declines in Asian selectivity.

As a result, Asian parents increasingly arrive in the U.S. with less education and job skills, which would have negative consequences for their children's education. To find empirical support for immigrant selectivity over time, our study compares the socioeconomic status and other related characteristics of two educational cohorts of adolescents born more than a decade apart. Not only do we find evidence of the change in immigrant selectivity over time, we also find its association with the decline in Asian students' advantageous academic achievement over White students.

DATA AND METHODS

We analyzed data of tenth graders from the National Educational Longitudinal Study (NELS: 88) and the Educational Longitudinal Study (ELS: 02) collected by the National Center for Education Statistics (NCES). Both databases gathered information every 2 years on students' family, neighborhood, and school characteristics from a nationally representative sample of high school students. NELS gathered information on a sample of students who entered eighth grade in 1988. Although there was attrition between eighth and 10th grade, the 10th grade NELS sample was refreshened such that it is nationally representative and can be compared to the base-year 10th grade sample in ELS, which was collected in 2002. Because both studies on high school sophomores were conducted 12 years apart, their data allowed for a cross-cohort comparison of student achievement. For methodological details, see National Center for Education Statistics (2007).

Sample

Our analysis focused on math achievement of Asian 10th grade students in 1989-90 (NELS) and in 2001-02 (ELS). We analyzed a total of 10,756 NELS students from 913 schools and 8,603 ELS students from 713 schools. The total number of Asian students in NELS and ELS analyzed in this paper were 910 and 1,397, respectively. The majority of the Asian sample in both cohorts had Chinese and Southeast Asian origins. Additionally, we observed an important prevalence of Filipino and Koreans in 1990 and 2002, respectively. Non-Hispanic native White students were included as the reference group. All other race/ethnicities and White students who have foreign-born parents were excluded from this study.

Variables and Measures

We measured math achievement using 10th grade *math test scores*. NELS and ELS 10th grade math tests were based on the same content areas (arithmetic, algebra, geometry/ measurement, data/probability, analytical geometry, and precalculus) and cognitive process (knowledge, understanding/comprehension, and problem solving). Common items in ELS and NELS allowed the construction of equated test scores based on the Item Response Theory (IRT). The ELS study reported the NELS-equated math scores that estimated how ELS students would have performed if they were given the NELS math test. Thus, the NELS 10th grade IRT math scores are comparable to the ELS 10th grade IRT math scores. These were the math scores we used to compare achievement patterns across cohorts.

Asian students' *generational status* was measured in four categories: 1st-, 1.5, 2nd, and 3rd-plus generations. Both the 1st and 1.5 generations were foreign-born individuals who were born to foreign-born parents. The difference is that the former came to the U.S. when they were 6 years old or more, while the 1.5 generation came to the U.S. when they were younger than 6. This classification is important because although 1.5 generation children were foreign-born, they were likely to have all their education in the U.S. Their academic achievement was expected to be similar to that of the 2nd generation who were children born in the U.S. to foreign-born parents. The 3rd-plus generation were U.S.-born children of U.S.-born parents. About 2% of either NELS or ELS Asian students in our sample were missing information about generational status. These students were kept in the sample and were specified by a dummy variable in multivariate analysis.

To capture Asian students' family, we analyzed the following family characteristics. *Family type* was measured by four dummy variables: child living with two biological parents (reference group); two parents, one biological; just one biological parent; or other (e.g., guardian or adoptive parents). The family structure was further measured by the *number of siblings*. *Parent's educational level* was measured as an ordinal variable with values from "1" to "6", where "1" indicates some high school and "6" indicates doctorate-level study. We also analyzed family *socioeconomic status* using a continuous composite measure (mean of 0 and standard deviation of 1) based on father's and mother's education, income, and occupation. To analyze the language environment at home, we included a dummy variable indicating whether the student lived in an English-speaking home. Finally, we measured *parent's educational expectations* for children's schooling based on a an ordinal measure indicating how far in school parents believed their child would go with values from "1" to "5", where "1" indicates some high school and "5" indicates graduate study. Less than 1% of students in our sample were missing information about socioeconomic status, family type, and parents' educational expectations, and less than 5% of students in our sample were missing information about number of siblings. These students were kept in the sample and are indicated by a dummy variable in multivariate analysis.

To capture Asian students' school environment we analyzed the following variables: sector, region, as well as socioeconomic, racial minority and immigrant composition of the schools. Students attending public schools were compared to those enrolled in private institutions and variables for urban, suburban or rural schools were studied. To measure school composition characteristics, we aggregated students' information within each school. Immigrant and racial minority compositions refer to the percentage of students living with foreign-born parents and Hispanics and Black students within each school, respectively.

Child-level variables included age in years, gender, and English proficiency. Age and gender were included in all regression models as control variables. Because the NELS and ELS study do not include an objective measure of English proficiency, we used a proxy based on students' subjective report of their ability (very well, well, not well, not at all) in understanding spoken English, speaking, reading, and writing English. Students in this study were defined as non proficient in English if they self reported below "very well" for at least one of the categories.

Analytical Plan

First, we conducted descriptive statistics of the main variables to understand the family and school environments of Asian children in 1990 and 2002. Second, we estimated several regression models using HLM software (Raudenbush & Bryk, 2002) to study the White-Asian achievement gaps and the association between family and school environments and changes in the achievement gaps. We used two-level hierarchical linear modeling (HLM) with students representing the level-1 units and schools representing the level-2 units. HLM gives valid and accurate estimates when dealing with nested data (as in this case where students are nested within schools) because it takes into account the complex structure of the error terms (Raudenbush & Bryk, 2002). With nested data, Ordinary Least Squares analyses tend to overestimate the levels of significance given that the assumption of independence of variables is violated. Individuals within social contexts—such as in schools, tend to be more alike than if the sample of students was randomly selected.

To analyze whether Asian students' math achievement changed between 1990 and 2002, we estimated two statistical models per time period presented in Table 2. We first analyzed the difference in achievement between White and Asian students (Models 1a and 1b). We then expanded this mode to include 1st, 1.5, 2nd, and 3rd-plus generations (Models 2a and

2b). Finally, we conducted multivariate hypothesis tests to test whether there were differences across time periods. To analyze whether family characteristics, English proficiency, and the school environment account for cohort differences in the Asian-White math achievement gap, we estimated four different models presented in Table 1.5. In model 3 we only included information about generational status and time period (i.e., 1990 and 2002). In model 4, we added family background variables (i.e., socioeconomic status, type of family, and number of siblings). In models 5 and 6, we added parents' educational expectations and language variables, respectively. Finally, in model 7 we added school variables.

RESULTS

Gaps in Math Achievement Between Asian and White Students in 1990 and 2002

As Model 1a Table 1.2 indicates, there was a statistically significant Asian-White achievement gap in the earlier cohort of 1990, with Asian students showing better math achievement than White students. The math achievement gap was 4.4 points in favor for Asian students in this year. When we disaggregated Asian students by their generational status, as in Model 2a, all Asian students with foreign-born parents had statistically significant higher math achievement than did White students, but Asian-origin students with U.S. born parents showed similar math test scores as did White students. The math advantage equaled 2.6 points for 1st generation, 3.8 points for 1.5 generation, and 7.6 points for 2nd generation Asian students, respectively.

In contrast, in the later cohort of 2002, the Asian students' math advantages observed in 1990 disappeared. Model 1b shows no statistically significant math differences between White and Asian students. A similar tendency of lack of math difference was observed for Asian students from different generational statuses. All Asian students, regardless of generation, had math scores that were not statistically significant vis-à-vis the mean score of White students in 2002.

We also tested the null hypothesis that the math achievement gaps between Asian and White students did not change between 1990 and 2002 (see Table 1.2, between cohort contrast column). With the exception of third-generation Asian students (the math achievement gap was not discernable between cohorts), all the Asian-White math achievement gaps have gotten worse between these two cohorts. Clearly, these results suggest that the model minority label does not apply anymore to the average Asian student and that the initial math advantage of Asian students

Table 1.2.   Gaps in 10th Grade Math Achievement by Generational Status (Unstandardized Coefficients)

	NELS 1990		ELS 2002		Between Cohort
	Model 1a	Model 2a	Model 1b	Model 2b	
Asian	4.35*** (0.49)		−0.03 (0.40)		a
1st generation		2.57** (0.87)	−1.19+ (0.69)		a
1½ generation		3.79*** (0.80)	−0.31 (0.71)		a
2nd generation		7.56*** (0.78)	0.58 (0.49)		a
3rd+ generation		1.29 (1.43)	0.11 (1.42)		

Note: Models 1a and 2a were estimated using only NELS data and models 1b and 1b were estimated only using ELS data. 3rd-plus generation Whites are the omitted reference group, so all coefficients are gaps relative to that group. The between cohort contrast tested whether the math achievement gaps between 1990 and 2002 were statistically significant (Significant at .05 level (or lower) are specified as: A). To analyze the between cohort contrast we created a person-cohort data with a dummy variable indicating whether the student was in the NELS or ELS sample. Robust standard errors in parentheses (SE). P-values are based on estimations with robust standard errors.

$+ p \leq .10, * p \leq .05, ** p \leq .01, *** p \leq .001.$

observed in 1990 disappeared in most cases by 2002. In the next section, we explored family, English proficiency, and school characteristics to try to explain why Asian students' math achievement decreased sharply between these two cohorts.

Asian Students' Families in 1990 and 2002

As Table 1.3 indicates, Asian students had socioeconomic advantages in the earlier cohort of 1990, relative to White students. These students were also more likely to live in two biological-parent families and were less likely to live in single-parent families. Asian students also had parents with statistically significant higher educational expectations than did White students.

After disaggregating Asian students by generational status, we found that 2nd generation Asian students experienced even greater family advantages than did foreign-born Asian students (we combined 1st and 1.5 generations here because separate analyses did not change the conclusions of our findings) in 1990. On average, 2nd generation students had statistically significant higher socioeconomic levels and showed a higher incidence of two-biological parent families than did foreign-born students. Similarly, 2nd generation Asian students had fewer siblings at home than did foreign-born Asian students.

In contrast, in 2002 a somewhat different pattern was observed when comparing Asian students' family characteristics to White students'. Asian students still had parents with higher educational expectations and were more likely to live with their two biological parents than White students. However, the fact that Asian students showed lower socioeconomic levels than White students may suggest that some Asian parents may have difficulty providing good educational opportunities and access to resources for their children in 2002. As in 1990, there were stronger disadvantages in socioeconomic status for foreign-born Asian students than for 2nd generation Asian students.

Moreover, there were important differences in Asian students' family characteristics between the two cohorts. The initial advantages of Asian students' family environment observed in 1990, diminished significantly by the later cohort. Although Asian students in 1990 still had parents with higher educational expectations and were more likely to live with their two biological parents than were White students, these advantages were less pronounced in 2002. In contrast, in 2002, Asian children lived in homes with fewer economic resources than did Asian students in 1990. These patterns were observed for all Asian students, regardless of generation.

Asian Students' English Proficiency in 1990 and 2002

As expected, Asian students were more likely to live in non-English speaking homes and not be proficient in English than White students in both cohorts (see bottom part of Table 1.3). In 1990, foreign-born and 2nd generation Asian students were equally as likely to live in English-speaking homes but a lower proportion of 2nd generation Asian students were nonproficient in English. In 2002, higher proportions of 2nd generation Asian students were living in English speaking homes and were also English proficient, relative to foreign-born Asian students.

After comparing the two cohorts of Asian students, we observed a higher incidence of English speaking homes but a lower incidence of English proficiency in 2002 than in 1990, which imply the existence of important linguistic disadvantages. This pattern was observed for both foreign-born and 2nd generation Asian students.

Table 1.3. Descriptive Statistics of Family Characteristics (Mean or Percentages)

	NELS (1990)					ELS (2002)					
	White	Asian	Asian Foreign	Asian 2nd Gen	Within Cohort	White	Asian	Asian Foreign	Asian 2nd Gen	Within Cohort	Between Cohort
SES	0.18 (0.74)	0.27 (0.89)	0.28 (0.87)	0.54 (0.89)	abc	0.24 (0.68)	0.01 (0.86)	-0.15 (0.89)	0.08 (0.85)	abc	Efg
% two biological parents	73.15 (44.32)	83.54 (37.10)	83.13 (37.49)	87.42 (33.21)	abc	66.26 (47.28)	70.44 (45.65)	68.84 (46.36)	70.96 (45.43)	ac	Efg
% two-parents, 1 biological	11.83 (32.30)	4.93 (21.66)	4.58 (20.93)	3.37 (18.08)	abc	14.68 (35.40)	11.45 (31.86)	11.01 (31.33)	11.47 (31.89)	abc	Efg
% single-parent family	13.56 (34.24)	9.07 (28.74)	9.16 (28.88)	7.98 (27.13)	abc	16.58 (37.20)	13.31 (33.99)	14.18 (34.92)	13.31 (34.00)	ac	Efg
% other	1.45 (11.96)	2.46 (15.51)	3.13 (17.44)	1.23 (11.03)		2.47 (15.52)	4.80 (21.38)	5.97 (23.72)	4.25 (20.19)	abc	Efg
# of siblings	2.06 (1.43)	2.10 (1.48)	2.35 (1.66)	1.75 (1.13)	bc	2.09 (1.39)	2.18 (1.70)	2.20 (1.75)	2.23 (1.67)		G
Parent's expectations	3.75 (0.90)	4.25 (0.87)	4.26 (0.89)	4.37 (0.80)	abc	4.22 (0.75)	4.45 (0.70)	4.44 (0.72)	4.49 (0.66)	abc	Efg
% English home language	95.62 (20.46)	19.12 (39.35)	8.77 (28.32)	9.73 (29.68)	abc	99.08 (9.53)	30.57 (46.09)	18.84 (39.14)	29.18 (45.49)	abc	Efg
%English nonproficient	1.35 (11.54)	28.19 (43.23)	32.94 (47.06)	16.41 (37.10)	abc	0.05 (6.75)	36.44 (48.14)	51.12 (50.03)	30.17 (45.93)	abc	Efg
Sample size	9,846	910	422	329		7,206	1,397	536	706		

Note: Descriptive statistics are based on nonmissing cases. Within cohort differences significant at .05 level (or lower) are specified as: a (White vs. Asian), b (White vs. Asian foreign-born students), and c (White vs. Asian 2nd generation). Between cohorts differences significant at .05 level (or lower) are specified as: e (Asian in 1990 vs. Asian in 2002), f (Asian foreign-born in 1990 vs. Asian foreign-born in 2002), and g (Asian 2nd generation in 1990 vs. Asian 2nd generation in 2002). Standard deviations are in parentheses.

Asian Students' School Environments in 1990 and 2002

Table 1.4 shows that although private school enrollment was similar between Asian and White students in the earlier cohort of 1990, Asian students were more likely to attend higher socioeconomic status (SES) schools than White students. Similarly, Asian students attended schools with a greater concentration of immigrant and racial minority students than White students. Further analysis showed that 2nd generation Asian students experienced important school advantages in terms of private enrollment and school composition, relative to foreign-born Asian students.

However, in 2002, Asian students were significantly less likely than White students to attend private schools and the schools they attended also have a higher concentration of poor students, compared with White students. Asian students in the later cohort also attended schools with a greater concentration of immigrant and racial minority students than did White students. In 2002, foreign-born and 2nd generation Asian students attended schools that were not much different from each other.

The schools children attend often reflect where their families reside and the socioeconomic resources their families have. Because Asian students' socioeconomic levels were less advantageous in 2002 than in 1990, we observed less desirable characteristics of the schools Asian students attended in 2002 than those schools attended in 1990. It is important to note that a greater concentration of poor or immigrant students is not less desirable in itself, but the main problem is that usually schools with a higher concentration of minority students are more likely to have less qualified teachers and fewer educational resources (Orfield & Lee, 2006). Asian students in the later cohort were less likely than Asian students in the earlier cohort to attend private school. Similarly, Asian students were more likely to attend higher SES schools in 1990 than in 2002.

Asian Students' Families, English Proficiency, and School Environments and the Asian-White Math Achievement Gaps

In this section we focused on analyzing whether family, English proficiency, and school environment impact changes in the Asian-White achievement gaps between the two cohorts (from 1990 to 2002). Table 1.5 shows the HLM results of the multivariate analysis on the combined samples of the two cohorts of Asian and White students. The 3rd-plus generation White students were the reference group. The upper part of the table (Cohort 02), showed the average differences in math text scores between 2002 and 1990 for all students. The next section of the Table 1.5 (Generational Status in 1990), showed the math achievement gaps between

Table 1.4. Descriptive Statistics of School Characteristics

	NELS (1990)					ELS (2002)					
	White	Asian	Asian Foreign	Asian 2nd Gen	Within Cohort	White	Asian	Asian Foreign	Asian 2nd Gen	Within Cohort	Between Cohort
Urban	21.06 (40.78)	43.63 (49.62)	44.79 (49.79)	43.16 (49.61)	abc	23.94 (42.67)	44.17 (49.68)	47.20 (49.92)	44.33 (49.71)	abc	
Suburban	41.38 (49.25)	45.60 (49.83)	45.26 (49.83)	47.11 (50.00)	ac	50.76 (50.00)	50.25 (50.02)	46.46 (49.92)	51.28 (50.02)		e
Rural	37.56 (48.43)	10.77 (31.02)	9.95 (29.97)	9.73 (29.68)	abc	25.30 (43.48)	5.58 (22.97)	6.34 (24.40)	4.39 (20.50)	abc	efg
Average SES	0.09 (0.50)	0.17 (0.56)	0.05 (0.54)	0.31 (0.56)	ac	0.15 (0.41)	0.02 (0.48)	-0.04 (0.46)	0.03 (0.49)	abc	efg
Private	14.09 (34.79)	15.28 (35.99)	8.29 (27.61)	20.97 (40.77)	bc	27.09 (44.45)	10.45 (30.60)	7.46 (26.30)	9.92 (29.91)	abc	e g
% Immigrants	10.61 (12.76)	37.46 (26.01)	42.23 (26.44)	37.03 (24.17)	abc	13.65 (14.76)	57.38 (28.77)	57.50 (30.23)	59.87 (27.15)	abc	efg
% Blacks & Latinos	10.86 (15.52)	20.43 (20.71)	25.21 (22.27)	16.79 (17.95)	abc	13.86 (15.93)	24.53 (20.39)	24.91 (20.43)	24.96 (20.57)	abc	e g
Sample size	9,846	910	422	329		7,206	1,397	536	706		

Note: Descriptive statistics are based on nonmissing cases. Within cohort differences significant at .05 level (or lower) are specified as: a (White vs. Asian), b (White vs. Asian foreign-born students), and c (White vs. Asian 2nd generation). Between cohorts differences significant at .05 level (or lower) are specified as: e (Asian in 1990 vs. Asian in 2002), f (Asian foreign-born in 1990 vs. Asian foreign-born in 2002), and g (Asian 2nd generation in 1990 vs. Asian 2nd generation in 2002). Standard deviations are in parentheses.

Whites and Asian students of different generations in 1990. The following section (Generation * Cohort 02), showed the differences in achievement gaps between Whites and Asian students of different generations between 1990 and 2002. The remaining two sections of the table showed the impact of family and school characteristics.

Model 3 indicates that math achievement decreased between 1990 and 2002. Regardless of race/ethnicity and generational status, students scored about 5 points lower in 2002 than in 1990 (see "Cohort 02" coefficient in Model 3). Particularly, Asian students' math achievement decreased between the two cohorts relative to White students; however, this finding applies only to Asian students with foreign-born parents (see "Generation * Cohort 02" coefficients where the only coefficients that were statistically significant are those for 1st, 1½, and 2nd generations). The math achievement gap between White and the 3rd-plus generation Asian students between 1990 and 2002 was 1.7 points, but it was not statistically significant different. The between-cohort analysis corroborated the findings presented in Table 1.2. The differences in math achievement between White and Asian students in 1990 and 2002 are represented in Figure 1.1.

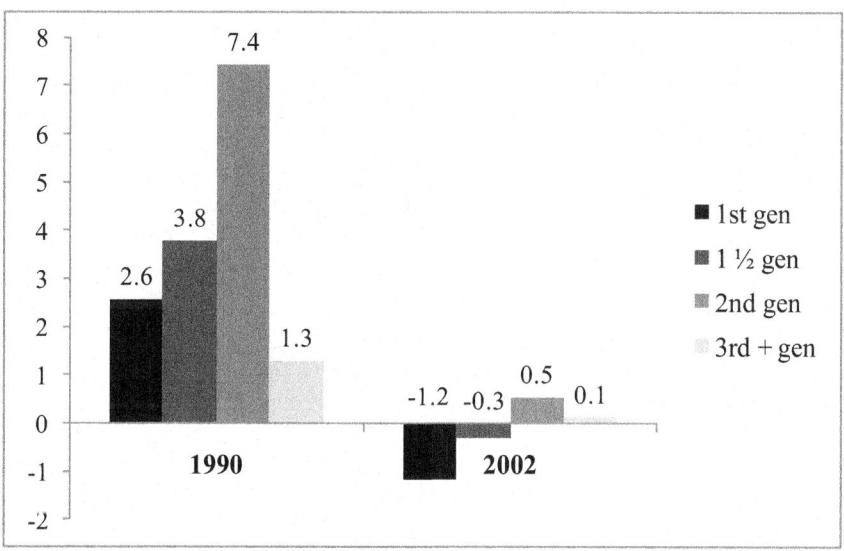

Figure 1.1.   Math achievement differences between White and Asian students, by generational status and Cohort (1990 and 2002)

In Model 4, we added family characteristics to the previous model to analyze whether these variables account for the decline in the Asian-White math achievement gaps from 1990 to 2002, signifying the decline of Asian achievement relative to White achievement. Family characteristics explain about 15%, 20%, and 30% for 1st, 1.5, and 2nd generation Asian students, respectively, of the over time decline in the Asian-White achievement gap. To estimate these percentages we compared the coefficients from Models 3 and 4 of the "Generation * Cohort 02" section (for example, for 2nd generation students, [(6.89-4.91) *100/6.89]). As seen in the descriptive findings in Table 1.3, the 2002 cohort had lower socioeconomic status than did the 1990 cohort. Therefore, after taking into account family socioeconomic status, the between-cohort achievement gap narrowed.

Additionally, parents' educational expectations further accounted for the reduction of the math achievement gap between cohorts for 1st and

Table 1.5.   Multilevel Analysis of 10th Grader's Math Achievement

	Model 3	Model 4	Model 5	Model 6	Model 7
Cohort 02	−4.95***	−4.74***	−6. 90***	-6.93***	−7.04***
	(0.31)	(0.23)	(0.23)	(0.23)	(0.23)
Generational Status (in 1990)					
1st generation	2.56**	5.14***	2.15**	3.35***	3.51***
	(0.87)	(0.84)	(0.83)	(0.92)	(0.92)
1½ generation	3.77***	4.41***	2.13**	2.79***	2.77***
	(0.80)	(0.80)	(0.74)	(0.83)	(0.82)
2nd generation	7.42***	6.26***	4.84***	5.52***	5.44***
	(0.78)	(0.67)	(0.67)	(0.75)	(0.75)
3rd + generation	1.28	−0.34	−0.29	−0.17	−0.27
	(1.43)	(1.33)	(1.32)	(1.31)	(1.30)
Generation * Cohort 02					
1st generation* cohort 02	−3.75***	−3.22**	−2.00+	−1.81+	−1.99+
	(1.11)	(1.10)	(1.07)	(1.07)	(1.07)
1½ generation * cohort 02	−4.08***	−3.25**	−2.79**	−2.69**	−2.74**
	(1.07)	(1.06)	(0.99)	(1.01)	(1.02)
2nd generation * cohort 02	−6.89***	−4.91***	−4.98***	−4.90***	−4.84***
	(0.92)	(0.81)	(0.82)	(0.82)	(0.82)
3rd + generation * cohort 02	−1.17	-1.06	-1.55	-1.51	−1.50
	(2.01)	(1.86)	(1.86)	(1.86)	(1.84)
Family Characteristics					
Socioeconomic status		5.69***	3.75***	3.71***	3.54***
		(0.13)	(0.13)	(0.13)	(0.13)

Two-parents, 1 biological	−1.47***	−1.23***	−1.24***	−1.16***
	(0.25)	(0.24)	(0.24)	(0.24)
Single-parent family	−0.43+	−0.69***	−0.70***	−0.67**
	(0.22)	(0.21)	(0.21)	(0.21)
Other	−2.03***	−1.80***	−1.75**	−1.64**
	(0.57)	(0.54)	(0.54)	(0.54)
# of siblings	−0.05	0.02	0.03	0.03
	(0.06)	(0.06)	(0.06)	(0.06)
Parent's expectations		4.51***	4.52***	4.51***
		(0.11)	(0.11)	(0.11)
English Home language			0.53	0.50
			(0.43)	(0.43)
English nonproficient			−1.58**	−1.63**
			(0.51)	(0.51)
School Characteristics				
Suburban				0.32
				(0.29)
Rural				0.24
				(0.34)
Private				1.44***
				(0.31)
% Immigrants				1.98**
				(0.71)
% Black and Latinos				−4.31***
				(0.66)

Note: Third-plus generation Whites are the omitted reference group, so all coefficients are gaps relative to that group. We included gender and age as control variables. Robust standard errors in parentheses (*SE*). *P*-values are based on estimations with robust standard errors.

+ $p \leq .10$, * $p \leq .05$, ** $p \leq .01$, *** $p \leq .001$.

1.5 generation Asian students (Model 5). Parents' educational expectations reduced the between-cohort difference in math achievement between White students and 1st generation Asian students by about 45% [(3.75-2.00) *100/3.75]. The Asian-White achievement gap in 1990 was no longer significantly different from the Asian-White achievement gap in 2002. The 1.5 generation Asian-White students math achievement gap between the two cohorts was reduced by 14%. Thus, the decrease in the Asian-White difference in parental expectations has important implications for the between-cohort achievement gaps.

In contrast, English limited proficiency did not seem to have a major impact in reducing the between-cohort achievement gaps, in the face of family characteristics and parents' educational expectations (Model 6).

Only for the 1st generation students, we observed a reduction of about 10% of the Asian-White achievement gap between 1990 and 2002. In Model 7, we added school variables. Although we observed some significant associations of school characteristics on math achievement, these variables did not help explain the between-cohort Asian-White math achievement gaps above and beyond the impact of the family characteristics that we observed in previous models.

Turning away from explaining the changes in math achievement gaps between 1990 and 2002, it is worth noticing that there were important contributions of some family and school characteristics to math achievement, regardless of the cohort analyzed. On average, students attending private schools showed better math outcomes relative to students in public schools. Also, students had lower math scores in schools with higher concentrations of Hispanic and Black students, but students had higher math scores as the concentration of immigrant students increased (after taking into account the presence of Hispanic and Black students in schools).

Additionally, student's math achievement increased by between 3 and 5.5 points as socioeconomic level increased. Students living in two-parent families but with only one biological, in single-parent families, or in other family arrangements displayed weaker math achievement, compared with students with two biological parents (the reference group). Parents' educational expectations were also positively associated with higher math achievement (increase of approximately 4.5 points) but nonproficiency in English was associated with lower math achievement (decrease of about 1.5 points). Schools' characteristics were also related to math test scores.

CONCLUSIONS

Our findings inform current discussions over Asian students' educational outcomes and the controversial label, "model minority." We further previous research on Asian students' education by analyzing their math achievement in two different time periods: 1990 and 2002. We then studied their family and school characteristics, and examined the impact of these variables on Asian and White achievement gaps. As a result, four important findings emerged from this study.

First, Asian students' math achievement significantly decreased between 1990 and 2001. In 1990, Asian students, particularly those with foreign-born parents, showed significantly better math achievement than did White students. However, in 2002 the Asian students' math advantages observed in 1990 disappeared. In the later cohort, no significant math achievement differences were observed between White and Asian students. Clearly, the educational advantage and the model minority image usually associated with Asian students do not uphold, at least for 10th graders.

Second, Asian students' family and school characteristics also changed between the two cohorts, especially in regard to their economic conditions. In 1990, Asian students, on average, not only experienced important economic and social capital advantages because of having additional material and parental resources at home, but their outcomes may also be positively affected by the encouragement and support that parents with high educational expectations usually provide for their children. However, the later 2002 cohort of Asian students had substantially lower family socioeconomic conditions. Although the later cohort was still more likely than White students to live with two biological parents and to have high educational expectations from parents, they tended to have lower socioeconomic status. In the case of Asian students, we found not only that their socioeconomic levels decreased between cohorts but we also found that their socioeconomic disadvantages were related to school disadvantages. After comparing the two cohorts of Asian students, we found a significant decrease in private school enrollment and an increase in attendance in schools with lower SES students and higher concentration of minority students. Thus, it is plausible that Asian students in 2002 were more likely to attend lower-quality schools (i.e., school with a higher concentration of poverty, less qualified teachers, or with fewer resources) than in 1990.

Third, Asian students' English proficiency also decreased between 1990 and 2002, although the proportion of Asian homes where English was the main language increased between the same time periods. The increase in limited English proficiency among Asian students is particularly problematic. Unlike Latino immigrants, most of whom communicate in Spanish, Asian immigrants are linguistically very diverse and they lack a dominant language resulting in a difficulty with offering bilingual education to Asian students. At the same time, many Asian students are limited in English proficiency and unable to follow English instructions in class. Furthermore, they are not able to participate in meaningful learning interactions, or to engage in inquiry processes that further learning.

Fourth, although English proficiency and the school environment somewhat account for cohort differences in the Asian-White achievement gaps, family characteristics, including socioeconomic characteristics and parents' educational expectations had the strongest impact. This finding corroborates previous research showing the pervasive effect of family socioeconomic conditions for learning outcomes when families live under poverty conditions. Overall, students from low socioeconomic environments are more likely to obtain lower grades, more likely to be retained, drop out of high school, and have lower levels of educational attainment than students from economically privileged families (Guo & Harris, 2000; Kao & Thompson, 2003; Lee & Burkham, 2002). However, our results also support the lasting and independent effects of parents' expectations on children's performance. It seems plausible that parents' expectations are indicative of the family norms and values that exist within the home context in which children are raised (Yan & Lin, 2005). Parents' expectations may also reflect parents' general attitudes toward schooling and their belief about the importance of education for social mobility.

It is important to note that although Asian students' academic achievement decreased between 1990 and 2002, relative to White students, these students still showed similar math achievement as did White students in 2002. We also know from previous research that White students as a whole tend to have stronger educational outcomes than other minority students. If the migration theory that we introduced earlier is correct that immigrant selectively tends to be negative for later waves of immigration, then the decline of Asian achievement may continue. Future studies should further explore whether Asian achievement decline is consistent and prevalent.

IMPLICATIONS FOR EDUCATORS

This study has provided evidence that Asian adolescent students in 10th grade experienced declining achievement relative to White students, from 1990 to 2002. Some of the achievement decline could be explained by cohort differences in Asian students' family characteristics, parental expectations, and English proficiency. These findings are based on math achievement scores so we may be providing an incomplete assessment of Asian students' achievement changes during this time period. Future studies are needed to analyze achievement patterns using alternative measures, including reading achievement scores, GPA, dropout rates and educational attainment. Future studies should also take into account the diversity of the Asian population and should not only focus on Asian American students as one pan-ethnic group. Regardless of these limitations, several implications for educators surface from these results.

First, educators and policymakers should pay more attention to the new sociodemographic trends among Asian immigrants. A significant demographic change in the characteristics of the Asian population seems to be affecting the educational experience of recently-arrived Asian children. Also, educators need to be trained to realize that not all Asian students are able to live up to the "model minority" label. Today's Asian students are much less likely to meet the expectation of the "model minority" image than Asian students a decade ago. Some Asian groups, such as Hmong, Cambodian, and Laotian students may have increased in population over time. These groups have high dropout rates (Rong & Preissle, 2009), and they lag behind other Asian subgroups in academic achievement (Harris et al., 2008). Appropriate remedial and supplemental education may help these students to catch up, and counseling services may assist them to fight the psychological pressure, such as depression or alienation, when these students cannot reach a high level of academic success as predicted by the "model minority" label.

At the same time, educators should avoid singling out the Hmong, Cambodian, and Laotian subgroups for their educational disadvantages. On the one hand, it may lead to negative labeling and stereotyping for these groups. On the other hand, educators should not overlook the socioeconomic and linguistic differences within groups. A salient example is the Chinese students who tended to concentrate in either end of the socioeconomic spectrum (Kasinitz, Mollenkopf, Waters, & Holdaway, 2008). Whereas many Chinese students have high income and educated parents, many others live in poor families with low parental education. Some Chinese students are fluent bilinguals, while a large number of them are not proficient in English. Recognizing that Asian students as a group are very diverse in socioeconomic status and linguistic background is extremely important for teachers and educational administrators, so that they do not lose sight of the disadvantaged Asian students who are overshadowed by their advantaged peers.

Our analysis reveals declining Asian parents' expectations for their children's education, relative to White parents' expectations, when we compared the two cohorts of students. The lower parental expectations from immigrant parents appeared to account for the narrowing of the Asian-White achievement gap. Epstein (2001) argued that the home and school constitute "overlapping spheres of influence" on children's development and academic achievement, and that the degree to which educators and family members maintain positive relationships with one another helps determine children's academic success. Therefore, school outreach efforts to reach Asian parents and to encourage family involvement may be an important way to influence parents' educational expectations and to improve Asian students' educational success. We recommend that schools should make a serious attempt to educate parents, particularly immigrant parents, by showing them the power of high expectations for their children. Vignettes based on the self-fulfilling prophecy (Rist, 2000) can be told, and workshops can be held for parents to help them overcome concerns about their children's future education.

Finally, one could argue that although Asian adolescent students' high degree of academic achievement has declined over time, the recent 2002 cohort still exhibited an achievement level as high as the level of White students who tend to outperform all other students. This may suggest that there is no need for educators to be concerned. However, we believe that this view encourages mediocrity. It is crucial that educators learn to identify all sources of excellent achievement. Good students should be rewarded and used as role models, and any useful information about reasons for high achievement should be used to design innovative curriculum and instructional strategies that aim at educational excellence for all.

REFERENCES

Bankston, C. L., & Zhou, M. (2002). Doing well: Self-esteem and school performance among immigrant and nonimmigrant racial and ethnic groups. *International Migration Review, 36*, 389-415.

Barnes, J. S., & Bennett, C. E. (2002). *The Asian population: 2000 census 2000 brief* Retrieved from http://www.census.gov/prod/2002pubs/c2kbr01-16.pdf

Blau, P., & Duncan, O. D. (1967). *The American occupational structure.* New York, NY: Wiley.

Borjas, G. (1985). Assimilation, changes in cohort quality, and the earnings of immigrants. *Journal of Labor Economics, 3*, 463-489.

Chen, C., & Stevenson, H.W. (1995). Motivation and mathematics achievement: A comparative study of Asian-American, Caucasian-American, and East Asian high school students. *Child Development, 66*, 1215-1234.

Chou, S. R., & Feagin, J. R. (2008). *The myth of the model minority: Asian Americans facing racism.* Boulder, CO: Paradigm.

Coleman, J. S. (1990). *Equality and achievement in education.* San Francisco, CA: Westview Press.

Epstein, J. 2001. *School, family, and community partnerships: Preparing educators and improving schools.* Boulder, CO: Westview Press.

Feliciano, C. (2005). Educational selectivity in U.S. immigration: How do immigrants compare to those left behind? *Demography, 42*, 131-152.

Kibria, N. (1993). *Family tightrope: The changing lives of Vietnamese Americans.* Princeton, NJ: Princeton University Press.

Fuligni, A. J. (1997). The academic achievement of adolescents from immigrant families: The role of family background, attitudes, and behavior. *Child Development, 68*, 351-363.

Fung-Arto, G. (2007). Academically at-risk English language learners of Chinese background: A pilot Study. In C. C. Park, R. Endo, S. Lee, & X. L. Rong (Eds.), *Asian American education: Acculturation, literacy development, and learning* (pp. 155-166). Charlotte, NC: Information Age.

Galindo, C. (2010). English language learners' math and reading trajectories in the elementary grades. In E. Garcia & E. Frede (Eds.), *Young English language learners: Current research and emerging directions for practice and policy* (pp. 42-59). New York, NY: Teachers College Press.

Glick, J. E., & White, M. J. (2003). The academic trajectories of immigrant youths: Analysis within and across Cohorts. *Demography, 40*, 759-784.

Guo, G., & Harris, K. M. (2000). The mechanisms mediating the effects of poverty on children's intellectual development. *Demography, 37*, 431-447.

Hao, L., & Bonstead-Bruns, M. (1998). Parent-child differences in educational expectations and the academic achievement of immigrant and native students. *Sociology of Education, 71*, 175-198.

Harris, A. L., Jamison, K. M., & Trujillo, M. H. (2008). Disparities in the educational success of immigrants: An assessment of the immigrant effect for Asians and Latinos. *The Annals of the American Academy of Political and Social Science, 620*, 90-115.

Hirschman, C. (2001). The educational enrollment of immigrant youth: A test of the segmented-assimilation hypothesis. *Demography, 38*, 317-336.

Hurh, W. M., & Kim, K. C. (1989). The "success" image of Asian Americans: Its validity, and its practical and theoretical implications. *Racial and Ethnic Studies, 12*, 512-538.

Kasinitz, P., Mollenkopf, J. H., Waters, M. C., & Holdaway, J. (2008). *Inheriting the city: The children of immigrants come of age.* New York, NY: Russell Sage Foundation

Kao, G. (1995). Asian American as model minorities? A look at their academic performance. *American Journal of Education, 103*, 121-159.

Kao, G. (2004). Parental influences on the educational outcomes of immigrant youth. *International Migration Review, 38*, 427-449.

Kao, G., & Thompson, J. S. (2003). Racial and ethnic stratification in educational achievement and attainment. *Annual Review of Sociology, 29*, 417-442.

Kao, G., & Tienda, M. (1995). Optimism and achievement: The educational performance of immigrant youth. *Social Science Quarterly, 76*(1), 1-19.

Kitano, H., & Sue, S. (1973). The model minorities. *The Journal of Social Issues, 29*, 1-9.

Lee, S. (2001). More than 'model minority' or "delinquents": A look at Hmong American high school students. *Harvard Educational Review, 71*, 505-528.

Lee, V. & Burkham, D. (2002). *Inequality at the starting gate: Social background differences in achievement as children begin school.* Washington, DC: Economic Policy Institute.

Lew, J. (2006). *Asian Americans in class: Charting the achievement gap among Korean American youth.* New York, NY: Teachers College Press.

Li, G. & Wang, L. (2008). *Model minority myth revisited: An interdiciplinary approach to demystifying Asian American educational expereinces.* Greenwich, CO: Information Age.

Liang, Z., & Morooka, H. (2004). Recent trends of emigration from China: 1982-2000. *International Migration, 42*(3), 145-164.

Liu, J. M., & Cheng, L. (1994). Pacific rim development and the duality of post 1965 Asian immigration to the United States. In P. Ong, E. Bonacich, & L. Ceng (Eds.), *The new Asian immigration in Los Angeles and global restructuring* (pp. 74-99). Philadelphia, PA: Temple University Press.

Martin, P., & Midgley, E. (2006). Immigration: Shaping and reshaping America. *Population Bulletin, 61*(4), 1-28.

Massey, D. S., Arange, J., Hugo, G., Kouaouci, A., Pellegrino, A., & Taylor, E. (1993). Theories of international migration: A review and appraisal. *Population and Development Review, 19*, 431-466.

McLanahan, S., & Sandefur, G. (1994). *Growing up with a single-parent: What hurts, what helps?* Boston, MA: Harvard University Press.

National Center for Education Statistics. (1999). *Generational status and educational outcomes among Asian and Hispanic 1988 eighth graders.* Washington D.C.: Office of Educational Research and Improvement, U.S. Department of Education. Retreived from http://nces.ed.gov/pubs99/1999020.pdf

National Center for Education Statistics. (2007). *Education longitudinal study of 2002 (ELS:2002) base-year to second follow-up data file documentation* (NCES 2008-347). Washington DC: Office of Educational Research and Improvement, U.S. Department of Education. Retrieved from http://nces.ed.gov/pubs2008/2008347.pdf

Ngo, B., & Lee, S. J. (2007). Complicating the image of model minority success: A review of Southeast Asian American education. *Review of Educational Research, 77*, 415-453.

Orfield, G., & Lee, C. C. (2006). *Racial transformation and the changing nature of segregation. report for the civil rights project.* Cambridge, MA: The Civil Rights Project at Harvard University. Retrieved from http://www.swannfellowship.org/research/files07/racialtransformation.pdf

Park. C. C. (2003). Educational and occupational aspirations of Asian American students. In C. C. Park, A. L. Goodwin, & S. J. Lee (Eds.), *Asian American identities, families, and schooling* (pp. 135-156). Greenwich, CO: Information Age.

Pong, S. (1997). Family structure, school context, and eighth-grade Math and Reading achievement. *Journal of Marriage and the Family, 59*, 734-746.

Pong, S. (2003). *Immigrant children's school performance*: Population Research Institute working paper series, Penn State University. Retrieved from http://www.pop.psu.edu/general/pubs/working_papers/psu-pri/wp0307.pdf

Pong, S., & Hao, L. (2007). Neighborhood and school factors in the school performance of immigrants' children. *International Migration Review, 41, 206-241.*

Pong, S., Hao, L., & Gardner, E. (2005). The proles of parenting styles and social capital in the school performance of immigrant Asian and Hispanic adolescents. *Social Science Quarterly, 86*, 928-949.

Portes, A., & Hao, L. (1998). E Pluribus Unum: Bilingualism and loss of language in the second generation. *Sociology of Education, 71*, 269-294.

Raudenbush, S. W., & Bryk, A. (2002). *Hierarchical linear models. Applications and data analysis methods.* Thousand Oaks, CA: SAGE.

Rist, R. C. (2000). HER Classis: Student social class and teacher expectations: The self-fulfilling prophecy in ghetto education. *Harvard Educational Review 70*, 257-301.

Rong, X. L., & Grant, L. (1992). Ethnicity, generation, and school attainment of Asians, Hispanics, and non-Hispanic Whites. *Sociological Quarterly, 33*, 624-636.

Rong, X. L., & Preissle, J. (2009). *Educating immigrant students in the 21st century: What educators need to know.* Thousand Oaks, CA: Corwin Press.

Rumbaut, R. G. (1995). The new Californians: Comparative research findings on the educational progress of immigrant children. In R. G. Rumbaut & W. A. Cornelius (Eds.), *California's immigrant children : theory, research, and implications for educational policy* (pp. 17-70). San Diego, CA: Center for U.S.-Mexican Studies, University of California.

Schwartz, A. E., & Stiefel, L. (2006). Is there a native gap? New evidence on the academic performance of immigrant students. *Education Finance and Policy, 1*, 17-49.

Steinberg, L., Dornbusch, S. M., & Brown, B. B. (1992). Ethnic differences in adolescent achievement. *American Psychologist, 47*, 723-729.

Stevenson, H. W., Lee, S. Y., Chen, C., Lummis, M., Stigler, J., Fan, L., et al. (1990). Mathematics achievement of children in China and the United States. *Child Development, 61*, 1053-1066.

Thao, P. (1999). *Hmong education at the crossroads*. New York, NY: University Press of America.

U.S. Department of Commerce. (1993). *We the Americans: Asians*. Washington, DC: Economics and Statistics Administration, Bureau of the Census. Retrieved from http://www.census.gov/apsd/wepeople/we-3.pdf

Vernez, G., & Abrahamse, A. (1996). *How immigrants fare in U.S. education*. Santa Monica, CA: RAND.

Walker-Moffat, W. (1995). *The other side of the Asian American success story*. San Francisco, CA: Jossey-Bass.

Wang, J., & Goldschmidt, P. (1999). Opportunity to learn, language proficiency, and immigrant status effects on mathematics achievement. *Journal of Educational Research, 93*, 101-111.

White, K. R. (1982). The relationship between socio-economic status and academic achievement. *Psychological Bulletin, 91*, 461-481.

Yan, W., & Lin, Q. (2005). Parent involvement and mathematics achievement: Contrast across racial and ethnic groups. *Journal of Educational Research, 99*, 116-127.

Zhou, M. (1997). Growing Up American: The challenge confronting immigrant children and children of immigrants. *Annual Review of Sociology, 23*, 63-95.

Zhou, M., & Bankston, C. (1998). *Growing up American: How Vietnamese children adapt to life in the United States*. New York, NY: Russell Sage Foundation.

Zhou, M., & Kim, S. S. (2006). Community forces, social capital, and educational achievement: The case of supplementary education in the Chinese and Korean immigrant communities. *Harvard Educational Review, 76*, 1-29.

CHAPTER 2

"GOOD KIDS,"
BUT "POOR STUDENTS"

The Academic Identities of
Refugee High School Students From
Vietnam's Central Highlands

Liv Thorstensson Dávila

This chapter explores the identity paradigms of a group of refugee high school students from the Vietnamese Central Highlands at a low-performing high school in the U.S. Southeast. Findings are drawn from student and teacher interviews and classroom observations and are analyzed through Holland, Lachicotte, Skinner, and Cain's (1998) notion of "positional identities." This study recognizes a specific academic identity among some inner city Southeast Asian refugee teens: the students generally view themselves and are viewed by their teachers as "good kids" who are hard-working and respectful in class, but "poor students," who struggle academically. Their identities not only help problematize dichotomizing discourse on Asian immigrants in U.S. schools, which tends to position them as either high-achieving and obedient or low-achieving, delinquent, and burden to teachers (Lee, 2005), but also reveals the wide range of academic identities among Southeast Asian students who fall between the stereotyped dichoto-

Asian American Education—Racial Issues, and
Languages, pp. 31–48
Copyright © 2011 by Information Age Publishing
All rights of reproduction in any form reserved.

mization. In addition, this study sheds light on the experiences of a specific group of Southeast Asian refugees who have heretofore received little attention in published academic literature.

> *"Why does he stay in school? His grades are so low!"*
> (Guidance counselor, Franklin High School)

The messages immigrant and refugee students receive in school play a particularly poignant role in their acculturation and in shaping their sense of belonging and aspirations in and beyond school (Suarez-Orozco & Suarez-Orozco, 2001; Valenzuela, 1999). Indeed, the sentiment expressed to me by a well-meaning yet overwhelmed guidance counselor regarding one of the students in my study during a visit to Franklin High School[1] (FHS) opened my eyes to a variety of contradictions in how students are often viewed and come to view themselves in school. More broadly, it underscores how the intersection of social factors (including race, culture, and language) and social contexts plays out in the daily experiences of many immigrant and refugee students in U.S. public schools.

This chapter explores the identity paradigms of a group of Vietnamese Central Highlands[2] Jarai and M'nong refugee students at a low-performing[3] high school in the U.S. Southeast. I specifically ask: How does positioning by peers and teachers influence the academic identities of these students? And, how do conditions within the context of FHS shape the identities the students transact? The students' histories as a marginalized ethnic minority in Vietnam and current circumstances as resettled refugees, along with the messages they receive from teachers and peers at the school they attend, combine to inform their academic identities and motivations beyond school. In exploring how a single group of Asian minority refugee students shape their identities in relation to these messages and conditions at FHS, this research helps to expand upon discourse on Asian immigrants and refugee students which tends to position them as either high achieving, respectful, and obedient or low-achieving, delinquent, and a burden to teachers (Lee, 2005). In response, the students' narratives underscore the importance of understanding identity in relation to local contexts and individual experiences and offer new directions for educational scholarship and practice. In addition, although recent scholarship has paid some attention to underrepresented Asian Americans (e.g., Ling, 2008), there is little published academic literature on refugee groups in the United States who are from Vietnam's

Central Highlands. This chapter meets this void by prioritizing the voices of a group of six Jarai and M'nong students.

POSITIONING(S) OF ASIAN AMERICANS

Scholarship has explored the multiple ways in which Asian Americans have been positioned within the U.S. racial landscape. At opposite ends of the spectrum are the model minority and problem minority paradigms. The model minority myth emerged in the 1960s and positions Asians as quiet, obedient, and smart and draws attention away from racial inequality. Lee (1996, 2005) has argued that the model minority stereotype obscures variation across ethnic groups and individuals and that students able to live up to the stereotype are hailed, whereas students unable to meet these standards are deemed failures or substandard for their race.

Recent studies have explored the model minority stereotype in reference to Southeast Asian immigrant student identities in school. For instance, Lee (2005) investigated the school experiences of Hmong refugee students and illustrated how teachers' misunderstanding of Hmong culture and adherence to the model minority stereotype pitted "obedient" first-generation and "delinquent" 1.5 generation students against one another. In addition, Centrie (2004) found that teachers and administrators at the school where he conducted his research valued what they perceived as a hard work ethic and high academic achievement among Vietnamese students relative to the majority African American and Latino students.

In contrast to the model minority stereotype, the problem minority image has typically been assigned to African American and Latino youth who live in impoverished urban centers, have high rates of teenage pregnancy, fall into gangs, and engage in criminal activity. However, statistics illustrate that Southeast Asian immigrant and refugee participation in the U.S. economic and educational system mirrors that of African American and Latino groups. For instance, 2000 U.S. Census data reveal that Southeast Asians residing in the U.S. are less likely to graduate from high school or college and have a higher rate of poverty than European Americans and Asian Americans as an aggregated group.

Statistical data in addition to the model minority and problem minority frameworks paint only a partial picture and in many ways fail to account for the diverse experiences of Asian immigrant and refugee students in U.S. schools. In response, I desired to build on existing scholarship by examining how a group of resettled Jarai and M'nong Vietnamese Central Highlands refugee students at a low-performing urban high school in North Carolina interpret and shape their identities in relation to these contradictory messages surrounding them.

CONCEPTUAL FRAMEWORK

I analyzed relational aspects of identity formation using the notion of positional identities (Holland et al., 1998) to situate the students' self-identities within the context of peer and teacher relationships, which themselves infer "deference and entitlement, social affiliation and distance" (p. 151). Holland et al. (1998) refer to positional identities as:

> how one identifies one's position relative to others', mediated through ways in which one feels comfortable or constrained, for example, to speak to another, to command another, to enter into the space of another, to touch the possessions of another, to dress for another. (p. 150)

C. Suarez-Orozco's (2000) notion of "social mirroring" provides a related explanation for students' self-understandings and adjustment in school. Social mirroring suggests that immigrant and refugee students absorb and internalize images and beliefs surrounding them in school that shape their academic and social identities either positively or negatively. Although they may enter schools with a strong motivation to succeed, these students often find it "extremely difficult to maintain an unblemished sense of self-worth for very long" (p. 213) because of negative institutional and relational messages conveyed to and about them.

Positional identities factor into Holland et al.'s (1998) notion of cultural or figured worlds, which are a "socially and culturally constructed realm of interpretation in which particular characters and actors are recognized, significance is assigned to certain acts, and particular outcomes are valued over others," and within which identities are created, enacted, assigned, and subverted (p. 52). In the figured world of schools, newcomers develop identities based on daily interactions—they identify themselves positively or negatively through acceptance or rejection from others. Students' self-identities are influenced by how they perceive their positions within the context of school. Conditions, such as student performance, curricular offerings, and teacher preparedness, also factor into the identities that students transact.

Holland et al. (1998) argue that newcomers:

> learn a feel for the game, for how such claims on their part will be received. They come to have relational identities in their most rudimentary form: a set of dispositions toward themselves in relation to where they can enter,

what they can say, what emotions they can have, and what they can do in a
given situation. (p. 143)

The concept of positional identities lends itself to an understanding of
how a group of newcomer Jarai and M'nong refugee students – as cultural, linguistic, and racial minorities—come to understand their identities within school.

SETTING AND PARTICIPANTS

In formulating my research questions and conceptual approach to this
study, I have attended to contextual, demographic and person-centered
factors which influence how the students either participate in or resist the
identities imposed on them. This necessitated gaining an understanding
of the broader context of their resettlement in North Carolina, and of
Franklin High School (FHS), where the majority of the data collection
took place.

As a state with a historically low immigration rate, North Carolina
has quickly become one of the nation's leading new immigrant gateway
states (Rong & Preissle, 2009). This study takes place in Bankston, one
of the largest cities in North Carolina and a transportation, financial,
and manufacturing center. As with other metropolitan areas in the
Southeast, Bankston, a historically White and African American city, has
seen tremendous growth overall and even greater increases in its immigrant population, particularly from Latin America. Bankston's Asian
population has also increased 20-fold in the last 40 years. By examining the school experiences of a group of Vietnamese Central Highland
refugee newcomer youth in Bankston, this study sheds light on the challenges and opportunities presented by resettlement in a rapidly growing and changing city.

Vietnamese Central Highlanders

North Carolina is home to the largest number of refugees from Vietnam's Central Highlands outside of Vietnam. Refugees within this group
are a marginalized ethnic minority in Vietnam and like many Hmong and
Lao refugees were recruited by the U.S. military during the Vietnam Conflict to fight against the communist North Vietnamese army. They saw
allegiance with the U.S. as an opportunity to gain political autonomy
from the repressive Vietnamese government. The resettlement of this
group in North Carolina began in 1986, and larger groups were resettled

in the state between 1992 and 2006 through an Orderly Departure Program agreement between the U.S. and Vietnamese governments. Most children and adults arriving in the U.S. since 2002 lived in rural areas in Vietnam, have spent time in refugee camps, and have had little or no formal schooling (Bailey, 2004).

Franklin High School (FHS)

I selected FHS as my research site because it enrolled the largest number of Vietnamese Central Highlands refugee students in the Bankston school system, which I believed would give me sufficient access to a variety of participants. Approximately 2,150 students attended FHS during the period of this study, and the school's demographics were 70% African American, 14% White, 8% Hispanic, 6% Asian, 2% multiracial and 1% Native American. Seventy-one percent of the school's students received free/reduced lunch, 17% were designated as students with disabilities, and 8% were designated as limited English proficient (LEP).

A 2005 state-wide school funding case threatened to close FHS and three other "lowest performing" high schools in Bankston. FHS was recently termed one of Bankston's four "challenge schools" in a local newspaper report because of its consistently low scores on No Child Left Behind (NCLB) tests and high poverty and drop-out rates.

The Participants

In this chapter, I present data from interviews with and observations of M'nong and Jarai students and school personnel at FHS. These participants included four male and two female students, four English as a second language (ESL) teachers, an assistant principal, and five content area (non-ESL) teachers.

I approached the students with the help of their ESL teachers who believed they would be interested in participating in this study and because they matched my criteria for selection. These criteria included a roughly equal representation of males and females with three or more years' residence in the U.S. In short, because I do not speak their native language(s), I desired a sample of students who could reflect on their school identities and experiences in English. Table 2.1 illustrates the general characteristics of the students.

To summarize, these students arrived in the U.S. in 2002 and 2003. Four of them spent time in refugee camps in Cambodia with their families, and two came to the U.S. as part of the Family Reunification Act to

Table 2.1. **Characteristics of Students in This Study**

Name	Gender	Age	Grade	Arrival to U.S./Bankston	Schooling in Vietnam (Yrs.)	Ethnic Group
H'Yin	F	19	12	2003	3	Jarai
Khuih	M	18	12	2002	2	M'nong
Sieng	M	17	10	2002	sporadic	M'nong
Luis	M	18	9	2003	1	M'nong
Vit	M	17	10	2002	1	M'nong
Gar	F	18	11	2002	0	M'nong

join family members who had received asylum status and resettled in Bankston in years prior. All of the students were English language learners (ELLs) with interrupted formal education, and all were also one or more years older than their grade-level peers at FHS. These characteristics influenced the ways in which they positioned their academic identities and were in turn positioned by their teachers and peers.

METHODOLOGY

This is a qualitative study that took place over the course of one school year. I drew upon principles of qualitative and narrative inquiry using ethnographic methods to develop a "thick description" (Geertz, 1973) of the school setting and the students' self and positional identities. As my primary method of collecting data, I conducted three separate hour-long interviews with each of the six students (one during the fall semester, and two during the spring semester). I believed it important to privilege students' understandings of their life stories—their thoughts, feelings, and ideas—and their identities as narrated by them. In addition, I conducted one 35 interview with 9 teachers and an assistant principal at FHS. I also briefly checked in with the teachers after observing their classes.

A sample of my questions for students included the following: How would you describe yourself? How do you compare to other students at FHS? How would a teacher describe you? Do you like school? Who are your friends at FHS? Do they like school? What is it like to go to school at FHS? What are your future goals? I interviewed teachers and the assistant principal to gain their perspectives on working with Vietnamese Central Highlands refugee students and their perceptions of how these students fit into the larger school context. My questions for these participants included: How is [student] doing in your class? What is your perception of him/her as a student? What is your perception of him/her compared to other students at FHS? These interview questions allowed me to gain a balanced perspective of the students' positional identities in school.

Narrative inquirers "settle in, live and work alongside participants, and come to experience not only what can be seen and talked about directly but also the things not said and not done that shape the narrative structure of their observations and their talking" (Clandinin & Connelly, 2000, pp. 67-68). In addition to interviews, I observed the students in various classes to better understand the school context and the students' lives within school, as well as their perception of particular classroom phenomena. I conducted observations in four ESL classes and five content area classes during the fall and spring semesters in which the students were enrolled. I observed the ESL classes on numerous occasions throughout the school year, and I conducted one observation of each of the five content area classes during the spring semester. During my observations, I sat at the back of the classroom taking field notes on the overall context and students' engagement with course materials. After my observations, I approached students and teachers to ask for their impressions about the classes. These instances offered opportunities to build detailed descriptions of the contexts, people and activities, but also to question my assumptions regarding what I observed. In my research, I continued to seek critical feedback regarding my research goals and interpretations from the students and their teachers.

Data analysis occurred in several stages. Following the methods outlined by Patton (2002) and Heath and Street (2008), upon transcription of interviews, I read through the data and generated codes from interview responses, background literature, and the conceptual framework. First, I organized details of students' descriptions in logical order and arranged them in a time-line (e.g., descriptions of life in Vietnam, departure, resettlement, schooling in the United States). From there I looked for specific events as told by the students that highlighted a particular meaning in relation to my research questions (e.g., H'yin's experience of being positioned as "innocent" by her math teacher, and students depictions of school violence). I then looked for patterns and deviations across all six participants. Finally, I synthesized the data and considered the implications of my findings beyond these specific cases. Using a constant comparative or recursive perspective, I juxtaposed data from observations and interviews with my underlying assumptions or hunches, as well as theories and concepts from the literature to create a dialogue between existing explanations and ongoing data collection and analysis (Heath & Street, 2008). Because the focus of my study was on the academic identities of the Jarai and M'nong students, I analyzed data in light of this objective.

DISCUSSION OF FINDINGS

Positioning by School Personnel

FHS has enrolled refugee students from the Vietnamese Central Highlands since the mid-1990s. When enrollment of Southeast Asian refugees from Vietnam and Laos increased in the early 2000s, an assistant principal and Vietnam veteran began offering teacher training sessions focusing on how teachers could best work with these students at FHS. He also invited Vietnamese Central Highland community members to talk about this group's history, culture, and experiences as resettled refugees. In spite of these training sessions, he noted a contradiction in terms of how teachers perceived Vietnamese Central Highland students:

> Teachers think they are quiet, no trouble, limited English, backward … but the squeaky wheel gets the grease. Because [these students] don't cause trouble in the classroom, they don't get help. Really, the biggest fallacy is that they are doing well.

The students are positioned by teachers as quiet and well-behaved relative to their American and predominantly Latino immigrant peers at FHS, and because of this they do not receive the help they need with grasping academic content.

The ESL teachers also remarked that Vietnamese Central Highland newcomers at FHS do not always receive the support they need in their content area classes, "because teachers are so focused on keeping the class under control," as one teacher explained. All believed that content area teachers are generally receptive toward these students. However, another ESL teacher shared:

> The other day I told a social studies teacher that some of my [Vietnamese Central Highland ESL] students needed more modifications on homework and in-class worksheets, and she just blew up at me. She rolled her eyes and said, "You want me to do more [for these students]?!"

And yet another ESL teacher commented, "At least in this school there are native U.S. students who perform poor academically because of family or other circumstances. So the [Vietnamese Central Highland newcomers] aren't the only ones having trouble."

A conversation with Sieng's algebra teacher further illustrates how Vietnamese Central Highlands students are positioned by teachers at FHS. "Sieng is a really good kid," the teacher related, "and he tries really hard. But he just doesn't get it. He seems like he understands the language, but he doesn't get the content." His teacher enjoys having Sieng as a student but is doubtful that he will pass the class. In addition, other content area teachers I spoke with related that although they are aware of the academic and linguistic needs of newcomer students at FHS, they are also overburdened by changes at the school, including increased class sizes, more discipline issues, a larger and more diverse ELL population, increased emphasis on state-mandated tests, and retaining their jobs during an economic downturn.

In summary, teachers at FHS generally hold contradictory views toward the students in this study. On the one hand, they embrace them for being "respectful" and "hard-working" relative to other students at FHS. On the other hand, many teachers doubt the students' ability to succeed academically, and in turn they are not always equipped or willing to help these students. In either case, in their positioning as a silent minority, the needs of these students are not always met, and their identities are not always affirmed.

Students' Mixed Perceptions of Their Academic Identities

I approached this study with the assumption that the way in which students believe they are viewed by teachers greatly impacts their sense of self and their success in school. I desired to uncover how these students understood their positional identities in relation to their teachers' perceptions of them. Their responses represent divergent identity paradigms.

I observed Sieng and Luis in an American history class, and field notes below illustrate a classroom environment in which these two students are positioned and position themselves differently:

> There are 28 students in this class—22 of whom are African American, four are Vietnamese Central Highlanders (VCH) and two are Hispanic. Students are sitting in assigned seats in rows facing the white board. Mr. Schwartz (White male teacher in his 30s) stands at the transparency projector and frequently reminds students in a loud voice to copy notes from his slide. He tells them that they will be quizzed on material tomorrow. Two students are out of their seats or shouting across the classroom to one another. Sieng and Luis sit quietly in front of two other VCH males in the back left corner. Sieng looks like he is taking notes, and Luis puts his head down. The two other VCH students talk quietly with one another. Mr. Schwartz passes out a worksheet for students to complete in groups. Sieng and the two other VCH boys are in a group together with Rosalia, a Hispanic student I recognize from Sieng's ESL class. The two VCH boys continue talking, while Sieng and Rosalia work on the assignment. Luis is still sleeping. Mr. Schwartz occasionally circulates the room, but does not approach Sieng and Rosalia.

Sieng embodies an identity shared by most of the students: a simultaneously "good" but low-achieving student. Like Sieng, these students believe they are good students because they "try hard and are quieter and nicer than American students," as Khuih noted. Being a good student means listening to the teacher, doing what is asked of them, and not talking in class. Luis, on the other hand, believes that he is a poor student who has little interest in learning, in spite of his desire to graduate from high school. "I sleep in class because I am so tired, and I don't want to learn about history. The teacher doesn't care" he told me after the class had ended.

Sieng believes that teachers find him quiet and cooperative and give him passing grades because he works hard and tries to do well. He does not believe he is ready to go on to the next level in some classes, however. Sieng attributes his low academic performance to his infrequent attendance in school in Vietnam, as illustrated by his comparison of Vietnamese Central Highland refugee and American students:

> How we feel is different from how American people feel. And American kids are smarter than me. In Vietnam I didn't even go to school, and that's why I'm not smart. But if American kids are born here, they are smart, maybe their parents are smart and they be smart too. I don't think I'm smart.

Although Sieng is aware of his struggles, he is emotionally unaffected by his setbacks. He does not believe that his survival is dependent upon acquisition of academic skills. Instead, he draws on his experiences of marginalization in Vietnam and in the U.S. as a means of transacting an identity in school. In a later conversation, he compared himself positively relative to his classmates at FHS, noting, "They speak one language, and I speak four. I am a refugee and they are not." Being a refugee is strong part of his self-identity. He shared:

> We had a hard time in Vietnam, so we had to leave. We didn't have no choice because we had no food and no land. And [the Vietnamese government] wanted my dad. So we came here. I want people to know about my life in Vietnam so they can know me and know why I am here—why I go to school. And so I can help other refugees too. I think many people don't know who I am, and I want them to know.

In his view, he has overcome many obstacles in his life, such as chastisement from ethnic Vietnamese teachers and students in Vietnam, flight to a refugee camp in Cambodia, resettlement in a low-income neighborhood in Bankston, and enrollment in school in the U.S. These experiences make up for the self-perception that he is not a good student.

H'yin offered a different account of how teachers and peers positioned her and how she positioned herself within this matrix. She related, "Other students think I am a mystery because I always do my homework and they don't. I like homework—it helps me to practice more, and I want to get good grades and graduate." She believes that teachers position her in different ways. In spite of having resettled in the U.S. as an adolescent, she noted, "Some teachers treat me like I was born here, like I speak English normally." Other teachers set H'yin apart from her peers. She explained:

> My teachers always say I am nice, hard working, and … innocent! I have math class, and my teacher is a White guy, and he always says that I am the only hardworking student in the class. I am the only Asian student in the class, and everyone else is Black or Mexican. I have a Black friend in the class who keeps on trying to get me in trouble. He says that I am trying to cheat in the class a lot. And the teacher says, "Why are you lying about your friend. She is a sweet, innocent Asian girl!" And the teacher always compares me to other students. He has our name on the board, like number 1, 2, 3. And last semester I was number one, then I went to number two when the class got harder for me, and I felt bad.

When I asked her about other students at FHS, H'yin shared, "I see a lot of students who don't care about school. They talk about what they do after school and they talk a lot in class. I don't really like talking in class." Although H'yin is concerned with doing well in school and articulates a "good student" academic identity against what she perceives as her apathetic peers, she is also reluctant to be positioned as a model minority.

Conversely, Luis believes that teachers at FHS generally show little concern for him. "[My ESL teacher] thinks I'm joking around a lot because I talk in class. Other teachers think that I'm the kind of person who doesn't talk much and that I don't make friends because I am quiet and I don't ask many questions," he shared. When I asked him why he does not ask questions in class, he replied, "Because if I ask, I still don't get it. And I am afraid to ask because people will say I'm stupid." Luis holds a negative self-identity in school, sharing:

> I'm not a good student now. I don't listen, my grades are not so good. Mostly math classes are hard. ESL class is OK—I can understand, and my teacher is good. Next year, I don't know. I have to retake a class—algebra—because I didn't pass.

In spite of his "poor student" identity, Luis also continuously positioned himself positively against students who "cause trouble" in school. He related:

It makes me mad [when kids fight]. When they fight then the school has to have a lockout. They locked the whole school one time because people were fighting. And I was kicked out of class onetime because I didn't make it to class before the lockout. I said "no way!" So I went to gym instead of going to ISS (in-school suspension). The gym teacher didn't care. If I could I would make the kids act better; change the school rules. If the students dressed the way normal people dressed, like what they wear to church it would be better. The clothes they wear are really bad—gangster and stuff.

In essence, Luis draws on aspects of his ethnic identity, such as respect for elders, and conservative dress, while simultaneously engaging in deviant behavior in school by sleeping in class, not completing his work, or not following directives to attend ISS.

To summarize, in many ways the students resist deviant behavior they see in their peers and shape their identities against this behavior. They actively project "good kid" identities in opposition to this behavior in spite of their generally poor performance in school. The students also transact divergent school identities: Sieng views himself and is viewed by his teachers as a "good kid" but a "poor student." H'yin's positional identity is that of a "good kid" and a "good student." Finally, Luis views himself as a "poor student" who is also socially withdrawn in school. The differences can be attributed in part to individual characteristics such as self-confidence, amount of schooling in Vietnam, and type of support received in school. Their differences are also due to the ways in which these students are positioned by teachers at FHS. More broadly, they illustrate the range of identities students from one ethnic group may inhabit.

Some students embrace what they perceive to be positive views of their teachers and peers, albeit for strategic reasons. For instance, Khuih related that a teacher encouraged him to apply for college and helped him apply for a scholarship because of his adequate academic performance and good behavior in class. He continued, "Students think I'm smart, too, because I do my work. And the teacher thinks I'm smart. Sometimes people ask me for answers and copy my work. I give it to them because I don't want them to get mad."

Vit resists being positioned as a model minority and instead wishes to be seen as equal to his classmates. He related, "My teachers think I am smarter than other kids because I do my work. But I don't want to be the smartest in my class. I want everyone else to be like me—to want to learn." Vit desires an academic context in which he does not stand out from other students. Alternatively, Gar noted that teachers in some classes have given her a passing grade whether or not she has grasped the content material because she is hard-working relative to other students. "They don't care about me because I don't cause trouble. But then I get to the next grade and I don't get anything. I am lost," she explained. Gar desires more individualized attention from teachers who wrongly assume that she understands the content presented to her. Paradoxically, Gar hesitates to approach teachers for help for fear of chastisement from peers.

To these students, behaving like a "good kid" is different from being a good student achievement-wise. In addition, although they believe that teachers value their behavior over other students, many of the students believe that teachers do not find them capable of achieving academic success in school. In summary, students' individual desires differ based on academic ability and general self-perception. They all, however, possess a strong motivation to graduate from high school and believe they would benefit greater and more consistent academic support in order to accomplish this goal.

DISCUSSION

This chapter underscores the importance of exploring the dialectic between identities offered to or imposed upon learners as well as how learners accept or resist those identities. Various factors complicate the self and positional identities of students in this study, including their experiences as a marginalized ethnic minority group in Vietnam, being ethnic and linguistic minorities at FHS, and in many cases believing they do not possess the intellectual capital to succeed in school. Conditions at FHS, such as student apathy, and teachers who are overburdened by state-mandated tests and classroom management issues contribute to the identities they transact. At the same time, they invoke a habitus (Bourdieu, 1977) which stresses respect for elders, a strong work ethic, persistence, and a collectivist value orientation which in many ways influences their being positioned by teachers as model minorities relative to other students at FHS in spite of their generally poor academic performance.

Ogbu (1991) has argued that, "[immigrant minorities] rationalize prejudice and discrimination by saying as 'guests' in a foreign land they have no choice but to tolerate prejudice and discrimination" (p. 21). The students in this study generally accept teacher apathy and being chastised or misunderstood by their peers as a condition of their existence as refugees. At the same time, they shape an academic identity against these conditions through which they filter their positions and motivations in school. This identity serves as a coping mechanism—as a reason to stay in school in spite of poor academic performance and inconsistent support from teachers at FHS.

In addition, the students' narratives suggest that neither the model minority nor the problem minority paradigms fully match their individual realities, and that, in fact, these polarizing discourses leave little room for alternative understandings of youth identity paradigms. The data presented in this chapter offer a more complex and local account of identity articulation and reveal some of the many academic identities for Asian Americans who fall somewhere between the model minority and problem minority frameworks. These identities are situated within the context of a low-performing, urban high school in a new immigrant gateway state (Rong & Preissle, 2009) which contributes to their being positioned in this way—as better behaved and more respectful, but lower achieving than many students at FHS. In addition, the narratives point to the shortcomings of imposing homogenizing labels on students who share many characteristics, such as race, class, and linguistic minority status, and whose past and current experiences in many ways overlap. It is clear that the academic identities of these students differ and that these students engage in different coping mechanisms to meet their individual needs. By the same token, although it would be easy to conclude that some students have progressed further than others, all students face uncertainties in school. Each identity offers implications for how scholars, teachers and policymakers might approach the education of students such as those in this study.

RECOMMENDATIONS FOR EDUCATORS

As the discussion in the preceding section reveals, the Jarai and M'nong students' identities are shaped by complex and contradictory processes involving interpersonal relationships and conditions within the context of FHS. As "good kids" but "poor students" these students are in some ways invisible minorities who are intentionally or unintentionally kept invisible by teachers who focus on disruptive students and passing state-mandated tests. One must ask, then, "What is the academic benefit to students who are viewed by teachers good kids whose academic needs are overlooked because they are less disruptive in class?" At FHS, an assistant principal attempted to inform teachers about Vietnamese Central Highland refugee students, their cultures and experiences. However in my observations, this awareness did not always translate into practical classroom application. Instilling in teachers a unified desire and the tools to help these students might increase their likelihood for academic success while simultaneously honoring their identities. School districts could assume some responsibility in training teachers to work with Vietnamese Central Highlands students and other smaller ethnic groups. The school district could also develop curricular materials to help these students catch up academically and linguistically with their peers. These materials might bridge aspects of students' culture and experiences in Vietnam with academic content material or topics relevant to their current contexts and future possibilities. FHS could also invite Vietnamese Central Highlanders who have graduated from high school in the United States, attended college, or entered a profession to discuss their experiences in school and the challenges they have overcome.

That many mainstream teachers at FHS are unwilling or unsure of how to work with students such as those in this study suggests that this group of students will continue to struggle in and beyond school. To counter this, teachers must engage in culturally responsive (Gay, 2000) and constructivist teaching that recognizes and validates the backgrounds of students. In addition, students may benefit from being taught strategies to help them become effective independent learners. Cooperative learning and peer tutoring may also be particularly beneficial on social and academic fronts and contribute to a more positive school climate more broadly. Afterschool tutoring programs for these students would provide needed academic support to help them succeed in school. In addition, an afterschool social club might provide opportunities to reflect on identity issues in school. Opportunities for different student groups to meet might foster understanding across racial and ethnic lines and provide opportunities for students to reflect on and transform broader tensions within FHS, such as student performance, school violence, and high teacher turnover.

In addition, new immigrant gateway states (Rong & Preissle, 2009), such as North Carolina, face specific educational challenges that must be met in part through teacher education. In particular, teacher education programs must build practicing teachers' and teacher candidates' awareness of smaller immigrant groups, differences between immigrant and refugee students, and expectations that may conflict with the needs of students. Teachers must also consider the implications of the perceptions they have of students and how this positioning translates into their interactions with students, and ultimately the identities the students inhabit. I suggest that teachers become dialogic researchers (Hones, 2002) who respect and bring to light the stories of their students while also exploring their own sense of cultural identity through ethnographic and narrative inquiry. This "border crossing," though time-consuming and often challenging, opens one's eyes to the experiences of students and how best to meet their needs.

In conclusion, the student and teacher data presented in this chapter direct our gaze to the complicated relationship between past experience, local contexts, wider structures, and interpersonal relationships. At the same time, while I do not intend to generalize the experiences of the students in this study, this chapter contributes to an understanding of how some Asian students in U.S. schools are "overlooked and underserved" (Ruiz-de-Velasco & Fix, 2000).

NOTES

1. All names of places and participants in this study have been changed to maintain confidentiality.

2. I use the term Vietnamese Central Highland(ers) throughout this chapter to refer to the collective origins of the students in this study, and where appropriate I use the students' ethnic group names (Jarai and M'nong), while also recognizing that there are several ethnic groups that fall within this broad category. The terms *Degar* (or *Dega*), *Montagnard*, or *Montagnard-Dega* are also used interchangeably in North Carolina (Pearson, 2009). Dega is thought to be an indigenous Rhade term, and Montagnard was the name given to indigenous groups in Vietnam's Central Highlands by French missionaries in the nineteenth century.

3. A low-performing school is one that does not meet the standards created and monitored by the state board of education. Low-performing schools tend to enroll students who come from impoverished backgrounds. Conditions prevalent in low-performing schools include high rates of truancy, low scores on state mandated tests, and high teacher turnover (Clotfelter, 2004).

REFERENCES

Bailey, R. (2004). *Montagnards: Their history and culture.* Retrieved from http://www.cal.org/co/montagnards/vtoc.html

Bourdieu, P. (1977). *Outline of a theory or practice.* Cambridge, England: Cambridge University Press.

Centrie, C. (2004). *Identity formation of Vietnamese immigrant youth in an American high school.* New York, NY: LFB.

Clandinin, J. D., & Connelly, F. M. (2000). *Narrative inquiry: Experience and story in qualitative research.* San Francisco, CA: Jossey-Bass,

Clotfelter, C.T. (2004). *After Brown: The rise and retreat of school desegregation.* Princeton, NJ: Princeton University Press.

Gay, G. (2000). *Culturally responsive teaching: Theory, research, and practice.* New York, NY: Teachers College Press.

Geertz, C. (1973). *The interpretation of cultures: Selected essays.* New York, NY: Basic Books.

Heath, S. B., & Street, B. V. (2008). *On ethnography: Approaches to language and literacy research.* New York, NY: Teachers College Press.

Holland, D., Lachicotte, W., Jr., Skinner, D., & Cain, D. (1998). *Identity and agency in cultural worlds.* Cambridge, MA: Harvard University Press.

Hones, D.F. (2002). *American dreams. Global visions: Dialogic teacher research with refugee and immigrant families.* Mahwah, NJ: Earlbaum.

Lee, S. J. (1996). *Unraveling the Model Minority stereotype: Listening to Asian American youth.* New York, NY: Teachers College Press.

Lee, S.J. (2005). *Up against whiteness: Race, school, and immigrant youth.* New York, NY: Teachers College Press.

Ling, H. (2008). *Emerging voices: Experiences of underrepresented Asian Americans.* New Brunswick, NJ: Rutgers University Press.

Ogbu, J. (1991). Minority coping responses and school experience. *Journal of Psychohistory, 18*, 433-456.

Patton, M.Q. (2002). *Qualitative evaluation and research methods.* Newbury Park, CA: SAGE.

Pearson, T. (2009). *Missions and conversions: Creating the Montagnard-Dega refugee community.* New York, NY: Palgrave MacMillan.

Rong, X. L., & Preissle, J. (2009). *Educating immigrant students in the 21st century: What educators need to know.* Thousand Oaks, CA: Corwin Press.

Ruiz-de-Velasco, J., & Fix, M. (2000). *Overlooked and underserved: Immigrant students in U.S. secondary schools.* Washington, DC: Urban Institute.

Suárez-Orozco, C. (2000). Identities under siege: Immigration stress and social mirroring among the children of immigrants. In Antonius Robben& M. Suárez-Orozco (Eds.), *Cultures under siege: Social violence & trauma.* Cambridge, England: Cambridge University.

Suarez-Orozco, C., & Suarez-Orozco, M. M. (2001). *Children of immigration.* Cambridge, MA: Harvard University Press.

Valenzuela, A. (1999). *Subtractive schooling: U.S.-Mexican youth and politics of caring.* Albany, NY: State University of New York Press.

CHAPTER 3

ETHNICITY, LANGUAGE, AND EDUCATIONAL INEQUALITY

Challenges Confronting Hmong Students in American Public Schools

Yang Sao Xiong and Min Zhou

This study shows how ethnicity intersects with polity to affect the educational outcomes of linguistic minority students. Using academic test scores and tracking data from California's Department of Education, this study identifies three structural processes that segregate and trap linguistic minority students: state-mandated classification, selective testing, and tracking. The results reveal that these processes jointly limit students' educational choices, their access to quality curricula, and their opportunity to advance beyond high school. Given Hmong students' lower socioeconomic status and their overrepresentation as English learners in California's public schools, we suggest that these processes and institutional practices reinforce Hmong students' educational disadvantages. We provide some theoretical and policy implications.

Asian American Education—Identities, Racial Issues, and Languages, pp. 49–72
Copyright © 2011 by Information Age Publishing

Hmong students and other linguistic minority students in California's K-12 public schools face a multitude of obstacles and problems such as low English literacy and low test scores which hamper their chances of academic success. While these obstacles and problems are linked to their disadvantaged socioeconomic backgrounds and refugee/immigrant status, efforts by the state and public schools to reform educational policy targeted at helping these students may sometimes have unintended effects. In this study, we show that the causes for academic success or failure are not simply rooted in an individual's family socioeconomic status (SES), ethnic background, ability and effort, or even school characteristics alone, but are intertwined in and related to broader historical and contemporary processes of class and racial stratification in American society. Using students' language census, academic test scores and tracking data from California's Department of Education, we explain how state-mandated classification, selective testing, and tracking inadvertently create new forms of segregation that disadvantage linguistic minority students.

In this chapter, we examine how ethnicity intersects with polity to affect the educational experiences of linguistic minority students, especially students of Hmong background.[1] We argue that it is important to distinguish between ethnicity and race, even though ethnicity and race connote similar meanings and sometimes even overlap. According to Max Weber (1968), an ethnic group may be defined as a "human [group] that entertain[s] a subjective belief in their common descent because of similarities of physical type or of customs or both, or because of memories of colonization and migration" (p. 389). A race, on the other hand, is "a human group defined by itself or others as distinct by virtue of perceived common physical characteristics that are held to be inherent" (Cornell & Hartmann, 1998, p. 24). We define polity as consisting of legal precedents, current state laws, ideologies, and policies that structure educational practices at the school district level.

We further argue that ethnic categorization is shaped by the polity to reinforce advantages or disadvantages associated with ethnicity. While we underscore the effect of ethnicity, we distinguish between an internal definition of ethnicity and an external imposition of an ethnic category. As Richard Jenkins (1994) points out, both processes of internal definition and external categorization help demarcate a group's ethnic boundary. However, the latter process involves the imposition of identity onto a group by another dominant group on the sole basis of arbitrary markers such as physical characteristics or language background (Jenkins, 1994). These distinctions are crucial for understanding the way social stratification reproduces educational inequalities among ethnic minorities and are particularly relevant regarding the tracking of Hmong and other students in public schools, which is usually based solely on their linguistic minority status.

First, we draw on prior research to present our central argument about the crucial sources of educational inequality that confront linguistic minority students. Next, we offer a general socioeconomic profile of Hmong Americans in the United States and discuss how initial disadvantages associated with immigrant/refugee status, such as poverty, low literacy, and the lack of English proficiency, create daunting challenges for refugee families and children. Third, and as the main contribution of our paper, we analyze the specific ways that the public educational system operates to structure and reinforce social class and ethnic disadvantages of Hmong American students. Finally, we discuss the long-term impacts that public policies and school practices of linguistic segregation have on the ethnic retention and mobility prospects of linguistic minority students. We conclude the paper with some theoretical and policy recommendations.

STRUCTURAL DISADVANTAGES AND UNEQUAL EDUCATIONAL OUTCOMES

A substantial body of empirical research has documented the persistent gap in academic performance between ethnic minority students and non-Hispanic White students in the post-Civil Rights era (Miller, 1995; U.S. Dept. of Education, 2000). In addition, research has shown that specific Asian ethnic groups differ in their overall levels of academic performance and that some perform at lower levels (Ngo & Lee, 2007). Socioeconomic background or class as well as race clearly have impacts on educational outcomes (Kao & Thompson, 2003; Mare, 1995). Existing research has also examined how race matters and how ethnicity is intertwined with class and race, showing that these factors together shape the structural contexts for student learning. School is one of such crucial structural contexts. Poor urban schools are often plagued by inadequate facilities, resources, and poorly trained and inexperienced teachers, making student learning difficult (Olsen, 1997).

Curricular Tracking

However, the conditions that perpetuate the achievement gap in the school setting include not only the location, quality of instruction, resources, and the perceptions and approaches used by school authorities and teachers (Anyon, 1997), but also high-stakes testing and systematic tracking. The Washington, DC-based Center on Education Policy has recently reported that in the 19 states that have high school exit exams, the percentage of English language learners who passed the math exit exam was 30-40 points lower than the average initial passing rates of 70 to 90% and that the gap in the reading exit exam was even larger (Sullivan et al., 2005, p. 90). In California, 49% of English Learners passed the math portion of the high school exit exam compared to 74% of all public school students that passed. Similarly, only 39% of English Learners passed the reading portion compared to 75% of all students that did so (Sullivan et al., 2005, p. 91). High-stakes testing has far-reaching consequences for low-income and linguistic minority students (Lucas & Good, 2001). One direct consequence of testing is tracking in academic curricula.

Empirical research has repeatedly shown that curricular tracking persists in urban schools, which are overrepresented by the poor and ethnic minorities. Ethnic minority students, especially resource-poor students, are disproportionately grouped as low-ability performers and tracked in remedial and non-college preparatory curricula for an extended period of time or even permanently (Lucas & Good, 2001; Oakes, 1985; Oakes, Gamoran, & Page, 1992). Compared to White students, Black, Hispanic, and Native American students reported lower enrollment in college preparatory courses, higher enrollment in vocational courses, and fewer opportunities for academic success (National Center for Education Statistics, 1997). Tracking also impacts students' long-term educational trajectories. The lack of equal access to college preparatory courses and advanced or honors courses hamper or even block their pathway to higher education (Alexander, Entwisle, & Horsey, 1997; Rosenbaum, 1980).

Empirical research has also found that the arbitrary classification of students into differentiated curricula can give rise to a number of sociocultural factors that exert independent effects on academic outcomes. Tracking generates self-fulfilling prophecies, which in turn inhibit students' motivation to learn, hold them back on track, and take away their chances of being reclassified into mainstream curricula (Braddock & Dawkins, 1993). Furthermore, tracking blocks students' access to positive social circles and role models (Byrne, 1988; Kubitschek & Hallinan, 1998). Moreover, tracking affects teachers' attitudes toward students and reinforces their differential expectations and instruction (Kerckhoff, 2001).

Classification by Language Proficiency

More recently, educational research on the new second generation—the children of Asian and Latin American immigrants—has examined the tracking system in K-12 schools and its differential impact on linguistic minority students (Gándara & Rumberger, 2003). These findings indicate that the achievement gap has become more severe in schools with disproportionately high numbers of low-income and immigrant minority students, and that students who are poor and do not speak English at home have a greater likelihood of dropping out of high school and that they often face a lifetime of diminished opportunity. Although linguistic minority students are considered one of the most academically needy groups, they have far less access to appropriately trained and qualified teachers than other students. Linguistic minority students are more likely than other students to be placed in classrooms where teachers are under-credentialed, if at all, and where most teachers hold "teacher in training" agreements (no certification) rather than hold full credentials such as the Bilingual Cross-Cultural, Language, and Academic Development and the Cross-Cultural, Language and Academic Development credentials (Gándara & Rumberger, 2003; Rumberger, 2000). In their study of teachers holding emergency credentials in California schools, Gándara, Rumberger, Maxwell-Jolly, and Callahan (2003) found that, even when controlling for poverty, "English learners are significantly less likely to have a fully credentialed teacher than other low- income non-EL students" (p. 9).

Structure Versus Culture

Empirical findings consistently confirm existing theories about the relationship between ethnicity and educational achievement. The structural approach to the effect of ethnicity on achievement focuses on the externally imposed ethnic categorization, which emphasizes the social positioning of the group so labeled and explains unequal educational outcomes in terms of the group's immigration histories (such as time since arrival), modes of incorporation (means of entry, official and societal receptions, and the strength of the preexisting ethnic community), and the average levels of human capital that the group possess, as well as the fit between their education and job skills and labor market requirements. This approach also views residential segregation as of paramount importance in determining groups' access to resources and upward mobility (Massey & Denton, 1987). The cultural approach, in contrast, focuses on the patterned—albeit not intrinsic—characteristics or behaviors of the group (Fukuyama, 1993; Sowell, 1981) and explains unequal outcomes in terms of the group's cultural repertoire which facilitates school success, including positive family socialization, high achievement motivation, industriousness, perseverance, future orientation, and ability to postpone immediate gratification for later rewards. Our argument falls somewhere between these two approaches to emphasize the interaction between structural and cultural components embedded in ethnicity. Although we recognize that a group's cultural repertoire often shapes how effectively group members deal with externally imposed institutional arrangements, we argue that structural factors such as linguistic categorization can exert profound impact on educational outcomes independent of individual family socioeconomic background. To understand the educational mobility of Hmong students, or of linguistic minority students more broadly, we examine the ways that state mandated classification, testing, and tracking operate as sequential and mutually reinforcing institutional practices to constrain educational mobility.

THE DISPLACED AND DISADVANTAGED: HMONG REFUGEES IN THE UNITED STATES

The massive Hmong refugee flight from highland Laos to the United States in the mid-1970s is directly linked to U.S. foreign policy and military intervention in Southeast Asia (Zhou & Bankston, 1998). In the aftermath of the U.S.-Vietnam conflict (1954-1975), hundreds of thousands of Vietnamese, Laotians, and Cambodians fled as political refugees to temporary camps in Thailand's countrysides and other parts of Southeast Asia. Hmong are a major ethnic group among the tens of thousands of Laotians who fled Laos after decades of war (Culas & Michaud, 2004).

The first wave of Hmong refugees arrived on United States in the late 1970s. Since that time, tens of thousands more Hmong refugees from Laos and Thailand were granted entry through the Migration and Refugee Assistance Act of 1975 and the Refugee Act of 1980 (Xiong, 2005). From 1990 to 2000, the Hmong population in the U.S. increased from 94,439 to 186,310, which represented a 97% increase (U.S. Census Bureau, 2000). In 2000, about 56% of the Hmong population in the United States was foreign born (U.S. Census Bureau, 2004). This is accounted for in part by the fact that Hmong persons under 18 years of age made up 55% of the Hmong American population while those 65 years and older made up only 3% (U.S. Census Bureau, 2004).

Despite Hmong's daily struggle to use whatever limited resources they can muster to make ends meet, they remain one of America's most underprivileged ethnic groups. As of 2000, nearly 60% of Hmong Americans aged 25 years or over had not completed high school, compared to 14% of non-Hispanic Whites, 19% of Asians, 28% of non-Hispanic Blacks, and 48% of Hispanics. Thirty-eight percent of Hmong Americans lived in poverty, compared to 8% of non-Hispanic Whites and 13% of Asians. While

Hmong's poverty rate was more than three times the national poverty rate, their poverty rate remained the highest among Southeast Asian refugee groups—Cambodians (29%), non-Hmong Laotians (19%), and Vietnamese (16%)—and higher than America's racial minority groups—non-Hispanic Blacks (22%) and Hispanics (21%). Nation-wide, Hmong's median family income was $32,384, compared to $54,698 for non-Hispanic White, $59,324 for Asians, $33,332 for non-Hispanic Blacks, and $34,397 for Hispanics.[2]

According to the U.S. Census Bureau, Hmong Americans in California displayed similarly low SES status. As of 2000, only 11% of Hmong adults over 25 years old had attained levels of an associate's, bachelor's or a graduate degree; Hmong men had a higher level of average education compared to Hmong women. Moreover, 38% of Hmong worked in 1999, which was much lower than the state's average employment rate (58%), but Hmong men had a higher employment rate (45%) than Hmong women (31%). The median family income in 1999 was $24,372 for Hmong in California, which was significantly lower than that for Hmong nation-wide ($32,384) and less than half of the state's overall median family income of $53,025 (U.S. Census Bureau, 2004).

Initial SES disadvantages associated with refugee status further exacerbate residential segregation among Hmong Americans. As a refugee group, Hmong's places of initial resettlement were largely decided by the government and sponsoring non-governmental organizations. Unlike other Asian immigrants who were assisted by families and preexisting ethnic communities and are thus geographically concentrated based on these family and ethnic networks, Hmong in the United States are highly concentrated in just three states—California (35%), Minnesota (22%), and Wisconsin (18%). Some of the negative effects of concentrated poverty were neutralized because many Hmong families resettled in semirural areas far removed from the urban core (albeit not completely isolated from working- and middle-class suburbs), or in urban peripheral areas sharing the same neighborhoods with other working-class Whites, Southeast Asians, Blacks, Hispanics, and Native Americans. However, given Hmong families' low SES backgrounds and persistent housing discrimination, they often found themselves in neighborhoods where other American families are poor, schools are inadequate, and parental access to political decision making positions are limited (even in urban spaces where their numerical size is substantial). In the next section, we analyze the specific ways that the public educational system operates to structure and reinforce social class and ethnic disadvantages of linguistic minority students. Specifically, we show how state policies, such as classification, selective testing, and tracking compound the class and ethnic disadvantages of 1.5 and 2nd generation Hmong students.

ETHNICITY, EDUCATIONAL POLICY, AND SCHOOL PRACTICES

English Learner Students in California's Public Schools

For more than four decades now, states, especially those most impacted by contemporary immigration, have faced the challenge of living up to the ideal of equal educational opportunity for all children regardless of race. In California, which has absorbed more than 30% of the total international migration flows into the United States since the late 1980s, the number of public school students requiring English language assistance is growing at unprecedented rates.[3] Mirroring the state's diverse demographic composition, California's 6.3 million K-12 student body in the public school system is made up of 46% Latino, 11% Asian, and 33% White; nearly half of the students come from low-income families.

California defines an English Learner (EL) student as "a child who does not speak English or whose native language is not English and who is not currently able to perform ordinary classroom work in English." In 1981, more than 376,000 students or 9% of all students enrolled in California's K-12 public schools were classified as EL students. Ten years later, this number increased more than twofold to over 986,000, constituting 19% of the total public school enrollment. Since 1998, EL students have consistently comprised 25% or more of California's public school enrollment. During the 2004-05 year, the number classified as EL increased further to 1.6 million, representing about a third of elementary school pupils and 21% of middle school or high school students in California (CA Dept. of Education, 2004b). In comparison, less than 10% (or 4 million) of all K-12 public school students in the United States as a whole were classified as EL students; about 40% of the EL students in the United States attended school in California (U.S. Department. of Education, 2005).

Moreover, data from the California Department of Education (2004b) show that over 90% of EL students speak one of the top five non-English languages: Spanish (85.1%), Vietnamese (2.2%), Cantonese and Mandarin (2.1%), Hmong (1.5%), and Tagalog (1.3%). Table 3.1. shows that of California's 1.6 million EL students, about 60% were enrolled in grades K-5, 20% in Grades 6-8, and 20% in Grades 9-12. Since most English Learners of all groups are enrolled in the elementary grades and academic tracking starts early on for linguistic minority students, we should examine students' disadvantages as the product of cumulative processes rather than simply as discrete factors or events.

Spanish speaking students, most of whom are of Mexican or Central American origins, are by far the largest group of English learners. They comprise more than three-fourths of all EL students in California since 1981 when the state began to use the term "Limited English Proficient" to

Table 3.1.   English Learner Students in California by Grades, Academic Year 2004-05

Rank/Language Name	Percent in K-5th	Percent in 6th-8th	Percent in 9th-12th	Total EL**	Percent Total
1. Spanish	60.3	20.0	18.3	1,357,778	85.3
2. Vietnamese	65.4	15.3	18.8	34,333	2.2
3. Hmong	51.5	23.8	24.7	22,776	1.4
4. Cantonese	64.2	14.4	21.0	22,475	1.4
5. Filipino (or Tagalog)	60.2	17.6	21.4	20,939	1.3
6. Korean	58.2	18.9	22.2	16,463	1.0
7. Mandarin (Putonghua)	56.2	15.5	28.2	11,825	0.7
8. Armenian	56.6	19.1	22.4	9,698	0.6
9. Khmer (Cambodian)	48.2	22.5	29.1	9,563	0.6
10. Punjabi	58.6	17.6	23.6	9,259	0.6
11. All Other Languages*	59.9	17.9	21.6	,76,416	4.8
Total	60.2	19.7	18.9	1,591,525	100.0

*Includes 48 other identified non-English languages and unidentified non-English languages.
**Includes a relatively few number of EL students reported as ungraded.

Source: California Department of Education (2004b).

classify linguistic minority students. Currently, they make up over 85%. Students of Asian, Pacific Islander, and Filipino languages comprise about 171,000 (not shown), or 11% of the state's EL population. It is also important to note that Southeast Asian students of Vietnamese, Hmong, and Khmer languages have remained among the top 10 largest groups of EL students in California since the mid-1990s. Furthermore, data from the California Department of Education's (2004c) Educational Demographics Office show that, from 1995 through 2005, of all the 10 major language groups, Hmong and Spanish students have consistency been the only two groups with the greatest ratio of English Learners to fluent English proficient students. Specifically, during academic years 1995-06, 2000-01, and 2004-05, the number of Hmong students classified as English Learners was 85% (of a total enrollment of 36,765), 80% (of 33,870), and 71% (of 32,225), respectively. In 2005-06, the most recent year for which data are available, 68% of all Hmong students were classified as English Learners while 32% were classified as fluent English proficient. A relatively high proportion of Spanish speakers was classified as English Learners—65% in 2005, down from 73% in 1995. In contrast to the Hmong and Spanish cases, during 2005, the proportion of students classified as English Learners for the Mandarin-speaking category was 25%; for Korean, 35%, Tagalog, 35%, and Cantonese, 38%.

Since most Hmong students, like their peers of Latino or Southeast Asian ethnicity, come from underprivileged family backgrounds, state-mandated classification and testing policies, which aim to help them, often actually have the opposite result. Next, we zoom in on the Home Language Survey (HLS) and the California English Language Development Test (CELDT) and discuss their effects on linguistic minority students.

State-Mandated Classification and Testing Policies

The federal No Child Left Behind Act of 2001 aims to ensure that all schools are held accountable for students' academic progress. In compliance with the Act, the California legislature modified its state education codes, mandating the use of the state-approved Home Language Survey to identify linguistic minority students and the development of the CELDT to assess the English proficiency level of students identified as linguistic minority students.4 Accordingly, all public school districts must administer the HLS to enrolled students and, based on the responses to this survey, determine if some of them must also be administered the CELDT. The HLS asks the student's parent or legal guardian to respond to each of the following questions: (1) Which language did your son or daughter learn when he or she first began to speak? (2) What language does your son or daughter most frequently use at home? (3) What language do you use most frequently to speak to your son or daughter? (4) Name the language most often spoken by adults at home. If a language other than English is listed on any of the first three questions, the student is required to take the CELDT. English monolingual speakers—those who speak only English at home—are exempt from taking the CELDT and are often automatically placed into mainstream curricula.

While the state's stated purpose is to use the HLS to identify a student's home language, California's Education Code does not actually define what "home language" means, nor does the Code take account of the real possibility that many ethnic minority homes use more than one language (e.g., adults and children speak English and a non-English language on a regular basis). Because the HLS is limited to four questions, it is reasonable to assume that schools sometimes use only the parent's primary language or only the language that adults in the home most often speak as the indicator of the student's home language. This occurs even if a child is born in the United States and resides in a home where his/her siblings speak, read, and write in English—which is often the case in many immigrant families. For example, a recent report from Fresno Unified School District reveals that 80 to 90% of the District's students classified as English Learners were U.S.-born children (Garcia, 2003). Given school-age children's frequent exposure to a multitude of bilingual and multilingual sources, including mass media, linguistically diverse neighborhoods and school environments, it would be unreasonable to assume that today's generation of children are monolingual speakers.

The CELDT, a test with no time limit, has three broad purposes: (1) to identify new students who are English Learners in kindergarten through Grade twelve; (2) to monitor EL students' progress in learning English; and (3) to help decide when EL students can be reclassified as fluent English proficient (FEP) (California Department of Education, 2004a). The CELDT tests students on different language skill areas depending on their grade level. Furthermore, state law requires that kindergarten students take the CELDT for "initial identification [purposes] only." However, the "initial identification" requirement warrants closer scrutiny. Current practices across school districts suggest that many kindergarten students, native born and non-native alike, by default become *preidentified* as English Learners even before they are administered the CELDT, because of their ascribed linguistic minority status. The CELDT tests kindergarten and first grade students on listening and speaking skills. For students in Grades 2 through 12, the CELDT tests listening, speaking, reading, and writing skills. Within these skill areas, there are five levels of English proficiency at which a student can achieve: beginning, early intermediate, intermediate, early advanced, and advanced. The State Board of Education establishes the cut-off points and criteria for determining English proficiency based on the CELDT. To be classified, or reclassified as fluent English proficient, a student must score at or above the "early advanced" level overall *and* must not score below intermediate proficiency level in any particular skill area (California Department of Education, 2004a, pp. 3-4).

Under current federal and state law, however, once a student has been identified as a language-minority, parents cannot have that child exempted from taking the CELDT. On the other hand, if responses on the HLS indicate that a student or his/her parents speak only English as a primary language such student is classified as "English Only" and automatically exempted from the CELDT. As mandated by the state, all students, whose home language is not English, must take the CELDT within 30 calendar days after they are enrolled in a California public school for the first time to determine if they are EL students. Once classified as an English Learner, a student must be given the CELDT once a year until he/she can meet reclassification criteria or be reclassified as FEP. Students with a disability who fall under the EL category must also take the CELDT (California Department of Education, 2004a, p. 3).

The practice of "initial identification" within the first 30 days of enrollment, therefore, indiscriminately targets students whose parents speak a language other than English without any regard for the child's actual potential as a *native-born* English speaker. Moreover, some English-fluent students, out of necessity, commonly, though not exclusively, speak a non-English language in the home (e.g., in order to communicate with parents who do not "fully" understand English). The HLS ignores these real possibilities. Given that Hmong as a group has been in the United States for less than 30 years, almost all Hmong children are members of the 1.5 and 2nd generations who are just coming of age. Since almost all Hmong students grow up in refugee or immigrant families where the home language is non-English, they are disproportionately affected by the state's practice of using the HLS to classify students as non-native English speakers.

These school practices ascribe linguistic minority status to students and subject them to mandatory testing, which even some native speakers may find difficult to pass,[5] and make it very likely that most of the linguistic minority students will end up being classified as English Learners during most of their early educational career. If a student is unable to demonstrate English proficiency as measured by the CELDT, he/she is placed in one of four possible instructional settings. Table 3.2 shows the types of

Table 3.2.   Number of English Learners Enrolled in Specific Instructional Settings

	1998-99 Statewide Total Number (Percent)	2000-01 Statewide Total Number (Percent)	2002-03 Statewide Total Number (Percent)	2004-05 Statewide Total Number (Percent)
(1) Mainstream Courses*	416,962 (28.9)	472,599 (31.3)	550,437 (34.4)	613,729 (38.6)
(2) Mainstream Courses upon Parental Request	44,947 (3.1)	44,921 (3.0)	42,400 (2.7)	32,132 (2.0)
(3) Structured English Immersion	702,592 (48.7)	720,948 (47.7)	773,132 (48.3)	755,137 (47.4)
(4) Alternative Courses of Study	179,334 (12.4)	181,455 (12.0)	153,029 (9.6)	120,849 (7.6)
(5) Other Instructional Settings	98,857 (6.9)	91,376 (6.0)	80,544 (5.0)	69,678 (4.4)
Total Number of EL	1,442,692 (100.0)	1,511,299 (100.0)	1,599,542 (100.0)	1,591,525 (100.0)

*Refers to regular courses where English is the medium of instruction.

Source: California Department of Education's (2006) CELDT Reports: http://celdt.cde.ca.gov/reports.asp/

instructional settings into which EL students have been placed since 1998. According to the California State Board of Education, 60 to 70% of EL students are *not* in mainstream classrooms where the English language is the medium of instruction. During 2004-05, about 63% of EL students were placed in structured English immersion, alternative courses of study, and other instructional settings. These settings are separate from the mainstream curriculum.

Reclassification Criteria and Long Term Tracking

California law states that school districts shall "continue to provide additional and appropriate educational services to EL students in kindergarten through Grade 12 until these EL students have demonstrated the level of English proficiency comparable to that of average native English speakers and have recouped any academic deficits which may have been incurred in other areas of the core curriculum as a result of language barriers."[6] The State Board of Education establishes a set of formal criteria for the reclassification of former EL to FEP status, requiring all school districts to develop student reclassification policy and procedures based on four reclassification criteria approved by the Board. These four criteria involve: (1) a review of an individual student's results on the latest California English-Language Arts Standards Test; (2) a review of the student's CELDT results from the annual assessment; (3) the teacher's evaluation of the student's academic performance; and (4) parent opinion and consultation (California Department of Education, 2004b, pp. iv-1 & iv1-iv3). EL students may be transferred from a Structured English Immersion Program to a Mainstream English Language Program when they have acquired a "good working knowledge"[7] of English *and* have satisfied all reclassification criteria.

Among English Learners, there were significant gains in the proficiency levels of EL students between academic years 2001 and 2005. As shown in Table 3.3, all EL students who participated in the annual CELDT assessments between 2001 and 2005 showed overall gains over time, with a much smaller percentage of students in the lower proficiency levels and a greater percentage in the higher proficiency levels. As shown, 48% of California EL students scored at early advanced or advanced in overall English proficiency, compared to 43% scoring at the same level in 2003, to 34% in 2002, and 25% in 2001—an increase of 23% between 2001 and 2005.

These results seem to suggest that California's state-mandated classification and selective testing of linguistic minority students appear to have some positive effects on test scores. However, we caution that behind the

Table 3.3.   Annual CELDT Assessments: 2001 to 2005
Percent of K-12 English Learners by Overall CELDT Proficiency Level

Overall Proficiency Level	2001-02 Percent of English Learners	2002-03 Percent of English Learners	2003-04 Percent of English Learners	2004-05 Percent of English Learners
Beginning	11	10	7	7
Early Intermediate	23	19	14	13
Intermediate	40	37	36	33
Early Advanced	21	25	32	33
Advanced	4	9	11	15
Total Percent	100	100	100	100
Total Number	1,262,296	1,297,435	1,357,754	1,342,954

Source: California Department of Education (2004d); CELDT Reports: http://celdt.cde.ca.gov/reports.asp/

seemingly optimistic statistics, three points are worth noting. First, California has the greatest number of students whose primary language is not English and the number of EL students enrolled in the State's public schools is disproportionately larger than any other state in the U.S. With respect to Hmong students, California also has the most number of Hmong students compared to states such as Minnesota, North Carolina, and Wisconsin. Thus, Hmong and other EL students in California are more likely than their coethnic peers elsewhere to be trapped in such a structural disadvantage.

Second, the percent of EL students who scored below early advanced level of English proficiency is still substantially high. For example, in 2004-05, the percent of EL students that scored below early advanced was 53%. Differences across grade levels and across language groups are significant. Examination of the CELDT annual assessment scores by grade levels (not shown) shows that during 2001-02, 82% of all first grade EL students scored *below* the early advanced level, compared to 86% of second graders, 90% of third graders, 81% of fourth graders and 72% of fifth graders. In that same year, 69% of middle school students (Grades 6-8) and 55% of high school students scored below early advanced.

Third, despite the apparent increase in the percentage of EL students scoring at or above early advanced since 2001, only a small percentage of EL students has been reclassified to FEP status. As Table 3.4 shows, the absolute number of students classified as EL steadily increased while the proportion remained at 25% between 1995 and 2005. Each year, the number of FEP students and that of EL students who were "tested out" of EL status increased slightly, but the proportions remained either unchanged or increased very modestly. Since the CELDT is the primary instrument used to determine student's "proficiency" in English, one would expect that as EL students' CELDT scores increase, the rate at which they become redesignated to FEP status should also increase. However, the percent of EL students reclassified has increased by only 1% during 2001 and 2005, even though the percentage of students achieving English proficiency status increased by about 23%.

As shown in the table 3.4, the overall reclassification rate remains below 10%. The evidence that over 90% of EL students consistently do not become reclassified raises serious questions about the concrete benefits, if any, that high CELDT scores actually have for students. The California Legislative Analyst's Office, using CELDT data from 2002, found in their simulations that "60 percent of those who begin attending schools in California after kindergarten, never become reclassified by twelfth grade" (Warren, 2004, p. 17). Next, we turn to discuss some major consequences of tracking and analyze how tracking limits EL students' access to college.

Language Tracking as an Obstacle to Higher Education

Tracking in California public schools takes many forms, one of which is English Language Development (ELD) placement. EL students who do

Table 3.4.   Percent Distribution of EL Students, FEP Students, and Redesignated FEP Students in California, 1995-2005

Year	CA Total K-12 Enrollment	Number of EL Students (% of Enrollment)	Number of FEP Students (% of Enrollment)	Number of Redesignated FEP Students (% of EL in Previous Year)
2004-05	6,322,167	1,591,525 (25.2)	1,064,578 (16.8)	143,136 (9.0)
2003-04	6,298,774	1,598,535 (25.4)	999,690 (15.9)	133,214 (8.3)
2002-03	6,244,642	1,599,542 (25.6)	931,869 (14.9)	120,122 (7.7)
2001-02	6,147,375	1,559,248 (25.4)	878,139 (14.3)	117,450 (7.8)
2000-01	6,050,895	1,511,299 (25.0)	844,387 (14.0)	133,964 (9.0)
1999-00	5,951,612	1,480,527 (24.9)	791,283 (13.3)	112,214 (7.8)
1998-99	5,844,111	1,442,692 (24.7)	758,363 (13.0)	106,288 (7.6)
1997-98	5,727,303	1,406,166 (24.6)	720,479 (12.6)	96,545 (7.0)
1996-97	5,612,965	1,381,393 (24.6)	682,004 (12.2)	89,144 (6.7)
1995-96	5,467,224	1,323,767 (24.2)	649,130 (11.9)	81,733 (6.5)

Source: California Department of Education (2004b).

not become reclassified into FEP status by ninth grade are usually placed in ELD classrooms when they enter high school. Such placement normally corresponds to their placement in other courses, such as a remedial or regular math course as opposed to a college-preparatory, honors or Advanced Placement (AP) math course. Other students not subject to ELD placement, including those formerly classified as EL, are generally placed in college-preparatory or AP English, math, science, and social studies courses. Moreover, schools commonly require students to demonstrate proficiency in English before they are given access to grade-level math and science courses or other regular courses.

As a result, many EL students are tracked into remedial or compensatory classes before they can access mainstream curricula and college preparatory courses (Berman et al., 1992, as cited in Heubert & Hauser, 1999). Evidence from one of California's largest school districts, Fresno Unified School District (FUSD), shows that there are disparities in the enrollment of EL students in college preparatory curricula, gifted programs, and AP or honors courses. At FUSD, more than three-quarters (79%) of the students received free or reduced lunch, 29% of the students enrolled (23,597) were classified as EL during 2004-05 (California Department of Education, 2004b). Spanish speakers make up 65% of all EL students, while Hmong speakers make up 25%.[8] At least 8,279 Hmong students were enrolled during 2003, comprising 10% of FUSD's student population, or more than 60% of the Asian Pacific Islander student body.[9] Data from FUSD show that, from 2001 through 2003, more than 80% of Hmong students were classified as English Learners, while 17% were classified as fluent English proficient (FUSD Office of Research, Evaluation and Assessment, 2003).

FUSD's Office of Research reports that, in 2003, only 8% of EL students in high school were enrolled in Gifted and Talented Education (GATE) programs, compared to 70% of English-Only students. Moreover, only 11% of EL students in high school were enrolled in honors or advanced placement courses, compared to 67% of English-Only students. Furthermore, the percentage of redesignated-FEP students enrolled in AP/honors was higher than that of EL students, but still lower than that of English-Only students. For example, in 1998, only 15% of R-FEP students were enrolled in GATE. That same year, 19% of R-FEP students were enrolled in AP/honors courses. Five years later, in 2003, the percentage of R-FEP students enrolled in GATE and AP/honors courses increased only slightly to 22% and 22% respectively (Garcia, 2003, p. 16). EL students are thus placed at a distinct structural disadvantage compared to non-EL and redesignated-FEP students.

The lack of access to college preparatory courses and AP courses seriously limits EL students' opportunity to enter higher education in direct and indirect ways. Directly, public four-year colleges, such as the University of California (UC) and California State University campuses (CSU), as well as other private 4-year universities, have stringent minimum academic requirements for admissions; however, meeting minimum requirements alone rarely ensures admission. FUSD's Office of Research reports that EL students have comparatively lower enrollment in college preparatory courses that meet the *minimum* course requirements for enrollment in the University of California and California State University campuses. In 2003, English-Only, redesignated FEP, and EL students comprised 61%, 11%, and 28%, respectively, of FUSD's total enrollment. Only 14% of EL students met the UC minimum course requirements compared to 32% of English-Only students (Garcia, 2003, p. 17).

Indirectly, the lack of access to college preparatory and AP courses implies that EL students are less likely to be in classes with highly qualified teachers who can provide students with college-level work and exposure to a pre-college culture that can prepare these students for college (Contreras, 2005). Moreover, being tracked in EL status reinforces the stigmatization of students' low ability and low performance, which has negative impact on EL students' college aspiration and motivation to do well. A student who does not or cannot enroll in GATE may think of him or herself as untalented, less smart, and less capable. Such a self-fulfilling process contributes to low expectation and low motivation, which may result in lower chances of applying to college.

Considering that college preparatory and AP courses can offer intellectually challenging contents, boost students' grade point averages and self-esteem, as well as learning skills, attitudes and habits expected in the college environment, and that colleges value these advanced courses more highly than regular courses, linguistic minority students' under representation in these courses translates to lesser chances of being admitted into college. Even if they get admitted to college, we think they may be less likely to graduate on time and at a higher risk of dropping out than other better-prepared students.

IMPLICATIONS FOR HMONG STUDENTS IN CALIFORNIA

What implications do these processes of state-mandated testing, classification, and tracking of linguistic minority students have for the children of Hmong refugees in particular? While we are concerned with the experiences of English Learners in general, we are especially concerned with English Learners of Hmong ethnic background, because of the overrepresentation of Hmong students in EL and ELD programs and because their ethnic communities have limited economic and political resources with which to counter educational disadvantages.

Hmong students in K-12 schools comprised approximately 22,000, or 4.4% of California's Asian student population and about 0.3% of the state's total K-12 student population (6,300,000) in 2003-04. Yet, of all linguistic minority students, only Hmong and Spanish-speaking students were overrepresented as English Learners and underrepresented as fluent English proficient. For example, in 2001, Hmong students made up 1.4% of the state's 2,355,686 linguistic minority students; yet, Hmong constituted 1.8% of all English Learners and only 0.8% of all fluent English proficient students (California Department of Education, 2004c). Since 1992, Hmong students have been reported year after year as comprising the third largest EL group statewide, trailing only Vietnamese and Spanish students. It is understandable that many of these students were placed in bilingual programs to help them acquire English language skills while also learning core curriculum materials.[10] However, it is unacceptable and discriminatory that virtually all Hmong children, including an overwhelming majority that was born in the United States, are continually selected for testing on the basis of their ascribed linguistic minority status.

The number of Hmong EL students continues to grow even when the number of U.S.-born among them increases each year. Given native-born peoples' rate of language acquisition and assimilation, it is hard to believe that native-born Hmong children would experience the same language deficiencies that foreign-born or immigrant children experience. That Hmong students experience institutional impediments to education rather than merely personal ones is suggested by California's Legislative Analyst's Office's (LAO) report on the number of years it would take for EL students to become reclassified as proficient. In 2004, the LAO projected that the number of years it would take until 50% of all Hmong EL students get reclassified is 7.4 years (Warren, 2004, p. 21). This projected length of time is longer than the projections for any other EL student population. Throughout the LAO's 31 page report, however, not a single question was raised about the selective classification, testing and tracking of ethnic-linguistic minority students. Nor was any question raised concerning the validity or legitimacy of the CELDT. Despite having ignored these issues, the LAO recognized the problem of long-term non-reclassification of English Learners.

Long-term or permanent placement in ELD curricula translates directly to denial of access to mainstream classroom instruction, to fully credentialed teachers, to programs such as GATE, and to college preparatory and advanced placement courses. The lack of access to these resources and services could result in severely diminished access to other tangible resources and opportunities beyond high school, such as higher education and high-prestige occupations. Of the 65,000 Hmong in California recorded in the 2000 U.S. Census, no more than 600 (less than 1%) Hmong undergraduate and graduate students are currently enrolled in the 10 campuses of the University of California.

CONCLUSION

We have shown that the economic disadvantages impeding Hmong students' chances of success are inadvertently exacerbated by educational policy and practices in California. We point out the unintended consequences of these policies, namely, that linguistic segregation is inherently unequal because it creates and maintains educational inequality. There are no straightforward remedies to these structural problems, however. Informed by our analysis above, we offer some provisional policy recommendations.

First, the processes of classification, testing, and tracking reinforce one another from very early on in a student's education and these processes can have irreversible effects on a student's academic opportunities and outcome. State policies on linguistic minority students must ensure that students and families are aware of what each step of the language classification, testing, and placement, and reclassification process entails, and provide appropriate opportunities early on in K-12 for parents and students to effectively intervene in a student's education. Many immigrant and refugee parents may not be informed about the socially recognized ways of intervening in their children's education, for example, requesting that their children be appropriately placed in rigorous curricula and ensuring their timely advancements. One way to address this issue is to regularly inform parents and students *in their native language* about specific and realistic channels through which they can contest academic placement decisions and request placement changes.

Second, the method of using the Home Language Survey to identify linguistic minority students for testing and subsequent placement in ELD, is biased. This survey does not take account of the real possibility that many ethnic minority and immigrant families speak English alongside their native language(s) at home. If the state's intention is to determine all students' initial English proficiency level in order to place them in the appropriate curricula, the minimum that the state should do is to require that all able students, not just linguistic minorities, be tested with the CELDT or some other valid, reliable test of English skills.

Third, tests are not always valid, reliable or unbiased measures of students' performance; classification and placement decisions based solely on test scores is flawed and unfair. The state must ensure that tests are fair and valid and that the decision to classify or place linguistic minority students is based on a review of multiple relevant factors, rather than test scores alone. Linguistic minority students' scores on the CELDT may be influenced more by their low socioeconomic status, their lack of exposure to the materials being measured, and/or their poor test-taking skills, than by their actual English skills and knowledge. Given the fact that the CELDT is normed on an English-speaking population and that "proficiency" is based on the number of questions answered correctly, *any* cutscore (other than zero) specified by the test maker can result in students, including English proficient students, being classified as English Learners (Rossell, 2000; Rossell, 2002). For example, before placing a student in an English Language Development course, a teacher should consult with previous teachers regarding a student's level of engagement and performance on other academic activities in the classroom besides speaking and writing English.

Fourth, the state's criteria for reclassification are illogical. Complicated reclassification criteria make the pathway out of the nonmainstream system extremely difficult, thus placing an undue burden on linguistic minority students. While a low score on the CELDT is used as the *primary* justification for classifying and tracking linguistic minorities, a decent performance on the annual CELDT often serves but *one* of the several criteria for reclassification into fluent English proficient status. Under current state law, there is yet another dilemma for EL students: an EL student may be "*re-enrolled* in a structured English immersion program" if he or she "has *not* achieved a reasonable level of English proficiency" (emphasis added).[11] What this means is that an EL student can be considered proficient in English at one point in time, and then be considered not proficient in English at a later period. This practice of reenrolling redesignated-FEP students in ELD curricula should be entirely abolished.

Last but not least, state policies on linguistic minority students must ensure that all EL students have equal access to English language mainstream curricula and quality instruction. This means that schools must ensure that an EL student enrolls in rigorous mainstream English language courses as well as mainstream math, science, social science and other core courses. If some students must be placed in ELD curricula, then states and school districts must improve the quality of the ELD programs, including teaches' qualifications and the rigor of curricula. For instance, they should ensure that teachers have proper training and preparation for teaching and assisting non-native speakers at each grade level. Regardless of whether they are part of "mainstream" or ELD curricula, low-level tracks with ineffective curricula should be entirely eliminated at all grade levels; all linguistic minority students should be enrolled, at a minimum, in rigorous, enriching courses, with bilingual assistance provided as necessary.

Although our study focuses on English Learners in California, it has broader implications for policy beyond California. We reiterate our argument that policy and institutional practices, especially state-mandated classification, selective testing and tracking may limit linguistic minority students' educational choices, their access to quality academic programs, and their opportunity to advance beyond high school. Thus, policymakers must be mindful of these unintended consequences.

NOTES

1. Throughout this article we use the phrase "linguistic minority students" to refer to all students whose primary home language is other than English.
2. U.S. Census Bureau, American Fact Finder http://factfinder.census.gov/
3. 2003 Statistical Year book of the US Citizenship and Immigration Services, Table 11.
4. CA Education Code §313, 60810, and 60812.
5. For example, when the Chicago Board of Education administered a widely used test, the Language Assessment Scales (LAS), to above-average students who spoke only English, almost half of these students were misclassified as non- or limited English proficient. Interestingly, 78% of the English monolingual 5-year-olds, but only 25% of the 14-year-olds, were classified as LEP (cited in Rossell, 2000, p. 146). CTB/McGraw Hill is the test contractor for the CELDT, which is, according to Rossell (2002), "purported to be an adaptation of the LAS to the new California ELD (English Language Development) standards" (p. 25).
6. CA Code of Regulations, Title 5, §11302.
7. CA Education Code §305 does not define what "good working knowledge of English" means. California Code of Regulations (Title 5, §11301) states only that these levels of English proficiency are to be measured by "any of the state-designated assessments approved by the California Department of Education, or any locally developed assessments."
8. Figures obtained from the Education Data Partnership website, under Fresno Unified School District. Retrieved from http://www.ed-data.k12.ca.us/welcome.asp
9. FUSD Office of Research, Evaluation and Assessment (2003) R-30 Primary Language Counts.
10. Debates on the effectiveness/ineffectiveness of "Bilingual programs" remain highly politicized and are beyond the scope of this article.
11. California Code of Regulations, Title 5, §11301.

REFERENCES

Alexander, K. L., Entwisle, D. R., & Horsey, C. S. (1997). From first grade forward: Early foundations of high school dropout. *Sociology of Education, 70*(2), 87-107.

Anyon, J. (1997). *Ghetto schooling: A political economy of urban educational reform.* New York, NY: Teachers College Press.

Berman, P., Chambers, J., Gándara, P., McLaughlin, B., Minicucci, C., Nelson, B., et al. (1992). *Meeting the challenge of language diversity: An evaluation of programs for pupils with limited proficiency in English.* Berkeley, CA: BW Associates.

Braddock, J. H., & Dawkins, M. P. (1993). Ability grouping, aspirations, and attainments: Evidence from the National Educational Longitudinal Study of 1988. *Journal of Negro Education, 62*(3), 324-336.

Byrne, B. M. (1988). Adolescent self-concept, ability grouping, and social comparison: Reexamining academic track differences in high school. *Youth and Society, 20*(1), 46-67.

California Department of Education. (2004a). *Media assistance packet for school districts/schools.* California English Language Development Test (CELDT), pp. 1-10. Retrieved from http://www.cde.ca.gov/ta/tg/el/documents/mediapkt304.pdf/

California Department of Education. (2004b). *Language census data 2003-04. DataQuest.* Retrieved from http://data1.cde.ca.gov/dataquest/

California Department of Education. (2004c). *Student demographics and enrollment. DataQuest.* Retrieved from http://data1.cde.ca.gov/dataquest/

California Department of Education. (2004d). *Glossary.* Retrieved from http://data1.cde.ca.gov/dataquest/gls_ElPart2.asp/

California Department of Education. (2006). *California English Language Development Test (CELDT) notes.* Retrieved from http://www.cde.ca.gov/ta/tg/sa/june06celdtnotes.asp

Contreras, F. E. (2005). Access, achievement, and social capital: Standardized exam and the Latino college-bound population. *Journal of Hispanic Higher Education, 4*(3), 197-214.

Cornell, S. & Hartmann, D. (1998). *Ethnicity and race: Making identities in a changing world.* Thousand Oaks, CA: SAGE.

Culas, C., & Michaud, J. (2004). A contribution to the study of Hmong (Miao) migrations and history. In N. Tapp, J. Michaud, C. Culas, & G. Y. Lee (Eds.), *Hmong/Miao in Asia* (pp. 61-96). Thailand: Silkworm Books.

Fresno Unified School District. Office of Research, Evaluation and Assessment (OREA). (2003). *R-30 2003 Primary language counts.* Retrieved from http://rea.fresno.k12.ca.us/District/R30PrimLang2003.pdf

Fukuyama, F. (1993). Immigrants and family values. *Commentary, 95,* 26-32.

Gándara, P., & Rumberger, R. (2003). The inequitable treatment of English learners in California's public schools. Working paper 2003-01. University of California Linguistic Minority Research Institute.

Gándara, P., Rumberger, R., Maxwell-Jolly, J., & Callahan, R. (2003). English learners in California schools: Unequal resources, unequal outcomes. *Educational Policy Analysis Archives, 11,* 1-54.

Garcia, P. A. (2003). *Annual English learner evaluation report 2002-2003.* FUSD. Office of Research, Evaluation and Assessment. Retrieved from http://rea.fresno.k12.ca.us/District/el0203eval.pdf

Heubert, J. P., & Hauser, R. M. (Eds.). (1999). *High stakes: Testing for tracking, promotion, and graduation.* Washington, DC: National Academy Press.

Jenkins, R. (1994). Rethinking ethnicity: Identity, categorization and power. *Ethnic and Racial Studies, 17*, 197-223.

Kao, G., & Jennifer S. Thompson. (2003). Racial and ethnic stratification in educational achievement and attainment. *Annual Review of Sociology, 24*, 417-442.

Kerckhoff, A. C. (2001). Education and social stratification processes in comparative perspective. *Sociology of Education, 74*, 3-18.

Kubitschek, W. N., & Hallinan, M. T. (1998). Tracking and students' friendships. *Social Psychology Quarterly, 61*(1), 1-15.

Lucas, S. R. & Good, A. D. (2001). Race, class, and tournament track mobility. *Sociology of Education, 74*(2), 139-156.

Mare, R. D. (1995). Changes in educational attainment and school enrollment. In R. Farley (Ed.), *State of the Union: America in the 1990s: Vol. 1. Economic trends* (pp. 155–213). New York, NY: Russell Sage Foundation.

Massey, D. S., & Denton, N. A. (1987). Trends in the residential segregation of blacks, Hispanics, and Asians. *American Sociological Review, 52*, 802-825.

Miller L. S. (1995). *An American imperative: Accelerating minority educational advancement.* New Haven, CT: Yale University Press.

National Center for Education Statistics. (1997). *Digest of education statistics.* U.S. Department of Education: Office of Educational Research Improvement.

Ngo, B., & Lee, Stacey J. (2007). Complicating the image of model minority success: A review of Southeast Asian American education. *Review of Educational Research, 77*(4), 415-53.

Oakes, J. (1985). *Keeping track: How schools structure inequality.* New Haven, CT: Yale University Press.

Oakes, J., Gamoran, A., & Page, R. N. (1992). Curricular differentiation: Opportunities, outcomes, and meanings. In P. W. Jackson (Ed.), *Handbook of research on curriculum* (pp. 570-608). New York, NY: State University of New York Press.

Olsen, L. (1997). *Made in America.* New York, NY: The Free Press.

Rosenbaum, J. E. (1980). Track misperceptions and frustrated college plans: An analysis of the effects of tracks and track perceptions in the National Longitudinal Survey. *Sociology of Education, 53*(2), 74-88.

Rossell, C. H. (2000). Different questions, different answers: A critique of the Hakuta, Butler, and Witt report, "How long does it take English learners to attain proficiency?" *READ Perspectives, 7*, 134-154.

Rossell, C. H. (2002). Dismantling bilingual education, implementing English immersion: The California initiative. Department of Political Science, Boston University.

Rumberger, R. W. (2000). *Educational outcomes and opportunities for English language learners.* Presentation to the Joint Committee to develop the Master Plan for Education Kindergarten through University. University of California Linguistic Minority Research Institute.

Sowell, T. (1981). *Ethnic America: A history.* New York, NY: Basic Books.

Sullivan, P., Yeager, M., Chudowsky, N., Kober, N., O'Brien, E., & Gayler, K. (2005). *States try harder, but gaps persist: High school exit exams.* Washington, DC: Center for Education Policy.

U.S. Census Bureau. (2000). *Special profile: Selected racial groups and specific origin of Hispanic or Latino*. Census 2000, Summary File 1.

U.S. Census Bureau. (2004). *We the people: Asians in the United States*. Census 2000 Special Reports. Issued December, 2004.

U.S. Department of Education. (2000). *The condition of education 2000, NCES 2000-602*. Washington, DC: Government Printing Office.

U.S. Department of Education. (2005). *Biennial evaluation report to congress on the implementation of the state formula grant program, 2002-2004*.

Warren, P. (2004). A look at the progress of English learner students. California Legislative Analyst's Office. Retrieved from http://www.lao.ca.gov/2004/english_learners/021204_english_learners.pdf

Weber, M. (1968). *Economy and society*. G. Roth & C. Wittich (Eds.). Berkeley, CA: University of California Press.

Xiong, Y. S. (2005). *An analysis of poverty in Hmong American communities*. Unpublished master's thesis, University of California, Los Angeles.

Zhou, M., & Bankston, C. L., III. (1998). *Growing up American: How Vietnamese children adapt to life in the United States*. New York, NY: Russell Sage Foundation Press.

CHAPTER 4

RACIAL TRANSFORMATIONS IN HIGHER EDUCATION

Emergent Meanings of Asian American Racial Identities[1]

Michelle Samura

This chapter examines shifts in Asian American racial identities—their meanings, importance, and utility—within the context of higher education. Particular emphasis is placed on students' interpretations of race-making processes. Drawing on frameworks, methods, and findings from a larger mixed methods study on the contradictory experiences of Asian American college students, this chapter investigates the uncertainties and varying experiences of students "from below." That is, rather than assuming that Asian American students, and Asian Americans more generally, are already located within the contemporary U.S. racial order, my perspective emphasizes their efforts to position themselves. This inquiry reveals how meanings of higher education space (i.e., freedom, opportunity, and mobility) converge with meanings of race (i.e., Asian Americans as a model minority with increased social mobility and high levels of academic achievement) and result in an emergent version of "Asian American-ness" that is primarily characterized by individual choice and ongoing dilemmas.

Asian American Education—Identities, Racial Issues, and
Languages, pp. 73–99
Copyright © 2011 by Information Age Publishing
All rights of reproduction in any form reserved.

The importance of Asian American racial identity for Asian American college students is changing. Racial identities were once a defining aspect of students' lives, and one's race often dictated experiences and determined opportunities. Although race is still a factor, Asian American college students today have an expanded set of possibilities that were not available to previous generations. For the Asian American students in this study, opportunities and possibilities unlike ever before are understood to be within reach. At the same time, they must still wrestle with past and present meanings of Asian American racial identity. What, then, does it mean to be Asian American in a "post-racial" moment and in a "space of opportunity?"

This chapter begins to address this question. In so doing, the "post-raciality" of the moment and the types of and extent to which opportunities are actually available to students come into question. Students' stories and images reveal that Asian American-ness, both what being Asian American means and what it looks like, is being remade. These students experience and engage with transitions between adolescence and adulthood as well as between former and emergent meanings of Asian American racial identities. In this transitional period, race still matters, but in different ways. Higher education continues to be a space of opportunity, but with limits.

In this chapter, I examine Asian American racial identity—its meanings, importance, and utility—within the context of higher education. Particular emphasis is placed on students' interpretations of race-making processes. Meanings of space (i.e., freedom, opportunity, and mobility) converge with meanings of race (i.e., Asian Americans as a model minority: increasing social mobility and high levels of academic achievement) resulting in a version of "Asian American-ness" that is primarily characterized by individual choice. Ideas of freedom and possibility associated with spaces of higher education affect various aspects of students' lives, including their racial identity formation. Much in the same way that they feel that they can choose their career paths and social circles, Asian American students increasingly view their racial identity as yet another option from which they may choose.

Because of this greater flexibility, Asian American students' articulation of the meanings and importance of their racial identities are, at times, contradictory. They have conflicted ways of understanding and experiencing their racial identities. These students are no longer bound or hindered by their racial identities, yet they cannot escape racialization. The dilemma of race for the Asian American students in this study involves negotiating when and to what extent to emphasize or de-emphasize their "Asian-ness." Students also determine what type or aspect of Asian-ness to embrace (e.g., stereotypical or nuanced) as well as what it would mean, or what the implications would be, if they chose to fully embrace or ignore their Asian-ness.

I begin by describing the landscape—the broader contexts and issues within which the investigated phenomena occur. Next, I briefly discuss the larger study from which this chapter draws. I continue by examining the main type of Asian American racial identity that is being made at a particular college campus, "West Coast University." This includes a discussion of norms and varying levels of Asian-ness as well as students' ties to ethnicity and culture. Shared symbols and material culture are explored to more clearly understand shared meanings of Asian American racial identity. Then I examine the variations, limitations, and contradictions that accompany the emergent version of Asian American-ness and make it a *transitional identity*. Finally, I discuss reasons for the version of Asian American-ness that is characterized by choice as well as contradictions. I argue that Asian American students experience a spatial duality of higher education as college simultaneously enables and constrains individual and collective processes of self reinvention. Moreover, as meanings of higher education space become transposed onto meanings of Asian American racial identity, Asian American racial identity is increasingly understood to be an individual choice. In many ways race becomes viewed as optional even while it remains inescapable.

CONTEXTS AND ISSUES

Locating Asian Americans

The face of Asian America has significantly changed over the past few decades. After 1965, Asia became a more significant source of immigrants to the United States. A number of factors, including compatibility of educational systems, discrepancy in wages between Asian countries and the U.S., and an increased demand for highly skilled workers in the U.S. that was not being filled by domestic labor pools, led a large influx of Asian migration into the United States (Ong & Liu, 1994). According to the U.S. Census Bureau, in 2000, 69% of all Asians in the U.S. were foreign-born and the majority (76%) entered the U.S. in the past 20 years (Reeves & Bennett, 2004). Previously, the majority of Asian Americans were U.S.-born and multigenerational.

These shifts in migratory patterns also have a profound effect on the meanings of Asian America. The cohort of recent immigrants from Asia who possess high levels of education and/or entrepreneurial tendencies seems to successfully transfer resources and knowledge to their children. This unique pattern of intergenerational replication has led scholars to suggest that there may in fact be something different about this group (Louie, 2004; Park, 2006). In other words, the combination of recent waves of highly skilled and highly motivated immigrants from Asia together with these immigrants' desire and ability to successfully transfer capital (cultural, social, and financial) to the next generation creates a perfect compound for which the "model minority" image seems to provide a reasonable explanation. Ironically, though understandably, a number of these 1.5 and second generation Asian Americans have little understanding of the dark side of the model minority stereotype and have instead appropriated this image (Louie, 2004). In many ways, it has become their shared, collective identity.

Kibria (1998) has suggested that the Asian American community has been "an instrumental and political one that stems from a shared racial location in the U.S." (p. 946). But given the recent, significant changes in demographics, it is less clear what the current, shared racial location looks like. Who fits in this panethnic racial category? Who *wants* to fit in? And in what contexts?

Meanings of race continue to be based on the position of a racial group within the U.S. racial order, and these racial meanings and the racial identities attached to them are fluid and shifting (Omi & Winant, 1994). Notions of race are developed and perpetuated as they are embedded in social institutions such as education and law (Kibria, 1998). Additionally, geographical contexts (e.g., within the U.S., the West Coast versus Midwest versus South) may also influence understandings and meanings of Asian American racial identities.

What has further complicated deep analysis of the racial meanings and racial positioning of Asian Americans has been a dominant discourse of race in the U.S. that is centered on a Black-White binary. Even though there are certainly shared connections among racial minority groups, Asian American experiences (as with any racial minority group) cannot and should not be made to fit within the limited binary. However, scholars of race still tend to advance a Black-White framework that overlooks, or worse yet, homogenizes other racial groups (Kim, 2001). A number of Asian Americanists have made efforts to tailor and even rework frameworks to better understand Asian Americans' unique and often awkward positioning within the current racial order (Dhingra, 2003; Kim, 2001; Kibria, 1998; Okihiro, 1994; Omi & Takagi, 1996; Wu, 2002).

In addition to understanding the role of immigration policies and patterns on Asian American college students' demographics, experiences, and perceptions, it is useful to examine the role of higher education, a space in which the popular understanding of Asian Americans as high academic achievers seems to particularly flourish. Because of what colleges and universities have meant (and continue to mean) to their students and to society, institutions of higher education are an ideal setting for analyzing processes of race-making.

Multiple Salience of Higher Education for Asian Americans

For Asian American students, higher education is a space in which the lingering dominant perception of Asian Americans as the model minority is perpetuated and certain depictions of Asian American racial identity are imposed. But higher education is also a space of contestation. Indeed, it was Asian American students and faculty who initially helped to create and articulate an Asian American panethnic identity (Chan, 1991; Espiritu, 1992). Today, Asian American college students continue to negotiate a variety of identities and associations. Furthermore, these students face a number of dilemmas that stem from their achievement, on the one hand, and their inability to escape processes of racialization on the other. However, examination of these tensions and dilemmas are further complicated because they are often concealed by a veil of success created by recent significant increases in Asian American college enrollment. Given all these changes, (i.e., shifts in Asian American demographics; uncertain political and economic climates; and fluctuating views of Asian Americans) how are Asian American students (and Asian Americans more generally) understanding what it means to be Asian American today?

One would imagine that the field of education would be ripe with investigations into the implications of the model minority stereotype on and interpretations by Asian American students and their communities. While some work has been done (e.g., Hune & Chan, 1997; Lee, 2005; Li & Wang, 2008), too often scholars automatically assume Asian American academic success or merely provide cultural explanations as the primary reason for these students' academic achievement. Worse yet, some of this research on Asian American achievement has implicitly (and unfairly) criticized the "failure" of other students of color.

The fields of education and ethnic studies generally lag behind in research that critically examines and challenges the portrayals of Asian Americans and their educational experiences (Ng, Lee, & Pak, 2007). Moreover, there is still a tendency for academics to theorize *about* Asian American experiences with minimal direct input from these individuals. There is an even greater absence of research on Asian Americans in higher education that considers broader U.S. racial politics. Racial politics in higher education have been primarily defined by Black and White experiences with Asian Americans as peripheral or even "invisible" (Osajima, 1995). Asian Americans continue to be the "wild card" in the racial politics of higher education, used (or not) in arguments for and against issues such as diversity, affirmative action, and educational achievement (Takagi, 1992). Given these realities, Asian American students are imagining and experiencing higher education in ways that are significantly different from before.

Re/locating Asian American College Students

We are in a post-civil rights, post-affirmative action moment—a moment in which race still matters yet the salience of racial identities varies depending on context. Racial minorities continue to carry the "double conscious-, ness" that Du Bois (1903) wrote about over a hundred years ago: "this sense of always looking at one's self through the eyes of others, of measuring one's soul by the tape of a world that looks on in amused contempt and pity" (p. 215). It is the dilemma that exists within an individual as she/he juggles and wrestles with multiple identities. It is an awareness of being this *and* that, of possessing a racial duality. Today's racial dualism, according to Winant (2004) is a universal racial dualism in which the meanings of race, and subsequently all racial identities, are problematized.

Indeed, Asian American college students find that their racial identities are problematized. In many cases, they are actively participating in the problematizing processes as they recreate, negotiate, and contest their racial identification(s). This is the first time in U.S. history that there are so many racial minorities in higher education, many of them Asian Americans. Moreover, this reality is impacting and even changing Asian American communities and Asian American panethnic identities. With new waves of Asian Americans coming through U.S. institutions of higher education, the ways in which Asian American students understand these changes are still unclear. Relatively little is known about these students' current experiences in college and the meanings of Asian American racial identity that they hold. Thus, this chapter draws on a larger study that aimed to: (1) examine how Asian Americans college students navigate through physical and social spaces of higher education; and (2) explore what it means to be "Asian American" in spaces where inclusion and mobility, while highly sought after, remain problematic.

OVERVIEW OF THE STUDY

The larger study examined how Asian American college students understand, contest, and negotiate seemingly inescapable racialization processes in higher education, a space assumed to be full of opportunity and possibility (Samura, 2010). The investigation intended to provide a snapshot of racial structures, racial spaces, and racial transformations in institutions of higher education in light of recent shifts in sociohistorical contexts. Institutions of higher education were examined as a particular kind of racial space in which meanings of the space and meanings of Asian American racial identity are conflated. In the public imagination, both have come to mean educational achievement. In the minds of Asian American students, the purposes of college as well as their own racial identities are about possibility and opportunity. As such, this study addressed how Asian American college students balance external and internal expectations, navigate through spaces of higher education, and subsequently remake themselves, remake race, and even remake space.

In addition to offering a different perspective (and subsequently, an updated framework) by situating this investigation of Asian American college students within larger social, historical, and political contexts, the larger study's approach was also different from other studies on these issues. This new orientation was examined and expressed "from below." That is, instead of assuming that Asian American college students and Asian Americans more generally were already situated within the U.S. racial order, my approach emphasized their efforts to position themselves. Particular attention was placed on students' processes of negotiation, contestation, and understanding of these experiences. As they wrestled with these dilemmas of race and space, Asian American college students strategically navigated through physical and social spaces of campus. The contradictory experiences of Asian American college students and the dilemmas with which they must wrestle offer insight into what is possible for their lives—who they will become and what they will do—as well as a window into the flexibility (and future) of Asian American racial identity.

A Blumerian-understanding of symbolic interactionism (Blumer, 1969) was utilized to reveal how interactions recreate meanings of race. Symbolic interactionism also highlighted the reflexive and self-reflexive capacity of these students, emphasizing students' agency in processes of race-making. Critical spatial theory (e.g., Delaney, 2002; Knowles, 2003; Lipsitz, 2007; Massey, 1994; Neely & Samura, n.d.) was also utilized to examine racial inequality by addressing issues of power on individual and structural levels and in material and intangible forms.

Data collection took place during the 2007-2008 academic year at "West Coast University," a large research institution on the West Coast of the United States. Asian American college students' experiences were examined in depth through qualitative analysis of semistructured interviews (Kvale, 1996) and quantitative analysis of data from a large scale longitudinal survey of undergraduate students' experiences. Additionally, visual methods (e.g., photo journals [Collier & Collier, 1986; Suchar,

1997]) were employed, and the analysis of student-created photographs allow for an extensive examination of students' experiences from their perspectives. Participants were undergraduate students who self-identified as "Asian" or "Asian American." Participants were recruited through verbal announcements made in classes, flyers posted around campus, and e-mail announcements sent directly to campus organizations and through Facebook pages. Snowball sampling allowed for further recruitment of participants. A total of 36 students participated in this study—18 interviewees and 19 photo journalers, with 1 participant doing both an interview and photo journal.

Of the pool of student participants, 69.4% were female and 30.6% were male. Although specific income data was not collected, almost all of the students described their families as either "middle class" or "upper middle class." Sixty-seven percent were born in the United States, and English was the primary language for 77.8% of the participants. The majority of the student participants self-identified as first or second generation. Ten of the 36 participants identified as first generation (27.8%), one identified as 1.5 generation (2.8%), and seventeen identified as second generation (47.2%). Approximately 28% of the participants self-identified as mixed race or ethnicity. Sixteen of the 36 participants (44.4%) self-identified as Chinese or part Chinese. The participant pool also included 7 students who self-identified as "Japanese" (19.4%), 7 who self-identified as "Vietnamese" (19.4%), 6 who self-identified as "Filipino" (16.7%), 2 each (5.6%) who self-identified as "Cambodian" and "Korean," and one each (2.8%) who self-identified as "Taiwanese," "Laotian," "Thai," and "Guamanian."

FINDINGS AND DISCUSSION

A Version of "Asian American-ness" Characterized by Individual Choice and Contradictions

Asian norms. Within any specific racial category, students must contend with various types of racial and panethnic identities. Students choose the particular type of racial identity to which they will adhere. For the Asian American students in this study, there were many versions of Asian American racial identity available. At the same time, these students did carry pre-existent notions of what it means to be "Asian" or "Asian American." Such ideas of Asian American identities can be understood as "Asian norms," many of which are stereotypical. It is useful to begin a discussion of the meanings of Asian American racial identity held by the students in this study by examining the common perceptions of who Asian Americans are and what they look like. This is an important first step because it is in relation to the Asian norms that students strategically position themselves.

Asian norms often emerged through students' inadvertent remarks. These were the moments in which students talked about one topic but would add additional commentary. For example, while talking about their choice of majors, several students mentioned how Asians are expected to be interested in and good at math and science. One student commented on how career paths in math or science fields were often expected by the "Asian community" and served as a marker of "real Asians." The idea that some Asians are not "real" Asian, or even less Asian, suggests that a number of the Asian stereotypes (e.g., "Asians are good at math") are still deeply embedded in people's minds. Moreover, even Asian American students continue to rely on these stereotypes to determine their type or level of Asian-ness.

Similarly, in explaining her discomfort around a part of campus that houses the physics, math, and engineering buildings, Leah, who self-identified as fourth generation Japanese American and third generation Chinese American, suggested that this discomfort had to do with her lack of skills in those areas. She then quipped: "How un-Asian of me." Evident in other parts of Leah's discussion were the more nuanced ways in which this student perceived and understood her Asian American racial identity. In other words, this comment in no way reflects this student's complete view of Asian American racial identity. At the same time, brief remarks such as the "un-Asian"-comment highlight some of the stereotypical ideas on which even Asian American students continue to draw in their talk about Asian-ness. Most of the time, Asian norms and stereotypes were referenced by students in this study as a way of talking about how they differed from these norms. For example, Ella, a third generation Chinese American, explained how being Asian American today required that she "not do what typical Asians do." Her reference to "typical Asians," and not doing what "they" (i.e., typical Asians) do, suggests that there are particular ways of being and acting from which some Asian American students are trying to distance themselves. Ella's statement also suggests that to *be* Asian American involves conscious choices about what to do and how to act. Thus, by not doing what typical Asians do, or not acting Asian, she would, by default, be *acting* American. Moreover, Ella's perspective on current meanings of and ways of being Asian American may indicate that Asian American students' transitional identities (from former to emergent meanings of Asian American-ness) involve bridging two seemingly separate identities. As a result, students would *be* Asian and *act* American. This was one way students worked to manage and understand the coexistence of Asian and American within themselves. And it speaks to the particular form of double consciousness and racial dualism (Du Bois, 1903) of Asian Americans. Nevertheless, management of various types and aspects of Asian, American, and Asian American identities is an ongoing struggle.

Managing Asian, American, and Asian American identities. There was wide variation among students regarding which aspects of their Asian or Asian American racial identities to emphasize. Students often attempted to strike a balance between embracing Asian-ness, on the one hand, and embracing American-ness, on the other. The disjunction between Asian identity and American identity suggests that an Asian identity means a racial or ethnic identity, whereas an American identity is understood to be a nonracialized and/or White identity. Students' pursuits of "diversity" were often their attempts to connect an American identity with their Asian identity. Another way that this Asian—American tension was manifested was through students' desires and attempts to "conform to" or "break away from" their racial and ethnic identities. Additionally, students vacillated between being "too Asian," on the one hand, and, on the other hand, "not Asian enough." This was the case for Violet, a self-identified second generation Vietnamese American, who explained the varying salience of her different identities. When I asked her which identities seemed to matter the most, Violet offered the following reply:

> Specifically to West Coast University, it would probably be my race. Just because I feel kind of like a minority here and sometimes I feel like I'm being judged sort of or like that I have this specific image I have to portray. So I guess that really matters to me that I'm not being too Asian or not Asian enough, so, and that and how I associate myself with like my white friends and, yeah, I kind of want to fit in too to that crowd.

Violet went on to explain how she acted differently depending on the crowd she was in and carefully managed her "Asian-ness" when she was with her non-Asian friends. She once again mentioned how she tried not to be "too Asian," and I asked her for an example of crossing the line between "too Asian" and "Asian enough." Violet explained:

> I guess, like the food that I eat, like with my other roommate who is Korean.... I could eat, you know, authentic Vietnamese food and she would enjoy the same thing. But if I feel like if I introduce that to my White friends or something like they would be like, "that's weird" or something, you know what I mean?

As students like Violet attempted to fuse Asian and American identities, they made choices about which aspects of their Asian identities they wanted to emphasize. "American" identities also were understood by students as exclusive of "Asian American" and remained void of specific ethnic or racial markers. Alternatively, students chose which aspects of their Asian ethnic cultures to de-emphasize. De-emphasizing of Asian elements is often understood as embracing American-ness. Embracing American-ness can also be understood as pursuing White-ness. It can also been seen as a move towards deracialization. Reasons for and implications of deracialization will be discussed later in this chapter.

Material culture and cultural markers. When trying to understand racial and/or ethnic identities, it is both useful and important to examine the cultural practices that produce these identities rather than assuming they are somehow set and predetermined (Lowe, 1996). And since culture is transmitted and learned through symbols (Charon, 2001; Shibutani, 1955), an effective way to examine Asian American culture and meanings of Asian American racial identity is to explore the shared symbols, objects, and material culture of Asian American students. Material culture functions as cultural markers, linking students to their racial and ethnic identities. Thus, by examining students' shared understandings of material culture, shared meanings of Asian American racial identity are also revealed. At the same time, my analysis focused less on the specific kinds of objects they chose to capture and more on the meanings they created and communicated through the objects. I also focused on the connections they were making between objects and their meanings of racial and ethnic identities. For example, I was less interested in the significance of a photograph of a rice cooker and more interested in the reasons why a student took the picture of a rice cooker as well as the ways she related the rice cooker to her racial identity.

The images captured by the student photo journalers are particularly useful in the analysis of symbols and shared meanings. Like written and verbal language, photographs are a form of symbolic communication. Images captured by the photo journalers offer insight into the meanings particular objects have for students. The images also provided insight into the ways the photo journalers infuse particular objects with racial and ethnic meanings.

Photo journalers' images included stereotypical "Asian" objects and practices as well as objects and scenes without explicit connections to Asian-ness. It was valuable to see the types of objects students chose to display, surround themselves with, and/or take pictures of. Images revealed the ways that students wanted to present themselves. There were also a number of symbolic images for which photo journalers' provided their interpretations. Some of the more explicit Asian objects included Chinese calligraphy, an Asian lantern, rows of shoes near the door, and a Hello Kitty alarm clock. Photo journalers also took numerous pictures of food. While the majority of the food images were intended to provide a general sense of students' everyday lives, some of the food images addressed connections to racial and ethnic cultures and identities.

For example, Buddy who, self-identified as a second generation Filipino and Guamanian American male, took a picture of a shelf in his pantry stocked with boxes of dried pasta and jars of marinara sauce as a way of emphasizing the independence (from his family and their cultural practices) he gained when he moved to college. Instead of rice, he chose to eat pasta. In so doing, he was exercising his freedom to develop his own tastes and preferences without being bound to his family's cultural practices. Alternatively, Melissa, a second generation Vietnamese and Chinese student, took a number of pictures of Asian food items, including an image titled: "pyramid & kimchee," to explain the links between students and their ethnic backgrounds. In fact, she explained that the image represented what it meant to be an Asian American today by focusing on individuals' ability or willingness "to embrace the culture we were born into and the one that identifies our ethnic background." Individual choice is still a factor, much in the same way as Buddy chose to assert his free will by veering from his family's preferences for food items often attached to Asian ethnic culture (e.g., rice). However, for Melissa it was more about choosing and even embracing Asian ethnic food while also managing "American" food items. In the same way that kimchee can share table space with an American microbrew, so, too, can the Asian and the American coexist within an individual.

On Jina's bedroom wall, among numerous pictures of friends and other mementos, were an ornate Buddhist shrine and a large Thai flag. She took a picture of these two objects in order to display her cultural and religious ties. Self-identifying as second generation Thai, Jina explained that they were "cultural reminders" that provided "a way of not forgetting roots and not being totally Americanized." As a mixture of Thai, Chinese, Cambodian, and Hungarian, Jina felt like she needed to emphasize her Thai culture. "Claiming my Thai heritage is important to my identity because I do not identify with the other ethnicities I am connected to," she explained. "If I do not emphasize my Thai culture people think of me as less Thai or label me mixed and believe that I have weakened links to my ethnicity." Ethnicity, according to Jina, was something that she could and needed to claim. By hanging the Thai flag on her wall, Jina reminded herself (and anyone who walked into or by her room—the flag was hanging on the wall just opposite of the door so that it would be the first thing people saw) that her ethnicity, particularly her Thai ethnicity, was important to her.

Jina's fear of being perceived as having "weakened links" to her ethnicity was shared by other participants. Other students talked about their actual weakened ties to their ethnicity by commenting on their embarrassment over not having full mastery of their Asian ethnic language(s). They also noted that while taking Asian American studies classes was often enlightening, they experienced some sense of shame for not knowing about their race and ethnicity. Some of the students who took Asian American studies courses were concerned that they would be viewed as culturally ignorant because they took these classes. They did not want to be perceived as not understanding their own culture.

Variations. The varying levels of strength or weakness of students' ties to their racial and ethnic cultures, or as some of the students have put it, how Asian they are or the extent to which they embrace Asian-ness, suggest that Asian American students are conflicted. On the one hand, the students in this study were concerned with losing connections to their Asian identity and being perceived by others as having lost ethnic ties. This is one reason they held on to and surrounded themselves with objects that symbolically, and at times, quite literally, connected them to Asian culture. Jina's decision to hang the Thai flag and Buddhist shrine on her bedroom wall is just one example of this. On the other hand, students also tried to reconcile the "Asian" with the "American." This often involved efforts to de-emphasize their racial and ethnic identities by emphasizing their efforts to join social groups or maintain circles of friends that were comprised of people of different racial and ethnic backgrounds. In fact, many of the students explained how being Asian American today meant that they could be friends with anyone.

Photo journalers, in particular, emphasized this desire to be diverse and multicultural primarily through their choice of social circles. Many of them captured numerous images of racially diverse groups of people as a way of depicting their social circles and the multiracial groups with whom they chose to spend their time. In fact, a number of photo journalers responded to questions regarding the places and people with whom their race does not matter with numerous images of their friends. Some of them chose to take pictures of or with their friends who were of different races. Others captured pictures of or with friends who were all White. All of those images, however, were meant to portray how race did not matter with their friends. In fact, one photo journaler explained how she "always tend[s] to be multicultural with friends."

Alternatively, other photo journalers captured images of racially diverse groups of friends, but instead of de-emphasizing the salience of their racial identities, these images were meant to comment on how they thought about their Asian American racial identity when they were among non-Asians. These students felt like their Asian-ness was emphasized, either by others or even in their own minds, when they were in racially diverse groups. This was especially true for the moments when they were one of a few Asian Americans in the space.

Other students, however, suggested that they thought about their race when they spent time with others of the same race. For example, Peter commented on how one could not help but think about his/her racial identity when spending time with members of race-based campus groups: "So it has to matter when you're in an Asian American club, cause that's why you're there. To represent. Either to represent or to learn about being Asian American, and so like I don't see how it wouldn't matter." In this situation, "to represent" meant students emphasized their racial or ethnic identities at Asian American club meetings. They highlighted their Asian American-ness as a way of connecting with same-race peers. Peter's comments also suggest that student had the ability to emphasize or de-emphasize their Asian American racial identities at will. In other words, they could choose "to represent" or not. On a related note, while there was a lot of discussion and images of "diversity," there were also a significant amount of discussion and images regarding race-based and ethnic-specific organizations or efforts. The prevalence of race- or ethnic-specific organizations, such as Asian fraternities and Asian ethnic cultural clubs, suggests that even as students were trying to engage in racial pluralism, they were still drawn to groups organized around shared racial or ethnic identification.

The wide variation of responses regarding the salience of students' racial identities is important to note because, although Asian American students would like to believe that their racial identities do not matter or that they minimally matter, they still must constantly negotiate their racial identification. Students thought about their Asian American-ness when they were non-Asian Americans, with racial diverse peer groups, and even with other Asian Americans. However, these variations also indicate that there was a limit to the type and amount of choice Asian American students had regarding their racial and ethnic identification.

Limitations. Students' overwhelming response to inquiries regarding contemporary meanings of Asian American racial identity was that Asian Americans today have the ability to be and do whatever they desire. In other words, Asian American racial identity is primarily a matter of personal choice. The fact that students see their ethnicity as something to search for, claim, or embrace suggests that ethnicity and race are somehow now claim-able and embrace-able. One student even suggested that Asian Americans today can "create their own version" of what it means to be an Asian American, thus generating a place for themselves in society. Yet this sense of choice in the creation, presentation, and even position of oneself in society is not without limitations. As some of the interviews and photo journaler images reveal, there were times when students had little or not control over how they were viewed by others.

Some students emphasized the continual importance of their racial identities in their everyday interactions. For example, Mika spoke of how people identified her racially in different ways depending on the setting. As a second generation Japanese and approximately sixth generation Irish American, Mika noticed that when she was in a group comprised of White people, her "Asian-ness will sort of shine out." Conversely, when she was around mostly Asians, her Whiteness was more salient. At West Coast University, in particular, Mika found that she had little control over which part of her biraciality was most salient to others. "That is a big thing ... and less of it, it's like, oh, that you're half. It's like you're Asian, like they're just, I'm just Asian, you know?" By default, the non-White part of Mika's biracial identity was the one people around her would notice. She had little control over how she was racialized.

While there were certainly variations among participants' responses regarding the salience of race in their lives, as well as recognition of the limitations of individual choice in their racial identifications, there were also variations *within* the course of one interview or within one collection of a photo journaler's images.

Contradictions. Just as noteworthy as students' perceived role of individual choice in the creation, presentation, and meanings of their Asian American racial identities are the contradictions tacitly expressed in students' interviews and photo journals. Contradictions most often occurred between students' ideals and their experiences. More specifically, contradictions emerged as students shared how, when, and why their Asian American racial identities seemed to matter in positive or negative ways.

John, who self-identified as second generation Vietnamese and "1/4 Chinese" provided a compelling example of how Asian American students at West Coast University often exist within a paradox. When asked if he felt like he belonged at West Coast University, John took a long pause and then responded: "I think I do because it really fits into my way of thinking, tò be more open-minded and to be more immersed in social circles and not just be restricted to your own culture based on your ethnic background." He even went on to talk about how he felt the most comfortable in the campus' surrounding city, so much so that he would like to settle down and relocate his parents to this city. I asked him to further explain why he felt this way, and he said:

> [This city] is a more open-minded place where it's there's not much tension as to like, "oh, you know, you're Vietnamese. You should stick with your own people." Or, you know, "you're Chinese, you stick with your own people." You know what, we're going to stick over here. Whereas everyone can be generally open-minded and not be biased to the point that it would affect like workplace issues or just living issues in general.

However, as John talked in greater detail about specific places in the city surrounding the campus in which he felt comfortable, he focused on his fraternity house. He explained how he spent most of his time in the fraternity house, an environment that was conducive to the high levels of socializing to which he was drawn. It is important to note, however, that John's fraternity was an Asian American fraternity.

John's choices and explanations of his choices are contradictory. On the one hand, West Coast University and the surrounding city was a place in which John felt comfortable, even more comfortable than in his hometown. His high level of comfort was due to the perceived open-mindedness that residents of the area had, even around racial issues. On the other hand, John chose to join one of West Coast University's few Asian American fraternities. And residents of John's fraternity house were mostly Asian men. If West Coast University was such an open-minded and comfortable place, why did he choose to join the Asian American fraternity and mostly spend time with his Asian American fraternity brothers? John attempted to explain:

> Because they're kind of like me. I guess we are open-minded and we do want to be like ... assimilated. And, you know, we do want to be in a place that's everybody's open-mindedness and like not be so clique-ish ... where it's hard to come up and talk to a group of white people. But at the same time, it is kind of hard

John and his Asian American fraternity brothers desired acceptance and inclusion with the majority (White) groups. To a certain extent, they did experience this, sometimes more than others. However, they also discovered that complete acceptance was not automatic nor could it be assumed. Subsequently, they searched for people with whom and places where they felt included. Similar to other students in this study, John and his fraternity brothers found or created spaces of comfort and belonging among coethnics, even while maintaining rhetoric of racial diversity and inclusion.

Emergent Meanings of Asian/Asian-American-ness

With all of the variations and contradictions among, and even within, interviewee and photo journaler responses, what can be concluded about Asian American racial identity? The uncertain and unsteady nature of students' responses is indicative of meanings of Asian American racial identity today, especially within the context of higher education. Racial meanings continually shift and fluctuate as a result of, and resulting in, the ongoing interplay between broader sociohistorical and political processes and everyday interactions among individuals. And yet the case of Asian American college students offers additional insight, not only into the navigational processes and experiences of an understudied racial minority group, but also into the dynamic nature of race and racial identities. Asian American college students' perceptions and experiences offer insight into the possibility of and potential for meanings of race in the United States.

Although individual choice, that is, students' ability to choose the elements of Asian ethnic culture they prefer or how students' present themselves as racial or deracialized beings, is part of the "version" of Asian American-ness emerging from higher education, it is only one part of the pattern. The version of Asian American-ness that is emerging from spaces of higher education is also an identity dominated by rhetoric. That is, the ideas of possibility and freedom do not align with the realities and limitations that students continue to face. Asian American racial identity today is conflicted and contradictory, unstable and shifting. In many ways, Asian American college students are negotiating *transitional identities*. Granted, *all* identities, in varying degrees, are transitional in that they are dynamic and not static. In the context of this study, however, "transitional" refers to the specific nature of these students' identities. Their identities are transitional, not only in the sense that they are moving from adolescence to adulthood (as all college students generally are), but also transitional in the sense that they are moving from that which was previously the standard to something "new." In other words, the experiences of students in this study are different from those of any earlier time. As a result Asian American students have limited ways of understanding these experiences. This is evident in the contradictions within students' responses as well as between students' words and actions. These transitional identities suggest that a paradigmatic change may be taking place that has implications for (racial) identity politics.

Making Sense of Contradictory Experiences: Reasons for the Emergent Version of Asian American-ness

Now that the particular "version" of Asian American racial identity has been examined, let us move on to a discussion of the reasons for this type of Asian American-ness as well as the implications of these emergent meanings of Asian American racial identity.

Multigenerational differences and expected patterns of integration. Some scholars of immigration and classic assimilation (e.g., Alba & Nee, 1997, 2003; Gordon, 1964) would likely explain Asian American students' contradictory experiences as resulting from multigenerational differences and the emergent brand of Asian American-ness as an indicator of students' movement toward greater assimilation and increased integration. From this perspective, the Asian American students in this study simply experience tensions associated with classic assimilation; they are drawn into mainstream society on the one hand and compelled to hold on to their culture on the other. If this is the case, Asian American students merely need to endure the discomfort associated with processes of integration. The expectation is that on the other side of it all, inclusion awaits.

Alternatively, a number of immigration scholars (e.g., Massey, 1995; Portes & Rumbaut, 2001; Portes & Zhou, 1993; Tuan, 2004; Zhou, 1997; Zhou & Xiong, 2005) contend that there are varying types and levels of assimilation. They suggest that new waves of immigrants, especially from Asia and Latin America, complicate more traditional notions of assimilation. Moreover, linear patterns of assimilation are a thing of the past and non-transferrable to non-White, non-European immigrants, particularly those who migrated to the U.S. after 1965 (Massey, 1995; Rumbaut, 1994). One of these perspectives on contemporary societal integration comes from scholars of segmented assimilation (Portes & Zhou, 1993; Zhou, 1997) who highlight the structural factors, particularly racial and class stratification, that affect the variety of directions and extent to which immigrants assimilate. Portes and Zhou's (1993) theory of segmented assimilation critiques and deviates from classic assimilationism by suggesting that the divergent paths taken by immigrant groups can be explained by interactions between individual-level factors, such as skills or networks, and contextual factors, such as political and economic climates. Segmented assimilation does offer some explanations for high numbers of Asian Americans in college. Namely, particular segments of Asian Americans (i.e., those who come from highly skilled and highly educated families) have the ability to pursue higher levels of education and to pursue such a path with the expectation of gaining upward mobility. The fact that there are significant numbers of Asian American in college also indicates that they are already becoming integrated, especially after gaining access to an important route for upward social mobility (i.e., college education and degree). High levels of Asian Americans college enrollment may serve as an indicator of Asian American upward mobility and potential for societal integration. However, as Tuan (2004) also points out, assimilation does not necessarily resolve racial, ethnic, and class inequalities, nor do high levels of acculturation automatically translate into inclusion or belonging.

If the U.S. remains, as Massey (1995) suggests, a "country of perpetual immigration," with large groups of people continually arriving, what will social inclusion look like? The experiences and interpretations of the students in this study reveal what some processes of integration look like, at least for Asian Americans at this point in time. The juggling of rhetoric (i.e., racial identity as cultural choice) and reality (i.e., varying levels of importance of one's race, often beyond one's control) indicates that things are in transition. Even in the midst of continued immigration, there are ways that some groups are able to gain mobility and greater inclusion.

At the same time, what these students express is more than a multiple generational pattern in which there is a conflict between the old and the new. They are caught between deciding what to shed and what to hold on to. In fact, the ways in which students express and emphasize personal choice as a primary element of Asian American racial meanings is reminiscent of how scholars suggest Whites have come to experience race and ethnicity. Waters (1990) offers the idea of "ethnic options" as a way of understanding the deracialization of White European immigrants during the twentieth century. Over time, Waters argues, these European immigrants became less concerned with race and ethnicity, to a point where Whites could pick and choose when and which aspects of their race or ethnicity to focus on. This notion of "ethnic options" of Whites in the U.S. raises some interesting questions regarding the availability of such options for racial minorities, particularly Asian Americans. For example, to what extent do Asian Americans have ethnic options? What do these ethnic options look like? And how are such options understood by Asian Americans?

Song (2001) points out that theorization on the ethnic options of racial minorities remains extremely limited as Waters' (1990) seminal work focuses on the ethnic options of Whites. Song also raises an important issue regarding recent scholarship (e.g., Kibria, 2000) that connects increased social mobility with increased ethnic options. In particular, Song aptly notes that is still unclear exactly *how* Asian Americans' social mobility would enhance their ethnic options. The findings from this study offer some insight. As a number of Asian Americans have gained access to higher education, they increasingly view their ethnic and racial identities as less important, at least to the extent that their ethnicity and race are not inhibitive. The perspectives of students in this study indicates that, because Asian Americans are attending college in greater numbers and attaining higher levels of education, they may now have increased ethnic options, or even *racial options*, previously unavailable.

However, these increased racial options need to be qualified. It is not a simple linear process whereby individuals increase their level of educational attainment and subsequently increase their ability to choose when and to what extent their racial identities matter. Instead, as the students reveal, individuals may actually play an active role in shaping and facilitating these racial options.

While existent research on cultural pluralism, immigrant integration, and racial identity politics provide some insight into the meanings of the Asian American racial identities emerging from spaces of higher education, this work still only offers partial explanations. How can we better understand, for example, why this "version" of Asian American-ness seems to be emerging from college campuses? And how can we make sense of the seemingly contradictory Asian American racial identity with which a number of Asian American students are currently wrestling? These Asian American racial identities are rife with contradictions between words and actions as well as rhetoric and reality. This indicates that there are multiple factors in play. The uncertainty and transitional character of Asian American racial identities explored here shows us where the interaction between race and space is most clearly worked out in students' lives. These students' understandings of increased racial options are more than just an outcome of their time in college and more than being only an Asian American phenomenon. Instead it is a combination of both. Meanings of campus space, including ideas of possibility and opportunity, become transposed onto meanings of race, more specifically Asian American racial identities, and vice versa. This results in Asian American college students experiencing transitional tensions and dilemmas among former meanings of higher education and Asian American racial identities and their current meanings.

Convergent meanings of race and space: The spatial duality of higher education. The spatial duality of higher education offers an effective way of understanding this transitional period and why this transitional identity—the particular "version" of Asian American-ness—emerges from higher education. As detailed above, Asian American college students wrestle with dilemmas that are a result of various negotiated expectations and experiences for which they do not have a sufficient paradigm. Asian American students juggle multiple identities. They wrestle with being Asian *and* American, too Asian *and* not Asian enough, and independent adults *and* children still responsible to parents.

In addition to the individual aspects of a transitional identity (i.e. adolescence to adulthood, multigenerational assimilation processes, etc.), Asian American college students also navigate through larger meanings of Asian American racial identities. In fact, these students problematize these identities as they negotiate between former and present meanings of Asian American-ness in their everyday college experiences. This is evidenced in students' notions of Asian norms and what they view as constituting Asian-ness. This also includes the popular view of Asian Americans' universal educational success. As higher education has increasingly become a site for Asian Americans to gain leverage and boost status, the college campus has become linked with meanings of Asian American racial identity. Thus the emergent form of Asian American racial identity can be explained by the convergence of meanings of space (i.e., higher education) and race (i.e., Asian American-ness).

Perhaps more than any other institution, higher education holds the greatest potential for individual and collective advancement. In theory, it functions as a space of inquiry and self-discovery and represents an attainable path toward upward social mobility. This is why I maintain that college campuses are not only the setting for reinventions of Asian American racial identities, but campus space itself contributes to this transformative process through the meanings it confers (i.e., possibility, choice, and the rewards of individual efforts). Of course these processes of self-discovery and transformation can occur for any college student, not just Asian American. What makes these processes particularly salient for Asian American students is the significant overlap of racial and spatial meanings and the compounded effect produced by Asian American students' interactions with and within higher education. In no other space is Asian American racial identity more salient than it is in higher education.

I argue that higher education operates as a spatial duality for Asian Americans. Higher education enables the transformation of individual and collective identities. This is due to the expectations associated with college as a space during which students can reinvent themselves. Additionally, college is generally understood to be a space of possibility and opportunity. It continues to be viewed as a primary key to upward social mobility. Thus for Asian American students who, like other students, intend to explore and pursue the possibilities, higher education becomes a space for multiple self-reinventions. Not only are they participating in the transition from adolescence to adulthood, and embracing and enacting the mantra of unlimited possibilities, even with regards to their racial identification. In their minds, race matters much less in this postracial moment, particularly in college.

It is also true, however, that higher education serves to constrain the extent to which any reinvention of self and group is possible. This limitation often arises as students experience something very different from what they previously expected. This may include their transitional to adulthood and independence. A number of Asian American students must continually negotiate their parents', families', or communities' expectations with their own. They also realize that their expectations regarding academics and career paths do not align with the reality of what is possible for them. In regards to race, students quickly come to realize that their racial identities still matter, even when they do not want them to. Despite this harsh reality, students still assert their agency as they continue to claim that their racial identification is mostly a cultural choice. Asian American racial identity, in their minds, is an option.

Thus, when meanings of race converge with meanings of space, the inner workings of Asian American racial dualities and the spatial dualities of higher education are exposed. Meanings of higher education space become transposed onto meanings of Asian American racial identity. This results in a view of Asian American racial identity as meaning freedom, choice, and possibility. This may be the primary reason why the rhetoric does not always align with students' realities. During college, Asian American students not only come to better understand their racial identities, but they also learn what it means to be Asian American in and through spaces of higher education. It is through their experiences with and within campus space that these students contend with various meanings of Asian American racial identities. Campus space especially highlights the stereotypical views of Asian Americans as somehow possessing a unique innate ability to attain high academic achievement and increased social mobility. In this way higher education operates as a space that intensifies and accelerates the formation of Asian American students' racial identities. This is because both higher education and Asian American racial identities have to symbolize academic success and the potential for upward mobility and greater social inclusion. At the same time, it is in spaces of higher education that these students are able to choose how to position themselves in relation to these ideas and even reinvent and transform meanings of Asian American-ness.

CLOSING THOUGHTS

Through this chapter, I have attempted to provide evidence of and possible explanations for a significant shift in meanings of Asian American racial identity—from an identity established out of political necessity to more individualized identities marked by personal choice. In this closing section, I will briefly discuss the implications that a version of Asian American-ness infused with choice may have for stakeholders (e.g., researchers, educational institutions, Asian American studies, and panethnic and inter-racial coalitions).

For researchers, this study's findings regarding shifts in racial meanings highlight the utility of this context (i.e., higher education) for work on racial theory. Scholars of race and ethnicity should give much more attention to college campuses because they offer a rich site for investigations of race-making processes and race relations. In turn, educational researchers who examine experiences of students of color should situate their inquiries within broader U.S. racial politics. The following are several questions to hopefully spur future research: How would geographical or regional differences affect students' meanings of Asian American racial identity? Are these meanings affected by the relative proportion of Asian American students on a campus and the social, cultural, political, and academic programs, events, and informal networks oriented toward Asian Americans? What would the effects of various intersectionalities of race, ethnicity, socioeconomic status, gender, sexuality, and generational status have on meanings of students' racial identities? Where do multiracial and multiethnic Asian American students fit into this discussion? What binds Asian American college students together? What is the utility of the pan-ethnic racial identity for these students?

As for programming, since college is a critical period for racial identity formation, ethnic studies and Asian American studies can play an important role in student development. Courses can offer a different, more critical take on the ways that Asian Americans are viewed. Indeed, a number of ethnic studies and Asian American studies programs and departments already address this issue in varying degrees. Through these courses students can learn about the various reasons for popular perceptions of Asian American academic success. Subsequently, Asian American students can gain a more nuanced understanding of how and why others might assume that they are high academic achievers, and other students can questions their own assumptions. As they learn to contextualize their experiences, students will be able to better understand and even question their own perceptions and assumptions about themselves—who they are and how they came to be where they are.

The emergent version of Asian American-ness is also a reminder that racial categories and identities are in constant flux. Racial categories and the meanings associated with these categories are constantly shifting. Ideas of Asian American racial identity and "Asian American community" cannot be relegated to the past. Therefore it is important that educational institutions, Asian American studies, and intra- and inter-racial coalitions examine, teach, and operate with this understanding. Additionally, the emergent version of Asian American-ness that is characterized by choice is a reminder that we should be careful not to assume belonging within the Asian American racial category. The boundaries of the Asian American racial category also continue to shift and it is not always clear as to who belongs or who wants to belong within this racial category. The extent to which an "Asian American" racial identity remains inclusive will determine the effectiveness and utility of this panethnic racial identity for organizing.

Finally, the dilemmas, tensions, and contradictions experienced by Asian American college students reveal the still tenuous racial landscape of higher education. This can even inform our understanding of the broader U.S. racial landscape. Through Asian American students' experiences, we gain insight into that which students of color still must contend, even after inclusion.

The contradictions and dilemmas experienced by the students in this study are evidence of the fact that space has not kept up with changes in rhetoric. Although there have been, to a certain extent, increased racial diversity of student populations and greater emphasis on racial diversity, how have these educational institutions have changed? On the one hand, racial diversity is promoted. On the other hand, a number of students of color do not experience college life with the same freedom and inclusivity that is talked about and imagined. Colleges and universities have the ability to propel individuals further up and into society as well as the ability to maintain a particular social (and racial) order. But without fundamental changes to the spatial conditions, which would involve a redistribution of power in more equitable ways, institutions of higher education will continue to reify the current racial order. This leads to a final set of questions for researchers, educational institutions, and policymakers to consider: What is the role of higher education in processes of race-making and race-relating? How has higher education space changed (or not) as a result of increased racial diversity? And how could higher education space be remade so as to more positively influence the race-making and race-relating processes that occur during this time in students' lives?

ACKNOWLEDGEMENTS

The author is extremely grateful for the generosity and enthusiasm with which the students in this study shared their lives, the invaluable feedback and support of Howard Winant, Hsiu-Zu Ho, and Jason Raley, and the generous research assistance from Tina Quan and Aiko Yamakita. The author also acknowledges the University of California All Campus Consortium for Research on Diversity (UC/ACCORD), the University of California Santa Barbara's Gevirtz Graduate School of Education and Graduate Division, and the Interdisciplinary Humanities Center for providing resources and support to complete this work.

NOTE

1.   All names used in this study are pseudonyms.

REFERENCES

Alba, R., & Nee, V. (1997). Rethinking assimilation theory for a new era of immigration. *International Migration Review, 31*, 826-874.

Alba, R., & Nee, V. (2003). *Remaking the American mainstream: Assimilation andcontemporary immigration.* Cambridge, MA: Harvard University Press.

Blumer, H. (1969). *Symbolic interactionism: Perspective and method.* Englewood Cliffs, NJ: Prentice-Hall.

Chan, S. (1991). *Asian Americans: An interpretive history.* Boston, MA: Twayne.

Charon, J. M. (2001). *Symbolic interactionism: An introduction, an interpretation, an integration* (7th ed.). Englewood Cliffs, NJ: Prentice-Hall.

Collier, J., & Collier, M. (1986). *Visual anthropology: Photography as a research method.* Albuquerque, NM: University of New Mexico Press.

Delaney, D. (2002). The space that race makes. *The Professional Geographer, 54,* 1.

Dhingra, P. (2003). Being American between and white: Second-generation Asian American professionals' racial identities. *Journal of Asian American Studies, 6,* 117-147.

Du Bois, W. E. B. (1903). *The souls of folk.* New York, NY: Penguin.

Espiritu, Y. (1992). *Asian American panethnicity: Bridging institutions and identities.* Philadelphia, PA: Temple University Press.

Gordon, M. (1964). *Assimilation in American life.* New York, NY: Oxford University Press.

Hune, S., & Chan, K. S. (1997). Asian Pacific American demographic and educational trends. In D. J. Carter & R. Wilson (Eds.), *Minorities in higher education 15th annual status report* (pp. 39-67). Washington, DC: American Council on Education.

Kibria, N. (1998). The contested meanings of "Asian American": Racial dilemmas in the contemporary U.S. *Ethnic and Racial Studies, 21,* 939-958.

Kibria, N. (2000). Race, ethnic options and ethnic binds. *Sociological Perspectives, 43,* 77-95.

Kim, C. (2001). The racial triangulation of Asian Americans. *Politics & Society, 27,* 105-138.

Knowles, C. (2003). *Race and social analysis.* Thousand Oaks, CA: SAGE.

Kvale, S. (1996). *Interviews: An introduction to qualitative research interviewing.* Thousand Oaks, CA: SAGE.

Lee, S. J. (2005). *Up against whiteness: Race, school, and immigrant youth.* New York, NY: Teachers College Press.

Li, G., & Wang, L. (Eds.) (2008). *Model minority myth revisited: An interdisciplinary approach to demystifying Asian American experiences.* Charlotte, NC: Information Age.

Lipsitz, G. (2007). The racialization of space and the spatialization of race: Theorizing the hidden architecture of landscape. *Landscape Journal, 26,* 1-07.

Louie, V. (2004). Being practical or doing what I want: The role of parents in the academic choices of Chinese Americans. In P. Kasinitz, J. Mollenkopf, & M Waters (Eds.), *Becoming New Yorkers: The second generation in a global city* (pp. 70-109). New York, NY: Russell Sage Foundation.

Lowe, L. (1996). *Immigrant acts: On Asian American cultural politics.* Durham, NC: Duke University Press.

Massey, D. (1995). The new immigration and the meaning of ethnicity in the United States. *Population and Development Review, 21,* 631-652.

Massey, D. (1994). *Space, place, & gender.* Minneapolis, MN: University of Minnesota Press.

Neely, B., & Samura, M. (n.d.). Social geographies of race: Connecting race & space. Manuscript in preparation.

Ng, J., Lee, S., & Pak, Y. (2007). Contesting the model minority and perpetual foreigner stereotypes: A critical review of literature on Asian Americans in education. *Review of Research in Education, 31*, 95-130.

Okihiro, G. (1994). *Margins & mainstreams: Asians in American history & culture.* Seattle, WA: University of Washington Press.

Omi, M., & Takagi, D. (1996). Situating Asian Americans in the political discourse on affirmative action. *Representations, 55*, 155-162.

Omi, M. & Winant, H. (1994). *Racial formation in the United States: From the 1960s to the 1990s.* New York, NY: Routledge.

Ong, P., & Liu, J. M. (1994). U.S. immigration policies and Asian migration. In P. Ong, E. Bonacich & L. Cheng (Eds.), *The New Asian Immigration in Los Angeles and Global Restructuring* (pp. 45-73). Philadelphia, PA: Temple University Press.

Osajima, K. (1995). Racial politics and the invisibility of Asian Americans in higher education. *Educational Foundations*, 35-53.

Park, J. S. W. (2006). Emergent divides: Class and position among Asian Americans. *CR: The New Centennial Review, 6*(2), 57-72.

Portes, A., & Rumbaut, R. (2001). *Legacies: The story of the immigrant second generation.* Berkeley, CA: University of California Press.

Portes, A., & Zhou, M. (1993). The new second generation: Segmented assimilation and its variants. *Annals, 530*, 74-96.

Reeves, T., & Bennett, C. (2004). *We the people: Asians in the United States: December 2004, census 2000 special reports*, Washington, DC: U.S. Census Bureau.

Rumbaut, R. (1994). The crucible within: Ethnic identity, self-esteem, and segmented assimilation among children of immigrant. *International Migration Review, 28*, 748-794.

Samura, M. (2010). *Architecture of diversity: Dilemmas of race and space for Asian American students in higher education.* Unpublished doctoral dissertation, University of California, Santa Barbara.

Shibutani, T. (1955). Reference groups as perspectives. *American Journal of Sociology, 60*, 562-569.

Song, M. (2001). Comparing minorities' ethnic options: Do Asian Americans possess "more" ethnic options than African Americans? *Ethnicities, 1*, 57-82.

Suchar, C. (1997). Grounding visual sociology in shooting scripts. *Qualitative Sociology, 20*, 33-55.

Takagi, D. (1992). *The retreat from race: Asian-American admissions and racial politics.* New Brunswick, NJ: Rutgers University Press.

Tuan, M. (2004). Assimilation redux. *Du Bois Review: Social Science Research on Race, 1*, 389-392.

Waters, M. (1990). *Ethnic options: Choosing identities in America.* Berkeley, CA: University of California Press.

Winant, H. (2004). *The new politics of race: Globalism, difference, justice.* Minneapolis, MN: University of Minnesota Press.

Wu, F. (2002). *Yellow: Race in American beyond and white*. New York, NY: Basic Books.

Zhou, M. (1997). Segmented assimilation: Issues, controversies, and recent research on the new second generation. *International Migration Review, 31*, 825-858.

Zhou, M., & Xiong, Y. S. (2005). The multifaceted American experiences of the children of Asian immigrants: Lessons for segmented assimilation. *Ethnic and Racial Studies, 28*, 1119-1152.

CHAPTER 5

ASIAN AMERICANS, "CRITICAL MASS," AND CAMPUS RACIAL CLIMATE

A CRT Case Study

Oiyan Poon

This article explores ways in which Asian American college students continue to be racially marginalized, based on their experiences of racial microaggressions, despite critical mass, due to a campus racial climate that maintains White dominance and privilege. In the *Grutter* and *Gratz* Supreme Court decisions, proponents of affirmative action claimed that a critical mass of minority students could effectively counter racial marginalization often experienced by students of color due to their racial status. On some campuses, Asian Americans as a panethnic population enjoy a critical mass in undergraduate enrollments and therefore present an opportunity for scholars to explore the relationship between critical mass and racial marginalization within the campus racial climate. Based on 25 in-depth interviews, the analysis identifies themes of Asian American student experiences with racial microaggressions. The article concludes with a discussion of implications for educational practice as well as future research directions.

Asian American Education—Racial Issues, and Languages, pp. 101–130

Critical mass, theoretically, is thought to counter the racial isolation, tokenism, and invisibility of a given group of students. In the 2003 Supreme Court cases of *Grutter v. Bollinger* and *Gratz v. Bollinger* (539 U.S. 306), the defense argued that, "the 'critical mass' admissions criteria supports the creation of a learning environment that combats the marginalization of underrepresented populations" (Anderson, Daugherty, & Corrigan, 2005, p. 53). On some college campuses, there is a conspicuous critical mass of Asian Americans among undergraduates, providing an opportunity for critical race examinations of the relationship between critical mass and racial marginalization in the context of campus racial climate.

This chapter identifies and discusses the unique ways in which Asian Americans at one large public university on the West Coast are racialized and negatively impacted by racism in the campus racial climate even though they represent over 40% of the undergraduate population. Although Asian Americans represent the largest racial group on this particular campus, they continue to be racially marginalized by a culture of White dominance. Using a critical race theory (CRT) framework, this study will determine whether and how Asian American students are racially marginalized on a campus where they represent a critical mass. In order to identify ways in which Asian Americans are racialized and impacted by racism, it will also examine Asian American experiences of racial microaggressions, which are daily experiences of subtle discrimination and racial assaults experienced by people of color that accumulate over time and contribute toward the maintenance of their racially subordinated position and White racial power in society (Solórzano, Ceja, & Yosso, 2000). By studying student experiences with racial microaggressions, scholars can "better understand how campus racial climate affects the educational experiences and outcomes of Students of Color" (Solórzano, Allen, & Carroll, 2002, p. 16). The experiences and perspectives of Asian American college students, especially stories about the hidden injuries of racism (Osajima, 1993) they endure, also provide critical insights into how systems of racial inequality in education shape race relations to privilege Whiteness.

After a brief review of literature on Asian Americans and campus racial climate and a summary of the study methods, this paper will summarize and discuss findings from in-depth individual interviews of 25 randomly selected Asian American undergraduates, who represent a diversity of ethnicities, genders, academic majors, and socioeconomic class. The study's findings indicate that numerical representation is not the sole indicator of racism in higher education. While the underrepresentation of minority students is a critical problem requiring significant attention in postsecondary education, it represents just one contributing factor that shapes students' racial contexts and campus racial climates (Hurtado, Milem, Clayton-Pedersen, & Allen, 1998). Minority status and racial marginalization in society are not only determined by numerical representation, but they are also linked to racial power. According to Kim (2000), racial power, "works via cumulative and interactive processes in the political, social, economic, and cultural realms to continuously reconstitute racial categories, meanings, and distributions in a way that maintains White dominance in American society" (p. 10). Despite the fact that Asian Americans represent a racial plurality on the campus in this study, their lack of White racial status maintains their racial subordination, which is often embodied by experiences of racial microaggressions. Therefore, it is important for discourse and policymaking related to racial diversity and campus racial climate in higher education to include an examination of racial microaggressions.

LITERATURE REVIEW

Asian Americans present an interesting and understudied population for campus racial climate studies. They represent a complex population consisting of a multitude of ethnic groups with many different sociopolitical histories, experiences, and languages; and as a result, there are great educational disparities among Asian Americans (Chang, Park, Lin, Poon, & Nakanishi, 2007; Teranishi, 2002). Given such intra-Asian American complexities, diversities and disparities, some scholars simply exclude Asian Americans from their research and discussion of data collected, while others just aggregate them with Whites, dismissing their unique experiences attributed to their racialized status. However, the unique ways in which they are racialized in higher education and throughout U.S. society in general provide a unique lens through which to understand processes of racial formation (Omi & Winant, 1994) in the campus racial climate.

Campus racial climate is broadly defined as the environment of race relations on a college campus (Solórzano, Ceja, & Yosso, 2000). Theories on campus racial climate have been developed to understand racial conflict (Hurtado, 1992), effects of affirmative action debates on students of color (Inkelas, 2003; Solórzano, Ceja, & Yosso, 2000), and student perceptions and experiences of campus racial climate (Ancis, Sedlacek, & Mohr, 2000). According to Allen and Solórzano (2001), "Understanding and analyzing the campus racial climate is an important part of examining college access, persistence, graduation, and transfer to and through graduate and professional school" (p. 239).

Hurtado, Milem, Clayton-Pedersen, and Allen (1998) recognize external and internal forces that shape student experiences and provide a framework for policymakers and educational practitioners to develop interventions for race relations on campus. In defining external domains, they state that, "Sociohistoric forces influencing the climate for diversity on campus are events or issues in the larger society, nearly always originating outside the campus, that influence how people view racial diversity in society;" they list state policies addressing financial aid, admissions, and state systems of higher education as examples (Hurtado et al., 1998, p. 282). Focusing on internal forces, Hurtado et al. (1998) identify four domains of the campus racial climate that influence race relations: the institutional context of historical inclusion or exclusion; institutional structural diversity; the psychological dimension and impact of campus racial climate on students; and the behavioral climate dimension, which encompasses interpersonal interactions and relations on campus. Racial representations among students, faculty and staff are included in the definition of institutional structural diversity. Therefore, while adequate representation of diversity on campus is an important internal dimension within the campus environment, there are many other external and internal factors that contribute toward the social construction of campus racial climate.

Through a review of 15 years of research on campus racial climate, Harper and Hurtado (2007) found that while Asian Americans were included in the majority of research on the perceptions of campus climate by race (7 of 11 studies and articles) and on the benefits associated with positive campus climates for cross-racial interactions (9 of 11), only 4 of the 13 articles on racial/ethnic minority student experiences with racism and prejudice included Asian Americans. Harper and Hurtado also indicate that Asian Americans, similar to White students, had a higher sense of social satisfaction on their campuses than Latino and African American students. However, the views and perspectives of Asian Americans on race are significantly different from those of other racial groups and more complex (Inkelas, 2006). The complexities of the relationship between campus racial climate and Asian Americans might not have been adequately captured by the studies reviewed by Harper and Hurtado (2007). For example, Inkelas (2006) found that certain subsets of Asian American students (immigrants, women, and those with high SAT scores) were more likely than others to believe that racial discrimination was a problem. Asian American students who more closely identified with White dominant culture were also more likely to oppose affirmative action.

Interestingly, in an earlier study, Inkelas (2003) also found that Asian American college students expressed a sense of being ostracized from race relations dialogues, which largely followed a Black-White paradigm. This last finding is reinforced in a study by Lewis, Chesler, and Forman (2000), who found that, "the dominant focus on Black-White relations in most discussions about campus racial/ethnic climate was sometimes found to create problems for the Latino/a, Asian American, and Native American students" (pp. 83-84).

Counter to what some may believe, Asian American college students often do cite racial oppression as a significant social problem (Chang et al., 2007; Inkelas, 2006). Ancis, Sedlacek, and Mohr (2000) found that like African American students, Asian American college students were less satisfied with the university than White students. Their study also indicated that Asian Americans reported more incidents of faculty bias and racism than Latino and White students (Ancis, Sedlacek, & Mohr, 2000). In a case study of the University of Massachusetts at Amherst, analysis of telephone survey data conducted by Kotori and Malaney (2003) found that Asian American students held a more negative perception of campus racial climate and experienced significantly more incidents of racial harassment than their White peers. Kotori and Malaney (2003) also found that Asian American students were less aware of their legal rights than White students to respond to racially harassing incidents. A study by Woo (1997) showed that Asian American college students reported experiencing subtle forms of racial discrimination on campus and struggled to negotiate what it means to be Asian American given the racial stereotypes they encountered. Moreover, analysis of data from the University of California Undergraduate Experience Survey indicates that despite their critical mass on the nine undergraduate campuses, Asian American students have lower sense of belonging than non-Asian American students (Samura, 2010).

Other studies have also examined how negative campus racial climates can result in significant stress on students' mental health. Solórzano, Allen, and Carroll (2002) examined campus racial climate through a CRT lens with individual experiences of racial microaggressions as units of analysis. Their study primarily focused on the perspectives of African American and Latino students with some incorporation of Asian American student experiences. Cress and Ikeda (2003) specifically studied the relationship between Asian American students and campus racial climates, and found that negative racial climate can lead to significant mental health consequences.

As the research on campus racial climate and Asian Americans slowly increases, it is interesting to note that none of the studies mentioned thus far focused on the relationship between "critical mass" and racial marginalization. Indeed, many campus racial climate studies begin with concerns about the "underrepresentation" of minority populations; and undoubtedly the lack of critical mass or experiences of racial isolation are important to address in campus racial climate assessments (Solórzano, Allen, & Carroll, 2002). However, on many U.S. campuses, the percentage of Asian

American undergraduate students often exceeds the local area's general population of Asian Americans.

Two studies have addressed campus racial climate on campuses with significant numbers of Asian Americans, where the population is no longer considered "underrepresented." At the University of Hawai'i-Manoa, one of the few majority Asian American institutions, Okamura and Tsutsumoto (1998) found that over one-fifth of undergraduates and staff had experienced discrimination, and 39% of student respondents reported knowing other students who had been the target of racist experiences. Additionally, their study found differences in experiences and perspectives by ethnic subgroup, demonstrating the importance of ethnic disaggregation when possible in research on Asian Americans. In another campus racial climate assessment at a large public Midwestern university with an Asian American enrollment percentage larger than the population's representation in the state, Lee, Lee, Mok, and Chih (2009) found that many Asian American students found an unwelcoming environment. Over one-third of their respondents indicated that they had experienced racially discriminatory incidents and had concerns about race relations on campus. Lee et al. (2009) also concluded from the survey data analysis that there were significant variations in how Asian American students were affected by the campus environment by ethnicity, student status (undergraduate vs. graduate), and generational status.

The findings presented by the campus-specific studies by Okamura and Tsutsumoto (1998) and Lee et al. (2009) reinforce the Hurtado's (1992) theoretical framework on campus racial climate, which outlines adequate enrollment representations of various racial groups as only one aspect of a positive campus environment. As Lee et al. (2009) concluded, having a racially diverse student enrollment is not sufficient for a positive campus climate. "Greater demographic diversity and meaningful cross-group interactions may affect psychological comfort on campus" (Lee et al., 2009, p. 207).

This brief literature review echoes Harper and Hurtado's (2007) acknowledgement that, "too few researchers have explored how Asian American and Native American students experience campus racial climates" (p. 12). In some studies, Asian Americans have been found to be similar to Whites in their satisfaction with campus environments. In others, they have been shown to experience negative racial climates. The contradictory findings on Asian Americans and campus racial climate indicate that the experiences of Asian Americans with race in college and in society in general present interesting, nuanced and complex research challenges. This study aims to contribute toward the campus racial climate literature by further exploring the relationship between the "critical mass" of Asian

Americans and racial marginalization. Does the critical mass of a given racial minority population mitigate racial marginalization?

STUDY AND METHODS

This study utilized a critical race theory (CRT) methodology. According to Solórzano and Yosso (2002), CRT methodology positions research as an epistemological project that generates knowledge about the experiences of populations that have been marginalized by past research. As discussed earlier, research on Asian Americans in education has been limited by the unique challenges presented by this diverse population. Additionally, in much of the existing literature on Asian Americans in education, Asian American voices and experiences have been largely silent, with research positioning these students and their families as objects rather than subjects. This study used CRT to overcome these difficulties and limitations. CRT methodology challenges scholars to conduct research in order to develop theories of social transformation and to intentionally address social inequalities. It also positions research to examine and understand the experiences of people of color with racism and other forms of oppression as well as their responses to these experiences. These experiences and responses can occur inside and outside the walls of schools and must be understood within the larger social context. Finally, research conducted using CRT methodology should be done through an interdisciplinary lens, and it must aim to counter dominant narratives.

This study was conducted at the University of California, Los Angeles (UCLA), a large urban public university, where approximately 40% of the undergraduates identify as Asian American. The prestigious reputation of the university and shifting enrollment demographics have led to intense debates that have shaped the campus racial climate and student experiences, especially since the 1996 passage of Proposition 209, a ballot measure that banned public institutions in California from utilizing race, ethnicity, and gender in admissions and hiring. When the interviews were conducted in Fall 2008, the campus was embroiled in an ongoing controversy over admissions policies directly and indirectly affecting Asian Americans.[1] During many of the interviews, as will be discussed in the findings section, students discussed the UCLA admissions debates, indicating that even though the admissions controversy primarily focused on the low numbers of African Americans admitted to the university, Asian American students were significantly affected by the public discourse.

Twenty-five random Asian American students who were at least sophomores were recruited for interviews, each lasting between one and two hours. In order to participate in the study, students had to identify as 1.5

or second generation Asian American. I defined 1.5-generation as Asian Americans who immigrated to the U.S. no later than the age of 12. I narrowed the focus of subjects to 1.5 and second generation Asian Americans because the research literature recognizes these two groups of youth generally as being similarly acculturated to and familiar with dominant U.S. culture and intimately familiar with the immigrant experience (Portes & Rumbault, 2001). They also make up the majority of Asian American youth population.

Table 5.1 summarizes the characteristics of the students interviewed based on data collected through the survey. Due to the self-selection nature of the sampling, the interview subjects' characteristics did not exactly match the patterns found among all Asian American undergraduates at the university. There was a larger representation of Southeast Asian American (28% vs. 17.8%) and Filipino American (16% vs. 9.3%) students in the study relative to the campus population. There was an underrepresentation in the study of East Asian Americans (48% vs. 59.8%) and South Asian Americans (8% vs. 13.1%). The gender balance between the subjects and the campus population was very close (56% vs. 55% women). Another difference between the subjects in this study and Asian American students at UCLA was in the distribution of academic majors. The students in this study were less likely than the overall population of Asian American undergraduates to be pursuing academic majors in the science, technol-

Table 5.1.   Characteristics of 25 Interview Subjects

	East Asian	South Asian	Southeast Asian	Filipino	% of Total
% of sample	48%	8%	28%	16%	100%
Female	6	2	3	3	56%
Male	6	–	4	1	44%
STEM	2	–	3	2	28%
Lib Arts	9	2	–	2	52%
Business	1	–	1	–	8%
Family Income					
<$60,000	5	–	4	1	40%
$60-$89,999	4	–	3	3	40%
>$90,000	3	2	–	–	20%
2nd generation	9	2	6	4	84%
1.5 generation	3	–	1	–	16%
Transfer students	2	–	–	2	16%

ogy, engineering, or mathematics (STEM) related fields in Fall 2008. Institutional data aggregates Asian Americans and Pacific Islanders (AAPI) and shows that Asian American and Pacific Islander students were the most likely (58%) to pursue STEM majors. Only 39% of White students, 38% of African American students, and 38% of Latino students were STEM majors. Interestingly, the distribution of majors for AAPIs at UCLA was very similar to that of international students, of whom 55% were STEM majors.

Prior to each of the scheduled interviews, I e-mailed the participants a one page outline of the themes of racial microaggressions experienced by Asian Americans developed by Sue, Bucceri, Lin, Nadal, and Torino (2007). Sue and his colleagues identified eight major themes of racial microaggressions that target Asian Americans. These include alien in own land, ascription of intelligence, exotification of Asian women, invalidation of interethnic differences, denial of racial reality, pathologizing cultural values/communication styles, second class citizenship, and invisibility. They also included a ninth theme of microaggressions that were undefined.

During the interviews, I asked subjects to discuss each theme and provide evaluation based on their personal experiences during their time in college. I encouraged the subjects to share memories and stories of their experiences that related to each theme. I also asked the subjects whether there were experiences of racial microaggressions they had experienced that were not detailed in the Sue et al. (2007) categories. Some were able to generate additional themes. Through their personal narratives, they were also able to critique the themes and discuss the themes in more detail, contributing toward a redefinition of the themes.

SUMMARY OF FINDINGS

Racial microaggressions, as past studies (Solórzano, Allen, & Carroll, 2002; Solórzano, Ceja, & Yosso, 2000) have shown, are outcomes of the social context and campus racial climate. Identifying and analyzing Asian American experiences with these racially marginalizing incidents can lead to a more complex understanding of how Asian Americans are racialized within the social context of the campus racial climate. All 25 of the interview subjects articulated and discussed racial microaggression experiences that fell under one of four categories of racial microaggressions that emerged from the study: exclusion, alien in own land, gendered racial microaggressions, and ascription of intelligence.

Racial Microaggression Category: Exclusion

Through analysis of interviews, I found that experiences of being treated as a second class citizen, denial of racial reality, invisibility, the invalidation of interethnic differences, and cultures and values being pathologized could be broadly categorized as experiences under a theme of exclusion from mainstream society. The interview subjects' discussion of these five themes, which were originally described by Sue et al. (2007), demonstrated that they were significantly interrelated. These five themes show how Asian Americans are racialized in a way that excludes and dismisses them from being recognized as a diverse population of individuals and U.S. citizens with valid and important perspectives and experiences.

Second class citizenship. Experiences of racial microaggressions under the theme of second class citizenship convey the message that Asian Americans are valued less than others, especially Whites (Sue et al., 2007). Students discussed experiences of being overlooked by faculty and other staff in favor of White peers, the demeaning nature of public commentary reducing Asian Americans to racial mascots, and observations of the institution reducing funding for academic curricula in ways that seem to target Asian and Asian American-related course offerings. Joe, a second generation Taiwanese American man majoring in business, discussed feelings of being treated like a second class citizen due to his racial status. As a marching band member for several years, Joe observed that the students in band and its student leadership, who were all selected by the band director and his staff, were overwhelmingly White and did not reflect the racial demographics of the rest of the university's enrollment. He stated:

> I know band is mostly White. The director, he's an old guy. He's a little bit old fashioned. A lot of times you feel like he does discriminate against certain races. For a really long time the only drum majors were White trumpet players. This year there was a kind of an exception.... A lot of people always said that he was racist or liked to discriminate. So I was always under the impression that he was going to no matter what. But sometimes, I guess perceptions change.

In sharing his thoughts, Joe noted that he and many of his peers had noticed that the band director, a White man, had rarely selected non-White men for the primary leadership role of drum major in the organization. Additionally, because membership in the band was by audition, the demographics of the band were an outcome of the selection process organized by the band director and his staff.

Students also expressed frustration over public discourse reducing Asian Americans to a discursive tool as "racial mascots" as a second way in which Asian Americans experience racial microaggressions characterized by the second class citizen theme. According to Cho (1998), "The adoption of a racial group or even an individual of color by a White political figure or constituency—a practice I refer to as mascotting—is necessary to deflect charges of racism and preserve the redeemed status of whiteness" (p. 169). Essentially, mascotting is a patronizing process, which two interview subjects particularly objected to because of how it reduced Asian Americans to discursive tools within the public discourse. Discussing the on-going campus controversy over race and admissions,[2] Kyle, a 1.5 generation Taiwanese American male studying ethnic studies and anthropology, shared:

> I do not think highly of Groseclose because he specifically targeted the Vietnamese Americans. He was the professor who wrote the article that basically pointed out the Vietnamese community. Like, "Oh it's so weird that Black student admissions went up, but Vietnamese admissions went down." So like it's obvious that is a blatant attempt to pit our two communities against each other. And also it just shows how he's basically saying that all Black students that got in didn't deserve it because there is something wrong with the admissions process.

EunJung, a second generation Korean American woman studying psychology and ethnic studies, also commented on the controversy, explaining:

> You shouldn't pit Asian Americans against other minority groups. It's just very misleading because data needs to be analyzed further to really get a full story. The way that some people frame it is … they're trying to pit the Vietnamese students against the African American students, which is divide and conquer. It's kind of the same thing as in the beginning of Asian American history, just manipulating Asian Americans to whatever policy that benefits the privileged.

EunJung recognized the larger implications of the professor's actions as a symptom of a larger historical pattern of pitting minority communities against each other and of a process of dividing and conquering in order to maintain White dominance.

Finally, students described experiences of racial microaggressions characterized by the theme of second class citizen committed by the institution through targeted budget cuts. During difficult budget times, all universities must make tough decisions for cost efficiencies. Seung, a 1.5 generation Korean American male majoring in communications, shared, "There was a budget cut, and the first thing they thought of getting rid of was Asian American studies and Korean classes. There was a big fight during the summer." He went on to explain that he and his peers suspected that the administration targeted Asian and Asian American-related curriculum because of a perception that Asian American students would not protest. Referring to the same proposed budget cuts, EunJung also asserted:

> If administration really values students' input, they wouldn't cut that. Things like language classes ... [cutting them] ... that's the idea that our cultures aren't valuable enough to maintain the higher levels of language. I don't know if they'll be cutting the lower levels, but it still ... it's the whole idea of promoting diversity and then slash what students actually want on campus.

On the one hand, the institution stood firmly behind a stated commitment to supporting diversity. Yet on the other hand, students observed the university cutting back on certain course offerings on topics like Asian languages and cultures, leading them to conclude that the university was insincere in its statements of diversity.

Denial of racial reality. Experiences with this type of microaggression convey the idea that Asian Americans do not experience discrimination or racial inequalities, essentially dismissing Asian Americans who claim that they have experienced racial discrimination. Amber, a second generation Chinese American female transfer student majoring in ethnic studies and political science, explained why others view Asian Americans as a model minority, "I can see how with the whole model minority, how our experiences don't matter as much, where some are doing so well, they're almost seen as economically where White people are at." Some students had experiences with racial microaggressions that directly questioned the legitimacy of Asian Americans as a racially marginalized group. Lee, a second generation Vietnamese American female majoring in art, shared:

> [The student-initiated retention office] tends to be a predominantly Black and Chicano space. It's kind of like the attitude of it ... as if their struggle is way worse than ours. It's kind of like this attitude like I'm more down than you or like my community's better than yours because I struggle more, which isn't even the case because oppression isn't even about comparability. So [Asian American organizations] were constantly left to legitimize our experiences and our struggle in that space. Because a lot of people are like "You're Asian. Why do you even need retention? Why do you even need these services? Look at your numbers!" 40%, right? Of course that 40% is an umbrella of like how many different ethnicities? And we're serving Southeast Asians specifically.

Even in these consciousness-raising and social justice dedicated spaces that Lee described, Asian American students continued to be marginalized, their racial realities denied.

Invisibility. Encounters with racial microaggressions characterized by the theme invisibility were also common. These incidents occur when Asian Americans are left out of discussions of race and inequality (Sue et al., 2007). As in incidents related to the denial of racial reality theme, Asian American experiences with racial inequality and discrimination are dismissed as irrelevant. In fact, the similarities between the two themes confused many interview subjects who did not see a difference. Experiences related to both themes effectively exclude Asian Americans from participating in dialogues on social inequalities related to racism.

Race in the U.S. has predominantly been understood and viewed through a Black-White binary framework (Takaki, 1989). However, Asian Americans continue to be excluded from the discourse on social problems stemming from racism. As Matthew, a mixed race second generation Asian American male transfer student majoring in history, stated:

> I talk with other people of color that just don't see problems for Asian Americans as being as real or important as theirs. A lot of it has to do with race in America being a Black or Brown versus White issue. Maybe certain types of racial issues aren't as tangible as like nooses hanging off a tree in a high school, but I mean these microaggressions, I would say, build up for people every day. A fantastic place to see this is ... have you ever been to juicy campus? It's the worst fucking thing in the world. People say shit that you wouldn't imagine people would say. There was one today. I go there to ... it keeps me inspired to keep doing work, for lack of a better word. Every time I think things are going better, I go there and some guy wrote ching-chong ching-chong for 30 lines. People say the most ridiculous racist things that like you know they would never say to somebody in a conversation, even if it was someone their best friend, they wouldn't say it, but with the anonymity of the internet like which isn't even that anonymous, you can trace this stuff. It seems virtually anonymous and people say terrible things. [looks for web site] Oh yea, this is it. Talks about the Asians last night at Jefferson. Someone was asking about why there was a big fight, and there was a bunch of cops. And then, "Ching chang chong I eat dog. I like rice. I come to UCLA and cheat on tests, go to med school so my papa won't beat me. I have small wee wee. Ching chang chong."

Indeed, Bonilla-Silva (2006) demonstrates that since the Civil Rights movement, White liberalism has defined racism as overt and blatantly violent incidents, leaving the subtler and less visible ways that racism operates go largely unexamined.

Although universities are often viewed as spaces that are more liberal and tolerant, interview subjects discussed incidents in classrooms when their experiences with racism and social inequalities dismissed as irrelevant. These experiences largely led to a silencing of Asian American students from participating in class discussions and from sharing their perspectives with others. Ken, a second generation Thai American male majoring in biological sciences, shared:

> In one of my classes, I tried to a take a comparative literature class over the summer and I ended up dropping it. In one of the discussions, there was an African American girl, and she was very outspoken. Throughout my life, I've never really complained about race in terms of academics or talked about it. Because of the model minority image, it doesn't seem like racism affects us as much in a negative way. So why should we even discuss it? I definitely feel like for other ethnicities, especially for African Americans and Latinos, race is a huge issue. I never want to be like that. I don't know ... I always viewed talking back in that way to be negative, so I just avoided it. As such, I guess I became invisible.

Ken's comments indicated that he has chosen to avoid publicly discussing how racism affects his life as an Asian American, which has led to his own invisibility and silence. Moreover, his comments suggested that he views "talking back" in ways that articulate injustices to be unpleasant, and that people of color who protest are targeting White racial power.

The overall, relative ignorance about social inequalities experienced by Asian Americans creates a burden for Asian Americans to educate their peers and others, even in spaces that value diversity. Lee, who is heavily involved in student-initiated retention organizations on campus with other students of color, shared:

> I explained to [the professional staff advisor] like the sentiment of Southeast Asian community feeling like delegitimized [sic], always having to prove ourselves and show people that we face adversities too. He was so surprised. He was like "Really? You feel that?" I'm really frustrated about it. As a person of color, I try really hard to educate myself to be conscious of what other communities' struggles are. I think it' really important to identify with the struggle and align myself with the commonalities. While we have different struggles, it's the understanding that within a political structure we're positioned, all of us are marginalized. It's really frustrating to feel that while I have people's backs, in certain moments when I need it, they don't have my back. But whenever I talk about Asian American experiences, other people are just blown away. They're like, "What? That happened to you in your lifetime? Your parents went through that?" They had no idea. It's good they're learning about it, but it also shows that people aren't taking the effort to educate themselves.

Perhaps due to their significant representation on campus, Asian Americans' experiences with racism are largely dismissed as irrelevant. Black and Latino experiences are used as the benchmark for racial oppression based largely on underrepresentation and other educational attainment factors. The narrow definition of racial marginalization further silences and excludes Asian American experiences in the campus racial climate.

Invalidation of interethnic differences. One of the most common experiences of racial microaggressions expressed by the interview subjects was the invalidation of interethnic differences. In the study by Sue et al. (2007), these types of microaggressions suggest, "that all Asian Americans are alike and that differences between groups do not exist and/or do not matter" (p. 76). Students not only felt annoyed in these circumstances, they also saw an East Asian centrality in the way Asian Americans are racialized, which also led to a systemic oversight in recognizing and addressing disparities experienced by Asian Americans who were not East Asian (e.g., Chinese, Korean, or Japanese).

Jason, a second generation Taiwanese American male studying psychology and arts, discussed his frustration over some people's lack of respect for his ethnic heritage as a Taiwanese American. He stated, "I identify as Taiwanese. I don't identify as Chinese. So there are times when I have to explain to people that it's different." Ignorance among peers over world politics and geography also frustrated Raakhi, a second generation Indian American woman majoring in economics, who shared, "I feel that people don't know the difference between Indian people and Middle Eastern. Also, I've had to deal with stuff like when people ask, 'Are you from Indonesia?' and ask 'What's the difference between India and Indonesia?' " While subjects recognized that these experiences are not the worst kinds of racist incidents, they found them annoying nonetheless. As Joe explained:

> I know the whole lumping all Asians together happens a lot. It's kind of like, "yeah, whatever, you're all Asian," sort of thing. They don't want to figure out which ethnic ... I can understand. There's a lot of Asians. But yea, Chinese are different from Japanese, are different from Koreans, etc. A lot of times, [my friends] like to do this joke because the marching band staff always mix me up with another Asian American. It's funny a lot of times ... well ... but, sometimes a lot of people do it too much.

Although experiences with the invalidation of interethnic differences seemed relatively harmless, some students explained that these assumptions connect to an institutional neglect of educational disparities faced by different Asian American ethnic subpopulations. Gary, a second generation Thai American male life sciences major, explained:

> If you lump people together, you kind of assume that there's this broader stereotype of how everyone doesn't have problems, but that's not really true for other groups. In many ways it could harm smaller under-represented

groups within the Asian American community. For example like the model minority kind of thing ... you see Chinese, Japanese or certain communities do well in the general population, but then Hmong, Khmer groups aren't. They're still struggling. So that's kind of harming people, grouping everyone together.

Lee further explained the challenges of the lack of ethnically disaggregated data on Asian Americans:

Part of the problem is that Asian Americans being an umbrella term and basically most think the population is really academically successful, socially mobile, all that stuff. They don't see a lot of the small issues within that umbrella, under that umbrella of the different communities. Like Southeast Asian communities are marginalized by refugee experiences, like undocumented status, and other problems.

These comments showed that the institution can also perpetuate the invalidation of interethnic differences by neglecting to collect ethnically disaggregated data so that educational inequalities are not overlooked and excluded from institutional attention.

Pathologizing cultural values/communication styles. Describing racial microaggressions that pathologize Asian American cultural values or communication styles, Sue et al. (2007) focused on classroom settings where teachers require all students to participate in discussion and argued that such expectations can be unfair to Asian Americans who are raised to value silence. In this theme, they also included experiences where Asian American cultural practices are derided for being strange, exotic, and outside of American norms.

As someone who is proud of her Hindu culture, Raakhi shared that some of her peers have asked her questions about her cultural practices in a way that made her feel uncomfortable. She explained:

People will ask me with this attitude, "You have a monkey god? You have an elephant god? What's up with that?" Our elephant god is seated on a mouse. People are like, "I don't get it." To me, I understand the significance. I don't know a lot about other religions like Judaism or Islam, but I'm not going to be like ... especially with that look on your face. I am very interested in religion, so I ask my friends questions like, "I'm not sure how to say it, but can you tell me more about that?" I feel like people don't have the politeness or sensitivity to phrase it right. Sometimes I'm just like, "Yea, we have a lot of gods" when I don't want to deal.

Raakhi's comments indicated that while she was willing to share about her religion and culture, she got tired and frustrated by negative and judgmental attitudes held by others about her heritage.

Lee's experiences in student-initiated retention programs offices were also indicative of cultural stereotypes that Asian Americans must face. Throughout her interview, Lee wanted to discuss her frustrations with how Asian American students and experiences were viewed by non-Asian American peers and professional staff. One of the problems that the Southeast Asian American students were facing, in Lee's opinion, was that the professional staff seemed caught off-guard by the voicing of concerns by students. Lee shared:

> It's finally coming out. That's why people are all surprised, like, "Why are they complaining?" They're not used to us, but what if it was African Americans. It would probably be totally different. But because it happened to us, it's because we're stepping so much out of our stereotype. Like we're demanding so much. We're being so outspoken that people are like, "What's your issue? What's your beef?" I don't know … maybe it's cultural. Maybe we've been socialized somewhat to take part in the role where anytime these issues happen to us we've been so compromising. We just want to resolve it with as little conflict as possible.

By articulating their concerns, the Southeast Asian American students may have been acting in ways that other students and staff did not expect from them. The lodging of complaints seemed to come after several incidents which were not addressed by Southeast Asian American students at earlier points in time. Lee admitted that perhaps it was possible that they had been socialized to avoid conflict. The avoidance of conflict coupled with the staff possibly being surprised by the students acting outside of the stereotypically passive behaviors of Asian Americans may have led to the significant clash experienced.

Racial Microaggression Category: Alien in Own Land

The historical legacy of exclusionary policies has led to Asian Americans remaining a largely immigrant population (Chan, 1991). Regardless of citizenship or generational status, Asian Americans continue to be viewed as foreigners. This leads to the second theme of racial microaggressions—alien in own land. Within the campus racial climate, it may contribute toward the low sense of belonging in the University of California (UC) expressed by Asian American undergraduates despite the large numbers of Asian Americans on the UC campuses (Samura, 2010). In addition to encountering individuals who assume that they are from outside of the United States, Asian Americans often have their cultural citizenship as Americans questioned, and Asian Americans studying non-STEM majors go through experiences that undermine their belonging in non-STEM fields. Interestingly, many subjects stated that they were often made to feel uncertain of their English language skills even when they were born in the United States and barely speak another language, if at all. These experiences can make Asian Americans question their sense of belonging in society, especially if the messages they receive from peers and others communicate that they do not belong in U.S. society.

Many of the subjects interviewed shared the common experience of being asked, "Where are you from?" When answering the questioner with a U.S. location, they next fielded the question, "No, where are you *really* from?" None of the subjects in this study discussed this experience in depth. Rather, they recognized it as part and parcel of the Asian American experience based on their racialization.

Some of the interview subjects discussed how, beyond their physical characteristics, some ethnic cultural practices also marked them as foreigners and outsiders to the U.S. mainstream. Raakhi shared experiences of being made to feel alien to U.S. culture even as a second generation American, often by Whites ignorant about non-White cultures. She explained:

> People ask me, "Do you speak Hindu?" I'm like ok; I guess I'll forgive that. It's not a language. It's a religion. Are you Hindi? Why do you wear a dot? Is the dot really cow feces? Or do you really have 1,000 gods? Do you have to worship them all? I'm like, that's OK, I can explain that to you. It's a polytheistic religion. That's fine. If you're interested in the culture, I'll tell you about it. Don't come at me with "Do you put cow feces on your head?" American people do a lot of disgusting things that I'm not mentioning.

Raakhi was frustrated over how people asked questions about her background. She was generally open to people's curiosity and even tended to accept what is essentially a burden of educating others about her cultural background as a cultural spokesperson. What is also interesting is that she also mentioned "American people" as being separate from herself, even though in another part of her interview she says, "I'm American-born," acknowledging that her frustration with people assuming that she is from a place outside of the United States. Her use of the term "American" may indicate a level of an internalized definition of "American" that does not include South Asian Americans.

Amber also shared stories about her experiences as one of the few Asian Americans studying political science. She stated:

> In the seminar classes I've taken there's so many people who are very political, who have very strong opinions. I have strong opinions, but I don't necessarily voice them. When I took a seminar class, I had the person next to me say, "Do you have any opinion about this? Because I don't see you Asian

people talking about these issues." It really struck me because I was sitting there, and I'm definitely interested in political science. Just because I didn't voice them out loud doesn't mean I don't have a strong opinion about it or that Asian people don't have a strong opinion about it. I was just taken aback. I didn't know what to say at that moment. It was weird because I looked around and I was like one of two Asian females in the class.

Although there is a critical mass of Asian Americans on campus, in certain academic departments they are not well represented. In Amber's case, it may have led to an experience of feeling alien in her class and being forced into serving as a racial spokesperson.

Interestingly, several interview subjects explained that they often experienced encounters with primarily White people that made them feel like their English language skills were not very good, even though they were either born in the U.S. or had spent most of their lives in the United States. Even though Shirley, a second generation Filipina American woman studying humanities, was born and raised in northern California, she often encountered incidents that made her feel self-conscious about her English speaking skills and made her feel like she was a foreigner. She shared:

> I still have kind of an accent way of talking but when I was little it was worse. It was a really strange accent too. It wasn't a Filipino accent. It's hard to explain. I guess I had a weird speech impediment. I couldn't say Rs correctly. So when I would talk, a lot of people would think I was from somewhere else, like I was foreign. And I'm like, "no I've been in California all my life." Then they'd be like, "Is English your first language?" And I was like, "Yea, I can't even speak Ilocano or Tagalog." Even last year, a friend of mine knew I was born here, but she was like, "Yea, I get confused because I know you were born here, but I don't know where your accent came from.

Even though her first language is English, people she met perceived some type of foreign accent in her speech.

Both Wilson, a second generation Thai American male studying arts, and Jill, a second generation Thai American woman majoring in anthropology, also felt self-conscious about their English speaking skills, mostly when they were around Whites and very assimilated Asian Americans. Wilson explained:

> I feel a lot more confident around Asian people, but then there's also a difference between white-washed Asians who grew up mostly in Caucasian areas, and they speak … but I guess I'm getting more confident. When I'm around Caucasians and white-washed Asians, they usually say "Huh? What?" So I assume they can't understand me. Or I might be mumbling or I might

not be speaking clear or I might be speaking too fast. So it makes me worry, especially since I notice it's mostly Caucasians who are like "What? Huh?"

Wilson's remarks indicated that past experiences had made him question his own level of acculturation as related to his speech patterns compared to "white-washed" or assimilated Asian Americans. Jill also remarked, "I feel like because the White people have been here longer … and my parents' English isn't so good. So sometimes I'll say something similar to them and I'll realize what I said wasn't grammatically correct." Although she was born and raised in California, Jill felt that being raised by immigrant parents put her at a disadvantage in her English skills compared to Whites.

Racial Microaggression Category: Gendered Racial Microaggressions

CRT also recognizes the intersectionality of one's racial identity with other social identities including gender. While Sue et al. (2007) found that Asian and Asian American women are exotified, the students I interviewed not only provided more details about racial microaggressions targeting Asian American women, they also identified gendered racial microaggressions that affect Asian American men. For many, college is a time to explore intimate relationships and their sexuality. For Asian Americans, how they are both racialized and gendered in U.S. society affects how others view them and in effect how and with whom they develop intimate relationships.

The interview subjects in the study provided details about how Asian American women are racialized and how it affects their lives. Many students shared their opinions about men with "yellow fever," which is a term they used to explain White men who exclusively dated Asian and Asian American women because of their assumptions and images of what Asian women are like. Interestingly, the term excuses the behavior of the men, who objectify and exotify Asian women, by explaining their desire for Asian women as an affliction.

Several students discussed how uncomfortable incidents characterized by the exotification of Asian women made them feel. Ruth, a second generation Chinese American woman majoring in biological sciences, shared:

I really feel that Asian women are exotified. It really bothers me. I don't want people to look at me and say, "Oh she'll be my little sex slave" or something. That's disgusting, and I really don't like it when men have yellow fever. I don't think I could date someone with yellow fever, just because all you see is the color of my skin. That really bothers me.

In the same light, Joe acknowledged:

> I know a lot of people who just love Asian women. I understand, you can have your preferences, but some people are just over the top. Sometimes when people say things like, "Oh I really love Asian women" or "I'd really love to be with an Asian woman" or "I'd really love to get with an Asian woman," it just makes me feel uncomfortable.

Even as an Asian American man, Joe is bothered by these incidents. While he could not fully articulate why these experiences made him uncomfortable, he knew that he did not like them.

Although Sue et al. (2007) did not describe racial microaggressions that especially targeted Asian American men, several interview subjects detailed how gendered racial microaggressions that emasculate Asian American men affected them. In relation to how some Asian American women preferred White men in dating, Mark, a second generation Filipino American male majoring in biological sciences, shared, "If you're going for an Asian American woman, and she says, 'I only want to date White guys,' it definitely affects you. People joke around about it, but sometimes it gets to you." These microaggressions can negatively affect the self-esteem of Asian American men, as Ken explained:

> There's a part of me as an Asian guy that's like, "Why can't the Asian guys get the Asian girls? The stereotypes of us are that we're socially awkward, always good at academics, but we can't approach women. That's why some of us are so bitter. We feel like we have a knife in our backs, like from the Asian girls who don't want us. As an Asian guy, I definitely feel it. We're just not really noticed. We're the nice friend who all the girls come crying to.

Subjects also described that Asian American men are characterized as effeminate and unassertive through these types of gendered racial microaggressions. Matthew shared:

> Emasculation of Asian males. I would say that people don't take me as seriously as if I was White and had the same type of communication style. I can be very forceful when I talk, and I can talk my way around most people. I think to a certain degree I would get more clout if I weren't Asian. Also physically, this always crosses my mind … is when I'm walking up Bruin Walk or somewhere crowded and I move my shoulder to not hit someone. I wonder why they didn't move their shoulder. Why did they wait for me to move? Because I'm pretty nice, but I'm not so nice to the point where I'm not going to knock someone down to prove a point, because sometimes over the years these things do irritate you. I think race affects the space people give you.

Matthew's description of his experiences, suspecting that his race affects how people treat him, included a brief discussion of how racial microaggressions can build up for people. Smith, Allen, and Danley (2007) describe this effect as racial battle fatigue, which refers to the psychological accumulation of the negative effects of racial microaggressions.

Racial Microaggression Category: Ascription of Intelligence

Because Asian Americans are racialized as innately intellectually gifted, especially in the STEM fields, some of the subjects' experiences with racial microaggressions may communicate that they should be academically self-sufficient and limited to STEM fields. This may also lead to an institutional ignorance of Asian American students' needs and a general negligence in conducting effective outreach to support their educational endeavors. Many of the interview subjects identified with this theme of racial microaggressions. For some of the students, academic achievement particularly in STEM fields was integral to being Asian American.

Some students found the stereotype of the academically gifted Asian American to be uncomfortable but were not sure how it was a negative stereotype. Ruth, on the other hand, discussed how even so-called positive stereotypes can harm people, and also critiqued how this type of microaggression can make some feel uncertain of their Asian American identity if they did not have significant academic achievements. She observed:

> The ascription of intelligence thing is definitely … I mean I guess some people consider it a positive stereotype or whatever, but I don't think there's such a thing as a positive stereotype. I think stereotypes in general just serve to trap people in these molds, and people will try to make them fit in the mold. If they don't, then they're suddenly ostracized. So for the intelligence thing … I remember there were Asians who didn't do well in my high school. They just really felt like they weren't Asian or something.

A second generation Chinese American woman majoring in ethnic studies, Delores' reflections on these types of racial microaggressions also indicate that being Asian American means being academically strong in STEM fields and how peers treated her for not being good or liking at math:

> My classmates would be like, "Oh, you're Asian. Why are you so bad at math?" I didn't really care, but our honors classes … everyone who was Asian was in the honors class. It was really easy for people who were Asian to get into honors classes. There was a lot more encouragement between us. My friend Joanie, she was in the regular class, and then senior year, her

friends ... I guess we were the big Asian group ... we were like, "Oh, take the honors class. You'll get in. They'll let you." And [administration] did let her, but I've always wondered like is it really that easy for anybody else? There was one Chicana student, and we were always telling her, "Oh yea, you're practically Asian because you're so smart."

The stereotype of Asian American students as being academically gifted may have allowed one of Delores' peers to easily gain entry into the honors classes. On the other hand, tracking positioned the one Chicana student in honors classes as a token, but due to her academic abilities Asian Americans labeled her an honorary Asian American.

Indeed, subjects seemed to indicate that Asian American identity was somewhat defined by academic success, particularly in STEM fields. Shih Ambady, Richeson, Fujita, and Grey (2002) have shown how this stereotype can be a boost to Asian American academic performance. Additionally, Conchas and Perez (2003) identify some benefits of the "model minority" stereotype for Asian American high school students. They found that teachers and parents had higher expectations for Asian American students, which also placed significant additional pressures on these youth. They described these students' experiences as "surfing the model minority myth," to indicate the tenuous nature of the phenomenon. While Shih et al. (2002) found that Asian Americans can experience a boost from a subtle activation of the stereotype that Asian Americans do well in school, they also found that a blatant activation significantly depresses their academic performance. Blatant activation of this stereotype can be enacted through racial microaggressions.

DISCUSSION AND IMPLICATIONS

College campuses and educational institutions in general are not immune to the pervasiveness of racial projects that reproduce social inequalities in society (Giroux, 1983). They serve as an important part of the "comprehensively racialized social structure" detailed by Omi and Winant (1994, p. 60). Within the settings of postsecondary education, racial projects define how Asian Americans are racialized within an unequal racial structure. The structures and processes of racial inequalities are manifested in daily interpersonal experiences through racial microaggressions in the campus racial climate, consequently shaping college access outcomes and student experiences. Thus, the college campus serves as an important space for lessons on racial meanings within the formal and informal curriculum. These lessons, both conscious and unconscious, socialize students to the broader social order (Harro, 2000).

In this case study at UCLA, Asian American students continue to be racially marginalized through experiences with racial microaggressions despite the critical mass of Asian American undergraduates. Specifically, student narratives of experiences on campus fit within four thematic categories of racial microaggressions: exclusion, alien in own land, gendered racial microaggressions, and ascription of intelligence. This finding is consistent with the assertion by Hurtado et al. (1998) that campus racial climate consists of multiple domains and shaped by external and internal forces. It also affirms the contention presented in Lee et al. (2009) that racial representations and diversity on campus alone will not automatically lead to positive campus racial climate. While critical mass may lead to a stereotype boost in some cases, it does not change the fact that Asian Americans remain a racially subordinated population due to the maintenance of White privilege.

The findings in this study also suggest that Asian Americans continue to be positioned in the middle of the U.S. racial hierarchy (Bonacich, 1973; O'Brien, 2008). As an aggregate, Asian Americans have attained higher levels of educational attainment than other racial minorities. However, findings in this study indicate that they continue to be racially marginalized. Positioned as such, Asian American students are challenged to navigate their social identities of race, gender, and class.

Therefore, it is important that student affairs professionals and social justice educators provide adequate and meaningful educational experiences for Asian American students to develop a critical understanding of racial diversity and what it means to be Asian American in society. Student services should provide learning opportunities, including intergroup dialogues and leadership training that intentionally include Asian American students. Gurin, Nagda, and Lopez (2004) have described an intergroup dialogue program and its positive effects on campus racial climate and learning outcomes for college students. Institutions should also offer ethnic studies and Asian American studies courses, from which all students can benefit. Saenz, Ngai, and Hurtado (2007) identified factors that promote crossracial interactions and learning outcomes that contribute to positive campus racial climate. For Asian American students, leadership training in college, precollege diversity education, and enrollment in diversity related coursework (e.g., ethnic studies) are all positive predictors of their willingness to engage in and learn about diversity in society (Saenz, Ngai, & Hurtado, 2007). Finally, educators should encourage Asian American students to also explore their identities through ethnic related cocurricular activities. Inkelas (2004) also found that Asian American participation in ethnic cocurricular activities increases their understanding of their ethnic identity.

It is the responsibility of institutional leaders and educators in general to ensure that sufficient and targeted services and programs are available for diverse student needs and that the campus climate is welcoming and conducive for positive educational experiences. As mentioned in the literature review, most campus racial climate studies are concerned with the well-being of students of color who are underrepresented. However, this study has shown that Asian American students, although well represented at UCLA, continue to experience racial microaggressions. As Cress and Ikeda (2003) found, negative campus racial climate may lead to adverse effects on the mental health of Asian American students. When institutions assess their campus environment for diversity, they must intentionally consider the unique experiences of Asian Americans. While they may not be underrepresented as a panethnic aggregate in college relative to general populations, Asian Americans continue to go through racially subordinating experiences that may negatively affect time to degree, persistence, and satisfaction with their college experiences.

Additionally it is important to note that some Asian American ethnic groups such as Cambodians, Laotians, Hmong, and other Asian Americans who are low income, first generation college-goers continue to face significant barriers to college access and persistence (Escueta & O'Brien, 1995; Teranishi, 2007; Yeh, 2002), but most colleges and universities collect data on Asian American groups as a panethnic aggregate. This practice reflects institutional views of Asian Americans as a uniform group. The invalidation of ethnic differences is not just found in institutional data collection functions, but it is also perpetuated through interpersonal experiences, as found in this study.

Therefore, as many other scholars have suggested, it is critical for institutions to conduct data collection and analysis through a meaningful lens of ethnic disaggregation, and to also examine data by class, gender, and immigration status (Lee et al., 2009; Ng, Pak, & Lee, 2007; Suzuki, 2002). Although Asian Americans share some experiences as a racialized panethnic group, there is great diversity in experiences and educational barriers among Asian Americans (Teranishi, 2007). The complexities of Asian American populations challenge institutional and academic researchers to conduct empirical studies on this population through a lens that reflects the diversity found among this growing population in post-secondary education.

Because this article is based on a larger case study with a limited number of subjects, it will be important to further explore the relationship between the growing numbers of Asian American college students and campus racial climate. The summary description of various ways in which Asian American college students experience racism in the academy suggests future research directions. It would be interesting to conduct an assessment of how institutional leaders perceive Asian American students and the availability of campus resources that target these students' needs. It would also be worthwhile to further examine how racial microaggressions can affect Asian American student lives in a more in-depth way. For example, how do "ascription of intelligence" microaggressions affect Asian American academic and vocational choices, if at all? Moreover, it is critical to identify and study ways in which Asian American students utilize their agency to respond to racial microaggressions. Asian American students' agency and choices in responding to racial microaggressions and other representations of systems of inequality also serve as forces of movement in processes of racialization, representation, and racial formation within college campuses and the broader societal context. Their actions, whether conscious or not, can redefine or reproduce the meanings of race and what it means to be Asian American in educational institutions and in society at large. Finally, it would be interesting to compare the ways in which Asian American students experience the campus environment in different institutional settings, including institutions at different levels and of different types as well as with different percentages of Asian American populations.

NOTES

1. Since Fall 2006, when the entering freshman class of over 4,800 students at UCLA in Fall 2006 included only 96 African Americans, UCLA has been at the center of on-going and intense public debates over the undergraduate admissions policies and practices in the University of California. These debates, while focused primarily on African Americans, have directly impacted and cast Asian Americans as unwitting participants in the racialized discourse. For example, in the heat of the public discourse, a commentary in the student newspaper called on the UCLA community to "Blame the Asians" for out-performing other students academically and contributing to the low numbers of other students (Levine, 2006). Given the alarmingly low numbers of entering African American students and encouraged by the Chancellor, the Academic Senate Committee on Undergraduate Admissions and Relations with Schools (CUARS) adopted a holistic application review process similar to the one at UC Berkeley, which was implemented in 2002. In the holistic comprehensive review process, each reader reviews applications in their entirety. Therefore evaluators are able to assess each application within the student's unique contexts for achievement.

2. Critics of holistic comprehensive review claim that the process allows for human bias in evaluations, or even violations of Proposition 209, as Professor Tim Groseclose claimed in Fall 2007, when the numbers of African American students admitted increased from 2.1% to 3.4 % of the students

offered admissions at UCLA. Groseclose (2007) questioned the ethics of other professors on CUARS and university administrators in the implementation of holistic review an accused them of conspiring in a cover-up of illegal activities in the admissions review process in order to increase African American admissions numbers. Some of the information he provided as evidence of foul play was that Latino and American Indian students admit rates decreased between 2006 and 2007. To Groseclose, the sharp decline in the Vietnamese American admissions rate was the strongest evidence of the problems of holistic review, which based on his understanding should privilege applicants with the most disadvantages. In his statement of resignation from CUARS he stated, "In terms of obstacles that can be precisely documented, it is not African-American applicants to UCLA who face the greatest life challenges. It is the Vietnamese. For instance, among UCLA applicants, Vietnamese parents, compared to African-American parents, tend to have lower incomes and they are less likely to have attended college" (Groseclose, 2007, p. 5). However, he did not acknowledge that the cause for increases in African American students could have been the result of intentional and sustained efforts by a University-community partnership, which began partly in response to the dismal numbers of entering African American student numbers in Fall 2006 (UCLA Newsroom, 2007).

REFERENCES

Allen, W. R., & Solórzano, D. G. (2001). Affirmative action, educational equity, and campusracial climate: A case study of the University of Michigan law school. *Berkeley La Raza Law Journal, 12,* 237.

Ancis, J., Sedlacek, W., & Mohr, H. (2000). Student perceptions of campus cultural climate byrace. *Journal of Counseling and Development, 78,* 180-185.

Anderson, G. M., Daugherty, E. J. B., & Corrigan, D. M. (2005). The search for a critical mass of minority students: Affirmative action and diversity at highly selective universities andcolleges. *The Good Society, 14*(3), 51-57.

Bonacich, E. (1973). A theory of middleman minorities. *American Sociological Review, 38*(5), 583-594.

Bonilla-Silva, E. (2006). *Racism without racists: Color-blind racism and the persistence of racial inequality in the United States* (2nd ed.). New York, NY: Rowman & Littlefield.

Chan, S. (1991). *Asian Americans: An interpretive history.* New York, NY: Twayne.

Chang, M. J., Park, J. J., Lin, M. H., Poon, O. A., Nakanishi, D. T. (2007). *Beyond myths: The growth and diversity of Asian American college freshmen, 1971-2005.* Los Angeles, CA: Univesity of California-Los Angeles Higher Education Research Institute.

Cho, S. (1998). Rethinking racial divides: Panel on affirmative action, APALSA symposium. *Michigan Journal of Race & Law, 195,* 233-234.

Conchas, G. Q., & Perez, C. C. (2003). Surfing the "model minority" wave of success: How theschool context shapes distinct experiences among Vietnamese youth. In C. O. Suarez & I. Todorova (Eds.), *Understanding the social worlds of immigrant youth* (pp. 41-56). San Francisco, CA: Jossey-Bass.

Cress, C. M., & Ikeda, E. K. (2003). Distress under duress: The relationship between campus climate and depression in Asian American college students. *NASPA Journal, 40*(2), 74-97.

Escueta, E., & O'Brien, E. (1995). Asian Americans in higher education: Trends and issues. In D. T. Nakanishi & T. Y. Nishida (Eds.), *The Asian American educational experience: A source book for teachers and students* (pp. 259-272). New York, NY: Routledge.

Giroux, H. A. (1983). Theories of reproduction and resistance in the new sociology ofeducation: A critical analysis. *Harvard Education Review, 53* (3), 257-293.

Groseclose, T. (2007, August 28). *Report on Suspected Malfeasance in UCLA Admissions and the Accompanying Cover-Up*. http://www.sscnet.ucla.edu/polisci/faculty/groseclose/CUARS.Resignation.Report.pdf

Gurin, P., Nagda, B. A., & Lopez, G. E. (2004). The benefits of diversity in education for democratic citizenship. *Journal of Social Issues, 60*(1), 17-34.

Harper, S. R., & Hurtado, S. (2007). Nine themes in campus racial climates and implications for institutional transformation. In S. R. Harper, & L. D. Patton (Eds.), *Responding to the realities of race on campus* (pp. 7-24). San Francisco, CA: Jossey-Bass.

Harro, B. (2000). The cycle of socialization. In M. Adams, W. J. Blumenfeld, R. Castañeda, H. W. Hackman, M. L. Peters, & X. Zúñiga (Eds.), *Readings for diversity and social justice* (pp. 15-21). New York, NY: Routledge.

Hurtado, S. (1992). The campus racial climate: Contexts of conflict. *The Journal of Higher Education, 63*(5), 539 -569.

Hurtado, S., Milem, J. F., Clayton-Pedersen, A. R., & Allen, W. R. (1998). Enhancing campus climates for racial/ethnic diversity: Educational policy and practice. *The Review of Higher Education, 21*(3), 279-302.

Inkelas, K. K. (2003). Caught in the middle: Understanding Asian Pacific American perspectives on affirmative action through Blumer's group position theory. *Journal of College Student Development, 44*(5), 625-643.

Inkelas, K. K. (2004). Does participation in ethnic cocurricular activities facilitate a sense of ethnic awareness and understanding? A study of Asian Pacific American undergraduates. *Journal of College Student Development, 45*(3), 285-302.

Inkelas, K. K. (2006). *Racial attitudes and Asian Pacific Americans: Demystifying the model minority*. New York, NY: Routledge.

Kim, C. J. (2000). *Bitter Fruit: The politics of Black-Korean conflict in New York City*. New Haven, CT: Yale University Press.

Kotori, C., & Malaney G. (2003). Asian American students' perceptions of racism, reporting behaviors, and awareness of legal rights and procedures. *NASPA Journal, 40*, 56-76.

Lee, S. S., Lee, M. R., Mok, T. A., & Chih, D. W. (2009) Looking beyond the numbers: Asian American college students perceptions of campus climate. In C. C. Park, R. Endo, & X. L. Rong (Eds.), *New perspectives on Asian American par-*

ents, students, and teacher recruitment (pp. 193-218). Charlotte, NC: Information Age.

Levine, J. (2006 October 10). A modest proposal for an immodest proposition [Editorial]. *The Daily Bruin.* http://www.dailybruin.com/articles/2006/10/10/iamodest-proposal-for-animmo/

Lewis, A. E., Chesler, M., & Forman, T. A. (2000). The impact of "colorblind" ideologies on students of color: Intergroup relations at a predominantly White university. *Journal of Negro Education, 69*(1/2), 74-91.

Ng, J. C., Lee, S. S., & Pak, Y. K. (2007). Contesting the model minority and perpetual foreigner stereotypes: A critical review of literature on Asian Americans in education. *Review of Research in Education, 31*(1), 95-130.

O'Brien, E. (2008). *The racial middle: Latinos and Asian Americans living beyond the racial divide.* New York, NY: NYU Press.

Okamura, J., & Tsutsumoto, T (1998). In R. Endo, C. Park, and J. Tsuchida (Eds.), *Current issues in Asian and Pacific American education* (pp. 99-124). S. El Monte, CA: Pacific Asia Press.

Omi, M., & Winant, H. (1994). *Racial formation in the United States: From the 1960s to the 1990s* (2nd ed.). New York, NY: Routledge.

Osajima, K. (1993). The hidden injuries of race. In L. A. Revilla, G. M. Nomura, S. Wong, & S. Hune (Eds.), *Bearing dreams, shaping visions: Asian Pacific American perspectives* (pp. 81-91). Pullman, WA: Washington State University Press.

Portes, A., & Rumbaut, R. G. (2001). *Legacies: The story of the immigrant second generation.* Berkeley, CA: University of California Press.

Saenz, V. B., Ngai, H. N., & Hurtado, S. (2007). Factors influencing positive interactions across race for African American, Asian American, Latino, and White college students. *Research in Higher Education, 48*(1), 1-38.

Samura, M. (2010). *Architecture of diversity: Dilemmas of race and space for Asian American college students.* Unpublished doctoral dissertation, University of California, Santa Barbara.

Shih, M., Ambady, N., Richeson, J. A., Fujita, K., & Grey, H. M. (2002). Stereotypeperformance boosts: The impact of self-relevance and the manner of stereotype activation. *Journal of Personality and Social Psychology, 83*(3), 638-647.

Smith, W. A., Allen, W. R., & Danley, L. L. (2007). Assume the position ... you fit the description: Psychosocial experiences and racial battle fatigue among African American male college students. *American Behavioral Scientist, 51*(4), 551-578.

Solórzano, D. G., Allen, W. R., & Carroll, G. (2002). Keeping race in place: Racial microaggressions and campus racial climate at the University of California, Berkeley. *Chicano-Latino Law Review, 23*(15), 15-112.

Solórzano, D. G., Ceja, M., & Yosso, T. (2000) Critical race theory, racial microaggressions, and campus racial climate: The experiences of African American college students. *Journal of Negro Education, 69*(1/2), 60-73.

Solórzano, D. G., & Yosso, T. J. (2002). Critical race methodology: Counterstorytelling as an analytical framework for education research. *Qualitative Inquiry, 8*(1), 23-44.

Sue, D. W., Bucceri, J., Lin, A. I., Nadal, K. L., & Torino, G. C. (2007). Racial microaggressions and the Asian American experience. *Cultural Diversity and Ethnic Minority Psychology, 13*(1), 72-81.

Suzuki, B. H. (2002). Revisiting the model minority stereotype: Implications for student affairs practice and higher education. In M. K. McEwen, C. M. Kodama, A. N. Alvarez. S. Lee, & C. T. H. Liang (Eds.), *Working with Asian American college students* (pp. 21-32). San Francisco, CA: Jossey Bass.

Takaki, R. (1989). *Strangers from a different shore: A history of Asian Americans*. Boston, MA: Little, Brown.

Teranishi, R. (2002). Asian Pacific Americans and critical race theory: An examination of school racial climate. *Equity and Excellence in Education, 35*(2), 144-154.

Teranishi, R. (2007). Race, ethnicity, and higher education policy: The use of critical quantitative research. In F. Stage (Ed.), *Using quantitative data to answer critical questions* (pp. 37-49). San Francisco, CA: Jossey-Bass.

UCLA Newsroom. (2007 May 24). *Background: African American Admissions at UCLA*. Retrieved from http://newsroom.ucla.edu/portal/ucla/Background-African-American-Admissions7977.aspx?RelNum=7977

Woo, D. (1997) Asian Americans in higher education: Issues of diversity and engagement. *Race, Gender & Class, 4*, 122-143.

Yeh, T. L. (2002). Asian American college students who are educationally at risk. In M. K. McEwen, C. M. Kodama, A. N. Alvarez. S. Lee, & C. T. H. Liang (Eds.), *Working with Asian American college students* (pp. 61-72). San Francisco, CA: Jossey Bass.

CHAPTER 6

TEACHING ON THE EDGE

The Life Story of an Asian American Woman Literacy Professor in a Rural, Predominantly White University

Keonghee Tao Han

In this study, I examine the life-work story of myself, a junior Asian American woman faculty member, while teaching and working in a predominantly White university (PWU). Employing qualitative methods, I analyzed undergraduate students' and administrators' evaluations of me for three years. Findings reveal that students "policed" my English language and physical/racial characteristics and resisted my authority and expertise. Administrators appeared to view diverse faculty from a deficit model, focusing on the cultural difference and demand in assimilation to the mainstream. This study breaks ground in higher education in three important ways: (1) race and culture issues are still among the most divisive concerns in education; (2) institutional-level policies and practices regarding the tenure and promotion process for faculty of color ought to be reassessed, and (3) there is an urgent need for global and multicultural awareness and practice among all participants in remote PWUs and general higher educational contexts.

Academic professors of color make up 17% of the total U.S. higher education faculty, and the numbers become even smaller for tenured and ten-

Asian American Education—Identities, Racial Issues, and
Languages, pp. 131–158
Copyright © 2011 by Information Age Publishing

ure-track faculty positions according to American Council of Education (Hune, 2006). Woman faculty members of color, in particular, are concentrated at the junior faculty level and the tenure rates and pre-tenure departure rates are disproportionate (Aguirre, 2000; Hune, 2006; Smith & Wolf-Wendel, 2005).

The paucity of diverse women faculty members has ignited research regarding the racial climate on campuses and relationships among racially different faculty, White students/faculty, and the university workplace (Aguirre, 2000; Hendrix, 2007; Hune, 1998; Li & Beckett, 2006; TuSmith & Reddy, 2002; Vargas, 1999, 2002). Many have looked at the social patterns of the university workplace: Some women faculty of color may feel that they are socially isolated due to cultural, linguistic, and racial differences (Aguirre, 2000; Lin, Kubota, Motha, Wang, & Wong, 2006; Vargas, 1999); White students often exhibit attitudes and behaviors of resistance toward faculty of color (Castaneda, 2004; Housee, 2001; Luthra, 2002; Perry, Moor, Edwards, Acosta, & Frey, 2009; Vargas, 1999), and White faculty may not include the minority faculty in social situations or provide them with mentoring (Aguirre, 2000). Typically, faculty members of color exist as "the strangers of the academy" (Hune, 2006; Li & Beckett, 2006; Lin, 2006, p. xiii).

As a non-native English speaker (NNES) and a junior Asian woman faculty member, I recount my subjective life story of teaching literacy methods classes to White undergraduate students in a predominantly White university (PWU) in the rural Mountain West. To describe the overall workplace environment and the collegial relationships in this particular setting, I also examine the administrators' evaluations of me and my interactions with senior faculty members. My overarching goals in this study are twofold: (1) to better understand and conceptualize the racial and cultural divide between my self-perception and evaluation and the White students' and administrators' views of me, and (2) to appraise the current institutional level practices for the tenure and promotion process in the case of minority faculty in this setting. In the next sections, I review previous research on diverse faculty that reflects the unfavorable administrative and institutional forces on them.

RESEARCH ON DIVERSE FACULTY IN THE HIGHER-EDUCATION WORK PLACE

Ethnicity, Race, and Teaching

The general presence and status of diverse faculty in U.S. higher education is dismal, and most acknowledge that the "glass ceiling" still exists

(Aguirre, 2000; Lim, 2006; Smith & Wolf-Wendel, 2005). Qualitative studies describe that faculty of color, including Asian faculty, experience outsider status due to Western-based theories and culture embedded in the historical and political climate of higher education (Aguirre, 2000; Lin et al., 2006; Muhtaseb, 2007; Smith & Wolf-Wendel, 2005; Vargas, 1999). Faculty members of color are often isolated as one unique member in their departments and they often leave professorships due to a lack of mentoring and opportunities for tenure and promotion (Hune, 2006). They tend not to be selected as leaders, are not on decision-making teams, but are assigned heavy teaching and clerical administrative duties such as diversity matters and events, and are sometimes singularly responsible for diverse students in their departments (Aguirre, 2000; Hune, 2006; Lin et al., 2006). By contrast, White faculty members have more access to their choice of teaching assignments and are in positions of power to maintain their scholarship and the pedagogical status quo (Aguirre, 2000; Smith et al., 2005). There is systematic and institutional resistance against accepting people of color as valid and credible authorities in university workplaces (Aguirre, 2000; Lin et al., 2006; Perry et al., 2009; Turner, 2002; Vargas, 1999, 2002).

White students, who are the largest demographic representative group in colleges, often resist the authority and credibility of the professor when s/he is the Other (Perry et al., 2009; Vargas, 1999). "Other" refers to anyone who is different in class, culture, gender, or race (Han, 2010b). White students from homogeneous neighborhoods often attend segregated secondary schools and traditional mainstream colleges (Jayakumar, 2008). In segregated areas outside of the university campus, White students often interact with people of their own race before, during, and after college (Braddock, 1985; Jayakumar, 2008). Without much exposure to and interaction with racially diverse people, White students, particularly in rural PWUs, seem to have negative reactions and resistance toward faculty of color and question their expertise and credibility (Braddock, 1985; Jayakumar, 2008; Perry et al., 2009).

On the linguistic and cultural front, there are culturally and linguistically incongruent teaching and learning mechanisms among diverse faculty and their White students, such as different communication systems, social relationships, authority structures, schooling content, and procedures (Green & Kim, 2005; Kim, 2005; Ma, 2008). Researchers (e.g., Muhtaseb, 2007; Vargas, 1999; Wei, 2007) explain that communication problems seem to exist between White students and faculty of color. Faculty members of color speaking English as a second language interact with students more formally and academically rather than jokingly and colloquially (Wei, 2007) and tend to speak with accents (McLean, 2007; Vargas, 1999). Language issues tend to cause communication problems, unconstructive comments, and negative evaluations (Fong, 2007; McLean, 2007; Muhtaseb, 2007). Moreover, disparate social and cultural expectations exist between faculty of color and White students (Vargas, 1999), and faculty of color's credibility and authority as professors are diminished by their devalued racial status. This devalued racial status calls for much more "extensive emotional management and increased amount of work in order to be effective" (Harlow, 2003, p. 350).

Gender and Teaching in Academia

In addition to race and ethnic bias, women faculty must adapt to fit the authoritative profile of the White professor (standard English use, cultural and racial norms of interactions, etc.), to which white students are accustomed (Fong, 2007). Beyond their routine duties, woman faculty of color face unique challenges to negotiate their racial and gendered identity. They are involved with increased emotional and tiring identity conflict while coping with White students' preconceived expectations of and resistance to them (Hendrix, 2007; Muhtaseb, 2007; Vargas, 1999). In many cases, Asians, as Other women faculty of color, are the only ones in their departments. Women faculty of color who are "first-generation academics lack knowledge about the 'rules of the game' to survive and thrive" (Hune, 2006, p. 30). In the case of Asian women, their ethnic/racial features often rouse unique student and faculty/staff reactions: Asian women are stereotyped as "exotic or dragon ladies" (p. 31) and, because of their petite physical size and youthful appearance, they are subject to sexual harassment and their authority is often undermined (Fong, 2007). Furthermore, due to Eastern cultural virtues of reticence and conformity to seniority and authority, Asian women tend to acquiesce to more teaching and administrative demands. The Eastern cultural tendency toward politeness and consensus building may also prevent these women from voicing and claiming their expertise; consequently they are often perceived as less competent (Hune, 2006). In their classrooms, Asian women faculty, along with all women faculty of color, have to engage with students to manage power struggles and discipline; yet, they are more likely to receive negative evaluations from White students (Aguirre. 2000; Fong, 2007; McLean, 2007; Vargas, 1999). As with other challenges unique to women, Asian women faculty in many cases take up and are in charge of household and child care duties more often than their male counterparts; these family duties can be a contributing factor to their dropping out of the demanding tenure track and resorting to work in part-time positions (Hune, 2006).

At the institutional level, woman faculty members are constantly subject to "systematic, institutional suppression of research and teaching" (Lin et al., 2006, p. 74), and have to fight to earn tenure and promotion. When their research centers on multiculturalism and diversity issues, their work is frequently disregarded as "repetitive" or considered subjective and without scientific evidence (p. 74). The process of women faculty gaining tenure and promotion has almost always been greeted with high levels of fear, anger, and despair (Hune, 2006). Known as traditionally normalized masculine space, the Ivory Tower tends to be a chilly and alienating workplace in which diverse women faculty members are often invisible, silenced, and marginalized beings (Aguirre, 2000; Hune, 1998, 2006; Lim, 2006).

Previous research clearly demonstrates that there are practices at a systemic level that are institutionally unfavorable to women of color as faculty members. Approached from the race-gender divide that exists in previous research, this study breaks ground in diversity scholarship in the higher education contexts in three critical ways: (1) it delves into the racial group dynamics among White students, faculty/administrators, and Others; (2) it examines the mismatched cultural values of Western-based and Confucian educational philosophies, and (3) it describes the tenure and promotion process and decisions that may have resulted from the long-forgotten lenses of individual and institutional influences of racism. I posed two research questions to guide this study: (1) How do I perceive the students' and administrators' views of and interactions with me? and (2) What possible institutional "rules of the game" (Hune, 2006, p. 30) are at play when an Other is the teacher and being evaluated for the tenure decision at one particular PWU? Before I discuss the study methods, I turn now to explain some concepts useful for data analysis.

CONCEPTUAL FRAMEWORK

To illustrate different cultural norms of my own and the White students' and administrators' attitudes toward Others in teaching-learning transactions, I draw on the theory of cultural models. James Paul Gee (2002, 2004) defines cultural models as beliefs, values, schemas, world views, and attitudes that people enact (un)knowingly in their talk and actions. These belief systems are situated within a specific cultural group and invoke particular meanings, which are mutually agreed and recognized among the members in that group. I use Confucianism (Kim, 2009; Koo & Nahm, 2007) to capture my cultural beliefs, while I review the theory of Status Characteristics (Berger, Fisek, Norman, & Zelditch, 1977; Cohen, 1982), prejudice and discrimination (Tate, 1999), and institutional racism (Stanley, 2006; Ture & Hamilton, 1967/1992) to explicate White students' and administrators' worldviews of and attitudes toward Others.

Confucianism as East-Asian Cultural Model

Confucianism is a significant cultural norm in the Confucius Heritage Culture (CHC) countries such as China, Korea, Japan, Taiwan, Hong Kong, Singapore, and Vietnam (Alon & McIntyre, 2005; Wong & Wen, 2001). Relevant to educational and social values, Confucianism emphasizes: (1) hierarchical social role division based on status, age, rank, class, and gender (Han & Scull, 2010; Koo & Nahm, 2007), and (2) education as one of the few keys to social mobility, thus equated with honoring a family's "face" (Aguinis & Roth, 2005; Han & Scull, 2010; Hidalgo, Su, & Epstein, 2004). The emphasis on education often revolves around a respect for proper teacher-student relationships. In Korea, for example, obtaining a teaching position is very competitive, ensures better pay, and comes with expectations of the highest moral standards (Kim, 2005). Educators have "absolute authority and are treated with high deference" (Aguinis & Roth, 2005, p. 149). Schools are structured hierarchically and emphasize top-down approaches in interpersonal relationships, organization, and management, using the teacher-centered transmission mode (Koo & Nahm, 2007; Litrell, 2005). Generally, students receive learning from the teacher, revere and depend on the teacher's authority, and seldom challenge that authority; they rarely contradict the flow of instruction (Aguinis et al., 2005; Liu & Littlewood, 1997; Litrell, 2005). To be sure, there is diversity within groups, and one cannot make a sweeping generalization for all Asian individual persons or families, or for all White individuals or families for that matter. My views of a good student and the process of forming social relationships with them and colleagues/administrators may differ from those of White faculty/administrators and students, since my social attitudes were rooted in Confucian teachings. I expect my students to be respectful toward me and do not anticipate any serious challenges regarding my curricular decisions or pedagogical practices. However, since I earned my master's and doctorate in the United States and also taught in U.S. public schools, my views of teaching, advising, and mentoring have been altered due to the acculturation process.

Status Characteristics Theory, Prejudice/Discrimination, and Institutional Racism: Mainstream Whites' Attitudes Toward Others

The theory of status characteristics explains that there are perceived power relations and rank/prestige orders that place people hierarchically in group settings based on race, class, and gender (Berger, Fisek, Norman, & Zelditch, 1977; Burke, Stets, & Cerven, 2007; Cohen, 1982). According to this theory, individuals of high status, usually White people, are considered more competent and as such they acquire leadership roles, invoke more initiation of interactions and more participation, and have more privilege to influence others (Berger et al., 1977; Cohen, 1982). In the case of course evaluations, White students' cultural models of "normal" professors tend to be limited to a White professor, and include "normal" language use, interactional styles, clothing, age, racial characteristics, body size, facial expressions, and gestures (Vargas, 1999, p. 366). An Asian female professor's "personal front places her outside the group of 'normal' (White) professors," and she is therefore often evaluated lower than the White professors (Vargas, 1999, p. 366).

In addition, two concepts closely related to the mainstream views and attitudes toward Others are prejudice and discrimination (Tate, 1999) and institutional racism. The term, institutional racism was first coined by Ture and Hamilton(1967/1992) and later expanded by critical race theory scholars (e.g., Ladson-Billings & Tate, 1995; Roithmayr, 1999; Stanley, 2006). The concept of prejudice and discrimination can be "defined in opposition to assessments of individuals on their merits" (Tate, 1999, p. 258). White persons can react with prejudice and discrimination or resentment toward the successes or socioeconomic advancement of persons of color (Bell, 2000). An example of personal prejudice relevant to this study is that White students persistently refuse to accept a faculty member of color as their professor. This is a case of a discrimination and prejudice specifically because the traditional roles are reversed and White students react to the role shifts with oppositional attitudes and prejudices: those normally in privileged status are asked to acknowledge the power over them from one who is not from a normally privileged group. In this shifted roles and expectations, White students have to listen not to their White professor but to the (immigrant) faculty of color, who they perceive to possess inferior English pronunciations, pragmatics, physical appearances, "awkward" interpersonal modes, and inferior racial status. Therefore, they resist accepting the faculty of color's authority and expertise (Perry et al., 2009; Vargas, 1999, 2002). Another example relevant to academics is the acceptance at face value of a logical or meritocratic explanation: When a faculty member of color receives student complaints and poor evaluations, the explanations are often documented with numerical ratings, with written comments from White students or administrators that might reveal personal biases. Conversely, if the faculty member of color is doing well, "ways must be found to bring him down a notch" (Gititi, 2002, p. 187): White students and administrators address the uses of the diverse faculty's language, "You can't understand their accent or so and so is a tough grader, you better not take that class" (p. 188). Arguing that instructors with accents provide poor language role models emphasizing a lack of leadership styles or communication skills is one of a few of signs of personal prejudice and discrimination under the logic of meritocracy.

Whereas prejudice operates within individuals' attitudes and personal bias against the advancement of people of color and ideas of social justice, the concept of institutional racism emphasizes the unconscious operation of institutional policies (Bell, 2000; Delgado & Stefancic, 2000; Stanley, 2006; Ture & Hamilton, 1967/1992). Institutional racism relates mostly to policies, procedures, and practices that operate, seemingly inadvertently, to the disadvantage of persons of color. This disadvantage does not result from the (c) overt bias or bigotry of individuals, yet policies and practices can have an equally or even greater oppressive or negative impact on groups of people of color. In debates about public schooling, for example, arguments have been made that the federal government should not provide funding for public schools, because public schooling is a local responsibility. However, the fact that most persons of color depend more heavily on public schools than do White persons means that cutting federal funding for schools will disproportionately disadvantage persons of color. In all higher educational settings, people of color are often much better represented in the ranks of maintenance and other support staff than on faculties (TuSmith & Reddy, 2002). The disparity between the lowest faculty member and most staff representation is so much that White persons are frequently tempted to assume that a person of color in a position of authority in their classroom is probably more likely to be an accident or a freak occurrence than a professional person placed in an authoritative position due to achievement or merit. In such cases, Ture & Hamilton (1967/1992) and critical race theory scholars (e.g., Delgado & Stefancic, 2000; Stanley, 2006; Villenas, Deyhle, & Parker, 1999) make it clear that the severity of the impact of institutional racism is different on the individuals of color: The damage derived from personal biases and prejudices can be relatively easily pinpointed and corrected, whereas institutional bias/racism carries long-term effects and is far more condemning to people of color. In other words, institutional change can be a more daunting mission than changing the behavior of one individual.

These three concepts—status characteristics, prejudice and discrimination, and institutional racism—can be useful in capturing the general attitudes of White students and superiors toward the faculty of color at the individual, group, and institutional levels. Therefore for this study, I examine how these three concepts can be played out and used as analytical lenses in the university workplace. For example, if the data can show: (1) individual students' consistent complaining and poor ratings on faculty of color using gendered/racial characteristics; (2) individuals (or a group of individuals) reacting with prejudice and discrimination when the teacher is Other, and (3) largely based on the student evaluation results, faculties' and administrators' condoning White students' complaints, and evaluating the faculty of color with narrowly merit-based arguments at the institutional level. Approaching from individual and institutional levels, this study demonstrates that racism can act to suppress the educational and social advancement of the faculty of color.

METHODS

Setting and Student Demographics

Located in a rural area of the Mountain West, near the home of the Aryan Nations group, my university houses a homogeneous, predominantly White student body and faculty. I was the only faculty member of color at the College of Education's main campus for 3 years, from 2007 to 2010. The percentage of White students in this university ranges from 86 to 94% in any given year. The students are undergraduates in the teacher preparation program. College of Education-wide, the demographic breakdown was much less diverse: There were approximately five non-White students in the literacy methods class I taught for 3 years. The elementary literacy methods course is required for juniors or seniors before their student teaching internship. The majority of them were females in their early twenties (21 to 23), several were in their mid-20s, and a few were middle-aged. There were approximately 25 students in the class, including two to three male students.

Study Design

In this study, I adopt the autoethnography genre to write about my work experience, incorporating my own life story as an "Outsider" (Collins, 2000) in a mainstream educational setting. Reed-Danahay (1997) stated that the genre of autoethnography should have two components: (1) "the auto-ethnographer is a boundary-crosser," and takes the role of dual identity (p. 3), and 2) the autoethnographer should "voice" and represent "authenticity" when writing about life stories and be straight about "who speaks and on behalf of whom" (p. 3). Denzin (1989) adds that in this genre of autoethnography, one writes from her own life experiences without adopting the conventional objective researcher stance. Although I was a graduate student, worked as a K-12 classroom, ESL teacher and ESL coordinator for over a decade, and later, a university professor in the

United States, I have always viewed myself as a cultural and racial outsider. As an outsider to the mainstream education, I write about my professorship by viewing and acting through a native Korean cultural lens, while my racial Others hold a worldview of Others needing to be as fully assimilated as a "normal" White professor (Vargas, 1999, p. 366). These inherently conflicting views fit the single case life experience of myself as a boundary-crosser and dual identity possessor. From this stance, I speak up to tell the "self-reflexive-field account" (Deck, 1990) of my professorship and my life story dealing with my White Others at this particular Mountain West PWU.

Data Sources and Data Analysis

I collected data for five semesters, including: (1) students' formal evaluations, and informal evaluations such as in-class anonymous comments/notes; the in-class notes were collected once every week for three years. The nature/purpose of these notes was to have my students make any comments about the content, the delivery, or the interactional modes so that I could use these comments to understand the students' reactions to my multicultural identity and views, check their content understanding, and get their straightforward feedback on my teaching in general without their having a fear of earning poor grades from me, and (2) my observations and interactions with the senior faculty and administrators and the departmental annual evaluations for 3 years. Using a thematic approach (Bogdan & Bicklen, 2007; Creswell, 2007; Emerson, Fretz, & Shaw, 1995), I first identified salient themes that emerged from the formal evaluations (five semesters worth of student evaluations and 3 years of administrator evaluations) and anonymous informal notes from students. Second, I examined the themes, identified the common themes, and grouped the similar ones thematically to answer the research questions. In the next section, I weave a thematic narrative based on the three themes: (a) policing my English use and personal front; (b) mismatched cultural expectations and blaming Others, and (c) student resistance and chilling workplace atmosphere.

FINDINGS

Policing English Language Use and Personal Front

Students made negative comments about my accent, language use, and grammar, the clarity of the assignments and instructions, and my ethnic/

racial characteristics. They expressed issues around my communication problems and their discomfort with listening to me lecture with a foreign accent, as a few examples of student evaluations revealed: "The professor was unclear 100% of the time," or:

> Teacher confused most of the students a lot and rarely clarified things to make them clear to the whole class until everyone was very confused ... with her language difference and the difficulty it takes for most students to understand her.

White students policed my language use, saying they could not understand my "broken English," that they wished I "did not have an accent," and that I "lacked pragmatics." It is certain that I do have a foreign accent and occasionally misuse pragmatics. I tend not to use jokes and colloquial expressions appropriately to smooth things out, since I am a NNES and use more formal, academic, bookish, and polite ways (see Wei, 2007).

Being consciously aware of my linguistic and racial identity, I had class agendas ready, sent them off before class, and prepared PowerPoint slides of the main ideas for each class I taught. A few of my White colleagues mentioned repeatedly, "I cannot put that kind of effort into teaching, I can't imagine doing what you do to prepare for the class." I honestly put my utmost efforts into teaching to compensate for my linguistic "deficiencies," both real and imagined.

I wondered whether my communication problems were largely due to my English language usage and pragmatics or at least partly to do with any prejudice/discrimination and the status characteristic theory's effect on me as someone gendered and racially different Other. That is, did my personal front, that is, "insignia of office or rank, racial characteristics, sex, body size, looks, speech patterns" (Vargas, 1999, p. 367), and nonstandard English use, get in the way of my students' views and evaluations of me? According to one student's in-class note:

> These guys [fellow students] don't know about other people's cultures and choose not to know. They are from here and raised with this kind of idea.... The teachers usually don't have difficulty, if they are from our own background, we have similar values and ideas, but when we have different teachers [diverse faculties], we put a guard up or have negative views on them. The students who sent notes to you, those were personal attacks and the underlying tones is prejudice or racism. They know that they can do that to you. They wouldn't admit it!

As this student mentioned, most of my students came from secluded European American cultural, ethnic, and racial circles. Although this monocultural life was not their own choice early on, they had become accustomed to keeping their homogeneous European American academic and social circles to themselves (see Braddock, 1985; Jayakumar, 2008). My students expected the image of the normal (White) professor from me: Standard American English speech patterns, pragmatics, and an enactment of the model image of the White professor's persona. Instead, my students had to listen to accented pronunciations, bookish and formal usage, and occasional awkward use of words and phrases. They viewed an Other professor's English use as inferior to theirs. It may have been natural for them to "put their guard up" when the teacher is the non-White Other and believe that they can behave in uncivil and hostile manners. The poignant problem with this phenomenon was that they "choose not to know" people different from them. By the same token, other students wrote informal group evaluations in class, "Many students took advantage of professor and didn't show respect—personal attack instead of constructive criticism," and "the fact that you are a small and Asian woman makes students sort of look down on you."

Along with the language pragmatics issue, my credibility as a professor was at stake, since the students scrutinized and policed my non-White physical and racial characteristics, as this student mentioned in an anonymous in-class note;

> They are used to the male faculty even if he did whatever in class; he has a control over students. You are small and minority, they [students] look at it and have already thought that they can do that to you.

Status characteristics theory demonstrates that race and gender issues do intervene in people's judgment and lower rating of Others' performance. My White students evaluated me negatively according to their uneasiness and inexperience with their only Asian faculty member's accent, language use, foreign speech patterns, pragmatics, and physical attributes (Fong, 2007; Lin et al., 2006; McLean, 2007; Wei, 2007). My racial/ethnic looks, size, and gender, along with my NNES identity, qualify as non-white, gendered Other. These racial characteristics (as explained in status characteristic theory) may have prompted their lower evaluations of me. Along with their views of my status characteristics, my credibility and expertise were questioned as they situated their complaints in the merit-based argument, "Tao does not have pragmatic skills," and "we cannot understand her because of her accent" and "broken English." The cumulative impact of these critiques amounted to what I came to see as my White students' personal prejudices.

Mismatched Cultural Expectations and Blaming Others

I do suspect that, occasionally and subconsciously, I must have enacted my cultural identity and expected my students to be respectful and compliant to me as "authority." For example, one semester I began the course by telling students, "I am not your friend. Don't you respect teachers here?" The class was silent. As I felt mismatched expectations between my students and me, many of my students also expressed this concern, noting, "I feel like at times there has been a lack of respect between students and professor. Yes, sometimes we are at fault but sometimes we are not";

> the teacher does not understand us, and is not open to our ideas or open to discussion and respectful of thoughts and ideas. It felt like there were two distinct cultures in the room and we did not understand each other.

On a similar note, students also commented, "She [the instructor] was completely biased, looking for only one answer when there could be multiple." "This instructor is not aware of what her students need or are expressing to her. She expects us to know everything without [sic.] very much if any explanation." Or "She was an extremely hard grader.... She definitely put forth a tremendous effort, but it has been rough." For five semesters, students in all cases wrote that I was a hard grader and that my expectations were "unrealistic." In most cases, the problem resided within me—that it was I who was biased and demanded too much of them.

On other occasions, when class disagreement occurred about a literacy strategy, I interjected correct information in the middle of discussions. When this happened, many students showed defiant attitudes and body language: some rolling their eyes, slamming the door and storming out of the classroom, etc. Regarding these incidents, several students complained in hostile voices:

> You are abrupt and take over when people are talking. They do not have time to fix what they say.
> If we are going to have co-teaching shouldn't we teach more than you do? Also I feel that you cut in when we are co-teaching rather than let us finish teaching and then add what you have to say. It's *rude*.

Even if some mismatches might exist at the cultural level, I could hardly have expected the tone of hostility and I felt that they went over and above student boundaries to reprimand the professor. It was clear that these students showed dislike and a disconnect between us, as one student noted:

> Dr. Han knew her information, there wasn't any doubt of that. But I got this feeling like it was her way or the highway ... she was very set in her ways. It seemed like if I didn't conform to the norm of the class and just sit then I wasn't looked at as a "good student."

This norm of a "good student" may be different for my students and me. The ideal, good student to me is probably a student who respects the teacher, speaks up only to raise intelligent questions/comments so as not to disturb the flow of the class activities, shows some sign of deference to the authority and peers in their talk and actions and especially toward the teaching profession, education, and their senior (age) professor (social status and rank). To my students, however, my direct interjections might have seemed as if I were imposing my authority on them, interrupting their efforts rather than respecting each independent learner's agency and allowing them opportunities to discover on their own. They wanted more freedom or agency from me, as expressed in their evaluations: more "breathing room," "more free choice for class assignments," "[instructors] be open to students' ideas and responses and give us opportunities to be independent learners," "students want to learn on their own, bring their own ideas to the class but they don't always feel supported in bringing up their ideas," "not a lot of room to be creative."

Upon reflection, I would admit that I may have been enacting my social values of hierarchical relationships, namely top-down management, teacher-centered teaching approaches, and central control of passing on correct knowledge, thus not actively promoting individual creativity through learner discovery methods and allowing freedom for their knowledge construction. Realizing what may have happened, I tried to better accommodate the students as I applied the notion of culturally relevant pedagogy (Ladson-Billings, 1994), only reversed in this case (i.e., diverse teacher with White students). Despite my efforts, I seemed to receive inferior evaluations and treatment from my students compared to those of the White faculty members (much lower than even the new White teaching assistants).

One significant mismatched expectation that surfaced was when a group of students reported their complaints to the department and college administrators. Without any notice to me, or a conference with everyone present, one senior professor told these students that "they are entitled to express their opinions and their voices should be heard," and advised them to go directly to the higher ups. The department chair and the dean met with the students. The department chair told them that they have rights and liberty to do well and make their opinions known. Following this incident, I was called in and talked to by the administrator. This administrator wrote in my annual evaluation, "Dr. Han is a below average teacher." I attempted to follow up with the petition and refute the evaluation but could not proceed. I received a letter from the Dean's office that the superiors in the college upheld this administrator's decision and that I must take up the formal procedure if I want to refute the annual analysis of this department chair's evaluation. Also written in the annual evaluation was that I had "practiced the more traditional Confucian transmission model" in my teaching practices. He went on to document that:

This model [Confucianism] is one with which she was trained and educated more than half of her life. It is this reversion to the more traditional model that causes friction between Dr. Han and her students. Students perceive her teaching, as a lack of respect and trust and this is evident in the qualitative course evaluation comments.

He used the student comments directly from the student evaluation and wrote these very statements in the second and third year evaluations, just as he had complaint sessions with grumbling students without my presence. These evaluations were devastating to my teaching career. In his annual evaluation, this administrator quoted student comments such as, "There were a few instances of unprofessionalism on her [Tao's] part, which caused a lot of tension in the class," and "She was also unwilling to answer questions and often blamed our lack of understanding on us being poor listeners not on her not teaching the information." The message was clear: I had failed in teaching and building relationships with the students. Without other substantiating documents and hard facts, or a single observation of my teaching in the classroom, the students' complaints were the final verdict he recorded; the other superiors supported him without further investigations. These incidents only encouraged my fearfulness as I thought about contesting the "below average teacher" judgment.

This series of events can be considered institutional racism. The department chair (un)consciously took the side of the students and listened to them without my knowledge, blaming my lack of understanding of the mainstream culture, and the "rules of the game," writing up in the annual evaluations that I was the one who went "back to the traditional Confucian" style, and thus it was I exclusively who did the students wrong! This administrator's annual report and the chain of command that deterred me from refusing to sign these documents—combined at all levels, institutional racism left psychological doubts within me about my teaching capability. I internalized some of the alleged deficiency and doubted my competence, and still today, teaching at a different university, I check with my students to see if I am making any sense when I lecture or give directions.

At the personal level, senior faculty and administrators never "threw a stone" at me. Interestingly enough, this administrator was appointed as a multicultural committee chair, and always spoke very favorably about multicultural education and internationalization on campus. My White colleagues often mentioned to me that the administrator was so kind and gentle to me in public and private meetings and at the personal level! Nobody ever doubted the administrator's or their own lack of intention of personal bias or racism. Instead, some senior faculty reminded me that the administration supported me, but I should be more understanding of the

146 K. T. HAN

students, try to work with them, and either change my ways or look for other positions elsewhere. Covertly, my White colleagues continued to support the officials in the department and the College of Education as they condoned the practices and policies of their superiors and the powerful officials.

"It is this reversion to the more traditional model that causes friction between Dr. Han and her students." This statement by this administrator did not reflect on his or any other party's personal bias or non-understanding of Others' cultural identity; it found fault solely with my not assimilating Western ideas about "student liberty and not forming trusting relationships." This practice, these Western-based rules of the game, excluding and silencing Others "would and do perpetuate institutionally racist policies" (Ture & Hamilton, 1967/1992, p. 5). This is a case of personal bias and discrimination operationalized at the institutional level, which limited my educational and social advancement as the only junior woman faculty member of color and kept me at the margin.

Student Resistance and Chilling Workplace Atmosphere

Five semesters' evaluations and informal in-class notes showed that students questioned my subject matter expertise and challenged my professorial authority by being unreceptive to how and what I taught. Students varied in how they questioned my expertise. Some compared me with White professors, some showed hostility toward me particularly when I included topics such as multicultural, struggling learners, and English learners (ELs) in my literacy methods classes, and a small number of students (one or two) appreciated the diverse perspectives and methods I brought to my teaching. Accusing me of teaching literacy methods inappropriately or repeating them, as these were also covered in other literacy classes, some students wrote:

> I think Tao needs to converse more with Dr. A [a White tenured professor] because she started teaching more reading than writing activities in her class, which is Dr. A's area. I understand that they both go hand-in-hand, but she [Tao] was teaching us reading activities like we had never seen them before.

This student went on to say that I was repeating the same literacy methods, even though these "methods were covered better in other classes." A few other students also wrote about my class; below is one example:

> We got a lot of the information taught in this class in [naming other course] and it felt like a repeat. However, what we were taught in that course contradicted sometimes with what she [Tao] taught.

How dare I contradicted the students' prior knowledge they had learned from other White instructors! Knowing the students' unreceptive and hostile attitudes, there was one instance when I captured a teachable moment to comment and interject during discussions, and the students revolted against the information, suggesting the correct version of the literacy method at hand. In this incident, many students overtly refuted information verbally and showed hostile body language:

> The instructor," wrote one student, "pointed out mistakes infront [sic.] of the entire class and was much of the time rude. THe [sic.] teacher would step in inappropriately when the students were presenting and force her theories upon the class even when the majority of the class felt as if she was the wrong one.

Another student stated, "It also caused some hurt feelings with professor and students alike ... there was some unprofessional confrontations in front of the class and with students." It was often attributed to my rudeness that I cut into their comments and that I did not respect their comments as these students stated. "It seemed with a lot of the strategies we were taught something different in one class and then when we came to this one [my literacy course], we were taught something different." Similarly, another student pointed out, "The information was things we have already learned and was not taught in appropriate ways ... I will not use the materials from this class in the future." Added another student, "This teacher should be looked into and the class should be evaluated." Comments like these suggested that no matter what I taught, the majority of the students disputed my subject-matter credibility and resisted my professorial authority. As Vargas (1999) stated in her research, "These students might find it difficult to accept" that women of color are their college professors and they may resist "that the university has bestowed on a woman of color the powers of surveillance and discipline over men and over whites" (p. 373).

The most resistance I received from the students was about the fact that I integrated multicultural and ESL methods as part of our integrated literacy methods classes. The theoretical bases and pedagogical strategies I brought to the classroom were probably very different from the mainstream European American Literacy professor's literacy theories/methods. Informing the students that the diverse student population will grow to be 50% by the year 2050, as reported in the U.S. Census and published research (e.g., Jayakumar, 2008), I integrated multicultural reading materials and discussions into my teaching after reading articles/chapters (e.g., Collier & Thomas, 1989; Gay, 2000; Han, 2010a; Heath, 1982; Hart & Risley, 1995; McIntosh, 1995; Rist, 1970/2000; Yoon, 2007). The ESL and multicultural topics seemed to ignite tremendous anger and resentment in many of my students. One student wrote in the evaluation:

> Many of the reading materials really did not seem relevant to the course. Many were very biased and many of us that are white middle class students felt like we were being targeted and criticized by what [our] ancestors [did] years ago. We are told we need to understand our ELLs culture and integrate it in the classroom.

Another student responded in a similar way:

> I think that you the instructor is [sic.] very passionate about subjects that may be irrelevant to teaching a general education classroom. Even though it is important to know about esl [ESL] and ell teaching strategies, I feel this should be taught in a separate class instead of teaching it in a language arts class. I would have liked to learn more material about language arts.

Still another student wrote:

> If 50% of the school population will be of the non white population then how are we going to teach to everyone? There will be people from over 50 nations who speak more than 30 languages and schools will start to segregate the students and put the white with whites and Spanish with Spanish because a teacher will not be able to tailor to all of them if they were in the same class.

Even though the multicultural and ESL strategies were integrated throughout the class, my focus had clearly been on providing a regular literacy foundation and methods. Many students disputed that I taught ESL and multicultural issues the entire semester. "This class was a waste of time and the professor did not teach anything at all. Tao wasted our time when we should have been learning language arts." Another student wrote, "The reading that we did was thought provoking but totally unrelated to the subject of teaching language arts. I learned new viewpoints about the world but again they were not related to language arts or teaching language arts." Another student angrily wrote, "We are wasting our valuable time talking about ESL or multiculturalism. When are we going to learn about language arts?" Furthermore, one student thought that I had a "mental block" about White students and that I was "closed-minded," noting,

> All Tao talked about was the poor multi-racial students. She has a mental block to the fact that there are poor White students as well. She was close-minded and judged us as a class, bashing us for not ever thinking about the

poor mult-iracial students.... Tao was a very poor teacher who was close-minded to a point of reverse racism.

This and other students' words (written in the formal evaluations) reacting to the multicultural and ESL issues revealed their personal bias and prejudice against the diverse content materials and social justice issues germane to Others. Their resistance to diverse worldviews led them to vehemently react and lash out not only at the content I taught but at me personally, accusing and attacking me as a "reverse racist."

At the same time, the administrator and two other senior faculty members concurred with these students' views of me. In writing the annual and third year review documents, the department chair, with two faculty members' support, recorded his view of the deficits of my third-year performance:

> Dr. Han's performance is marginal when teaching Literacy Methods class.
>
> Dr. Han was assigned to teach graduate courses with limited numbers of students ... Dr. Han must improve her quantitative evaluation to match the college and department average [3.5] and qualitative evaluations for EDCI Integrated Language and Literacy.

These demands sound reasonable in terms of finding solutions within the individual's merit and accountability. In my five semester student evaluation records, my graduate course evaluations ranged from 3.8, to 3.7, 3.5, and 4.0, averaging 3.7, while the undergraduate course averaged 2.7 on a scale of one to four, four being the highest. The department chair, with the support of two senior faculty members, wrote the third year review. He minimized the excellent record of the graduate students' evaluations, stating that these classes did not have "large numbers of students" or describing them as "graduate courses with limited numbers of students," accentuating the undergraduate course ratings as "marginal," or "below average teacher." The problem with his conclusion describing me as "marginal" is that it was solely based on the student evaluations. He never observed my teaching, formally or informally, nor did he or senior faculty offer to provide any mentoring.

As for the scholarship, three of my papers had been published (i.e., the *Urban Education* article in 2007, the *College Teaching and Learning* article in 2010, and the article in the *International Journal of Learning* in 2010) by the third year. I was told to publish a minimum of six articles by the sixth year for the tenure review. I also had a few research projects under review with "revise and resubmit" requests from several journal editors. Without giving this due recognition, the administrator commented on one of the diversity manuscripts I wrote as, "Dr. Han wrote Diverse faculty and White students' attitudes from her subjective standpoint without much evidence." In order for me to gain promotion and tenure, he stipulated five conditions: "publish five to sixteen peer-reviewed articles in the national or international journals within the next two years, and seek grants to support her research and outreach activities, etc." In summation, he declared, "It is my professional opinion that Dr. Han has marginally performed to meet expectations...gaining tenure and promotion will be very difficult for Dr. Han."

Official documents such as formal student- and annual- and third-year tenure evaluations single-handedly claimed that I did not meet the standard expectations in the higher educational meritocratic system. The administrators and senior faculty members were quick to point out my "marginal achievement," linking their deficit views of me to narrowly focused merit-based arguments. Based entirely on the Western-based theoretical stance and undermining Other's cultural values, these administrators and senior faculty displayed similar attitudes to my White students. They "do not want to hear" Others' perspectives. Just as my White students resisted and refuted my credibility, authority, and expertise as their professor, the administrators and senior professors consistently revealed their deficit views of a woman faculty member of color. This racial climate was not conducive to accepting Others, or multicultural and global education for all involved; this atmosphere resulted in grumbling White students and complaint sessions with the administrators and ended in singling out the problem residing within the junior faculty member of color. In this setting, I was the only one who was not able to open to the mainstream cultural models, as I "reverted back to the traditional Confucian transmission model" (Translation: I could not assimilate to the system). This is reasonable sounding, yet its invisible effect of institutional racism robbed the faculty member of color of the opportunity to obtain tenure and promotion in this particular PWU.

DISCUSSION

In this paper, I examined the pedagogical practices of an Asian woman junior faculty member reflected in annual department and student evaluations and anonymous, informal class notes over five semesters at a remote Mountain West university. Throughout the paper, I have recounted my self-reflexive story of working as a solitary faculty member of color in a traditionally homogeneous classroom and work environment. Three points worth further discussion and implication are: (1) the overarching and persistent student resistance to the cultural mismatch and racial tensions that surface when people of color are their professors (i.e., in positions of power); (2) the responsibility for change at the institutional level in policies and practices for the tenure and promotion of faculty members of color, and (3) the urgent need for global and multicultural education.

One persistent phenomenon is the cultural and racial mismatch between diverse faculties and White students/faculties/administrators. This phenomenon still stands as one of the most divisive factors when faculty members of color hold positions of power not only within rural settings but also in urban classrooms and other types of workplaces, as shown in much previous research (Bishop, 1997; Hune, 1998; Li & Beckett, 2006; Perry et al., 2009; TuSmith & Reddy, 2002; Vargas, 1999). Regarding my English language use, I have a foreign accent and may occasionally misuse pragmatics. Culturally, I continue to adapt to the American culture, but I know this deeper level of internalizing American cultural models does not come overnight; in fact, it takes 10 of years or even a lifetime (Cummins, 2001; Gee, 2004). Having grown up in a different socioeducational environment, I enact my cultural model (Confucianism) in demanding student attentiveness, compliance, hard work, and deference to authority and subject matter expertise. In addition, I also come from a generation older than that of my teacher education students. Because of these different backgrounds I bring with me, I may not have always granted opportunities for my students to be creative and independent learners and let them discover knowledge their own. Even though I am educated and trained in U.S. graduate schools that encouraged student-centered learning, I am a Korean at heart, and this cultural identity is something I am not able to and do not desire to eradicate. This is one area where my students have to accept my diverse generational/linguistic/cultural/racial background. As I need to reflect and shift my thinking and values to consider my White students' cultural identities, I strongly feel that the students (as well as faculty and administrators, for that matter) should also meet me halfway and be open-minded about Other worldviews and values. As I critically check my language/literacy use, interactional modes, and teaching practices, my students (faculty/administrators) should also check their biases against diverse Others. As it takes more than one hand to clap and make music, we should understand implicitly that persons from both mainstream and NNES cultures must adapt together if real change is to occur. As Ture and Hamilton (1967/1992) and critical race theory scholars (Bell, 2000; Delgado & Stefancic, 2000; Ladson-Billings & Tate, 1995; Stanley, 2006) pointed out, it is crucial to have the individuals in organizations recognize and correct personal biases. They also posited that personal transformation is a relatively easy task compared to institutional change. This brings us to the goal of the social justice movement, that is, the chief concern of most social justice leaders is transformation at the larger social or institutional level.

A second point comes to mind regarding the responsibility for change. Personal reflections and transformations are the precursor conditions for larger groups and organizations to transform. Civil rights and social justice movement leaders such as Ture and Hamilton, Bell, Tate, Stanley, and others feel that the primary concern is the transformation at the level of institutional and larger societal change. In the higher education contexts, culturally sensitive policies are far from being practiced. As I have worked in three different universities, I have asked senior faculty and administrators whether they consider cultural and racial factors when it comes to tenure and promotion decisions for faculty members of color. All three university senior faculty members and administrators informed me that they do not.

At the institutional level, universities should consider implementing culturally sensitive policies to account for the unconscious cultural and racial biases on the part of students, senior faculty, and administrators, particularly when it comes to the tenure and promotion process. How much does the student evaluation count for good teaching? How can young developing minds such as college students (21-23 of age) evaluate cultural and racial Others, and how much weight should their opinions carry? There should be measures that place the cultural/racial biases against Others in a balanced perspective at the larger institutional level.

If we acknowledge that student and peer evaluations are forms of faculty assessment, then it seems that we need to consider basic assessment principles. The context in which these assessments are applied to faculty, particularly faculty who are NNES and faculty of color, is crucial. If student and peer evaluations are used to help faculty grow, consistent with the idea of formative assessment, evaluations are more meaningful to the NNES faculty or faculty of color. However, if student evaluations are used in the spirit of summative assessment, in order to make evaluation scores/comments a permanent record influencing merit pay increases, or promotion and tenure decisions, then student and peer evaluations can be pernicious. Stifling the ability of faculty of color and NNES faculty to deal with controversial issues in college classrooms, such as those relating to race, class and gender, or asking students to go through painful processes of academic skill building or professional self-criticism or self-reflection, all are possibilities under a summative assessment context for student and peer evaluations. A summative mindset also empowers department chairs and other administrators who might not have the skill sets to help junior NNES faculty and faculty of color to adopt superficial and short-term applications. Just as in a K-12 classroom, where it is tempting for a frustrated monocultural-monolingual teacher to refer a struggling NNES student for "special education" services, so is it tempting for White administrators and faculty members from a monolingual-monocultural background to use student and peer evaluations as a way to explain what they might feel to be the merits or demerits of a junior faculty member of color or NNES faculty member, so care must be taken in applying student evaluations in a more balanced context. Perhaps if there are patterns across classes and groups of students or faculty (e.g., across undergraduate and graduate), conclusions about an NNES faculty or faculty member of color can be made at the individual department and college levels. New policies and practices regarding tenure and promotion should be set up, such as faculty mentoring, multicultural group conversations, and tenure and promotion steering committees to implement policies/practices regarding student evaluations/teaching, scholarship, and service expectations.

Third, there should be some mentoring system to set up multicultural group conversations on a regular basis for students, faculty members, and administrators with the faculty of color. Mandatory workshops and dialogue around the topics of ESL, and multicultural and internationalization issues can be helpful for all participants. Ture and Hamilton (1967/1992) asserted in their book *Black Power* that well-meaning individuals do smile at people of color, but they will tacitly support their superiors and the policies and practices that benefit them. From my work experience in this PWU, it seems to me that universities serve as a factory model when it comes to multicultural education and internalization, that is, they recruit diverse faculty to show "we have our multicultural person" or recruit international students to increase student enrollment as a way to defray the financial and cultural deficit. The factory model of learning can only result in political rhetoric, and may backfire on the diverse students and faculty because it is they who pay directly for the consequences of institutional racism. As shown in this study, when superiors exclusively insisted "to blame the victim" and demanded that a faculty member of color assimilate to the mainstream norms and cultural models, the consequence was to bring forth a "mock-multicultural environment, in which ethnic and cultural minority students and [faculty] are given attention primarily as tokens of difference, but rarely allowed their own cultural voice" (Nykiel-Herbert, 2010, p. 13). With administrators operating according to meritocratic arguments and a deficit mindset, a junior faculty member of color was defeated and her desire to pursue petitioning the case was suppressed by the power structure.

As a cultural/racial outsider, I have reason to believe that it is imperative for all participants in education to take part in creating equity, hope, and possibility when working with Others. Without culturally sensitive views of Others operating at the institutional level, the individual level of awareness of Others and supportive practice for Others is not often warranted in day-to-day teaching/learning situations. In teacher education programs, it is crucial to expose multicultural, critical, and new literacies to all students (and faculty members and administrators), including critical media literacy and multimodal genres (Han, 2010b). College is the time period when postsecondary students develop a critical awareness of diverse issues (Jayakumar, 2008). Students and faculty do not often acquire cultural awareness and global citizenry on their own. This responsibility belongs to university educators (Jayakumar, 2008; Han, 2010b). University educators do indeed have a need for global/multicultural education to adapt and modify our attitudes and practices for future students and faculty members. If students, faculty and administrators have difficulty relating to NNES faculty, what does this say about their abilities to be global citizens and, furthermore, what consequences do we face if our preservice teachers are ill equipped to prepare their future students to be global citizens?

The responsibility for change toward socially just practices for faculty and students of color must come from the universities. Universities must deal with the lack of faculty and student diversity and the apparent lack of sensitivity toward, understanding of, and valuing of diversity. Leadership on socially just policies and practices will help White students and White faculty/administrators to meet NNES faculty members and students halfway and adopt Other cultural models equally. In a more general context than just this remote PWU, we know that racial and cultural divides still exist in the higher education. Without rethinking current practices, therefore, discrimination, prejudice and institutional racism will not fade away; the Ivory Tower will continue to foster a Eurocentric atmosphere, an atmosphere that is most certainly detrimental not only to untenured immigrant and language minority faculty, but also to our societal well-being and prosperity as a nation.

REFERENCES

Aguinis, H., & Roth, H. A. (2005). Teaching in China: Culture-based challenges. In I. Alon & J. R. McIntyre (Eds.), *Business and management education in China: Transition, pedagogy, and training* (pp. 141-164). Hackensack, NJ: World Scientific.

Aguirre, A. (2000). *Women and minority faculty in the academic workplace: Recruitment, retention, and academic culture.* San Francisco, CA: Jossey-Bass.

Alon, I., & McIntyre, J. R. (Eds.). (2005). *Business and Management Education in China: Transition, pedagogy, and training.* Hackensack, NJ: World Scientific.

Bell, D. A. (2000). After we're gone: Prudent speculations on America in a post-racial epoch. In R. Delgado & J. Stefancic (Eds.), *Critical race theory: The cutting edge* (pp. 2-8). Philadelphia, PA: Temple University Press.

Berger, J. Fisek, M. H., & Norman, R. Z. (1977) Status Characteristics and Social Interaction: An Expectation State Approach. New York, NY: Elsevier.

Bishop, R. S. (1997). Selecting literacy for a multicultural curriculum. In V. J. Harris (Ed.), *Using multiethnic literature in the K-8 classroom* (pp. 1-19). Norwood, MA: Christopher-Gordon.

Bogdan, R. C., & Biklen, S. K. (2007).*Qualitative research for education: An introduction to theory and methods.* Boston, MA: Allyn & Bacon.

Braddock, J. H. (1985). School desegregation and Black assimilation. *Journal of Social Issues, 1*(3), 9-22.

Burke, P. J., Stets, J. E., & Cerven, C. (2007).Gender, legitimization, and identity verification ingroups.*Social Psychology Quarterly, 70*(1), 27-42.

Castaneda, C. R. (2004).*Teaching and learning in diverse classrooms.* New York, NY: Routledge.

Cohen, E. G. (1982). Expectation states and interaction in school settings. *AnnualReviewof Sociology, 8,* 209-235.

Collier, P. V., & Thomas, W. P. (1989). How quickly can immigrants become proficient in school English? *Journal of Educational Issues of Language Minority Students, 5,* 26-38.

Collins, P. H. (2000). Black feminist thought: Knowledge, consciousness, and the politics of empowerment. New York, NY: Routledge.

Cresswell, J. W. (2007). *Qualitative inquiry & research design: Choosing among five approaches.*Thousand Oaks, CA: SAGE.

Cummins, J. (2001). The entry and exit fallacy in bilingual education. In C. Baker & N. H. Hornberger (Eds.), *An introductory reader to the writings of Jim Cummins* (pp. 110-138). Clevedon, England: Multilingual Matters.

Deck, A. A. (1990). Autoethnography: Zora Neale Hurston, Noni, Jabavu, and Cross-Disciplinary Discourse. *Black American Literature Forum, 24*(2), 237-256.

Delgado R., & Stefancic, J. (2000). Images of the outsider in American law and culture: Can free expression remedy systemic social ills? In R. Delgado & J. Stefancic (Eds.), *Critical race theory: The cutting edge* (pp. 225-235). Philadelphia, PA: Temple University Press.

Denzin, N. (1989). *Interpretive biography.* Newbury Park, CA: SAGE.

Emerson, R. M., Fretz, R. I., & Shaw, L. L. (1995). *Writing ethnographic field notes.* Chicago, IL: The University of Chicago Press.

Fong, M. (2007). The permeable and impermeable wall of expectations. In K. G. Hendrix (Ed.), *Neither White nor male: Female faculty of color* (pp. 35-45). San Francisco, CA: Jossey-Bass.

Gay, G. (2000). Culturally responsive teaching: Theory, research, & practice. New York, NY: Teachers College, Columbia University.

Gee, J. P. (2002). *Discourse analysis.* London: Routledge.

Gee, J. P. (2004). *Social linguistics and literacies.* New York, NY: RoutledgeFalmer.

Gititi, G. (2002). Menaced resistance: The Black teacher in the mainly white school/classroom. In B. TuSmith, B. & M. T. Reddy (Eds.), *Race in the college classroom* (pp. 176-188). Piscataway, NJ: Rutgers University Press.

Green, D. O., & Kim, E. (2005). Experiences of Korean female doctoral students in academe: Raising voice against gender and racial stereotypes. *Project Muse, 66*(5), 487-500.

Han, K. T. (2010a). English Learner Status and social relationships in a predominantly European-American School: A Korean Student's Story. *Journal of College Teaching & Learning, 7*(3), 65-78.

Han, K. T. (2010b). *Seeing through the eyes of others: Films, anime, and manga in teacher education programs.* Unpublished manuscript.

Han, K. T., & Scull, W. R. (2010). Confucius culture in the mainstream classroom: A case study of an Asian American student. *The International Journal of Learning, 17*(1), 601-616.

Harlow, R. (2003). "Race doesn't matter, but...": The effect of race on professors' experiences and emotion management in the undergraduate classroom. *Social Psychology Quarterly, 66*(4), 348-363.

Hart, B., & Risley, T. R. (1995). *Meaningful differences in the everyday experiences of young American children.* Baltimore, MD: Brookes.

Heath, S. B. (1982). *What no bedtime story means: Narrative skills at home and school.* New York, NY: Cambridge University Press.

Hendrix, K. G. (2007). *Neither White nor male: Female Faculty of color.* San Francisco, CA: Jossey-Bass.

Hidalgo, N. M., Siu, S. F., & Epstein, J. L. (2004). Research on families, schools, and communities: A multicultural perspective. In J. A. Banks & C. A. McGee Banks (Eds.), *Handbook of research on multicultural education* (pp. 631-655). San Francisco, CA: Jossey-Bass.

Housee, S. (2001). Insiders and/or outsiders: Black female voices from the academy. In P. Anderson & J. Williams (Eds.), *Identity and difference in higher education: "Outsiders within"* (pp. 109-124). New York, NY: Peter Lang.

Hune, S. (2006). Asian Pacific American women and men in higher education. In G. Li & G. H. Beckett (Eds.), *Strangers of the academy: Asian women scholars in higher education* (pp. 15-36). Sterling, VA: Stylus.

Hune, S. (1998). *Asian Pacific American women in higher education: Claiming visibility & voice.* Washington, DC: Association of American Colleges and Universities.

Jayakumar, U. M. (2008). Can higher education meet the needs of an increasingly diverse and global society?: Campus diversity and cross-cultural workforce competences. *Harvard Educational Review, 78*(4), 615-651.

Kim, K. H. (2009). Cultural influence on creativity: The relationship between Asian culture (Confucianism) and creativity among Korean educators. *The Journal of Creative Behavior, 43*(2), 73-93.

Kim, K. H. (2005). Learning from each other: Creativity in East Asian and American education. *Creativity Research Journal, 17*(4), 337-347.

Koo. H. S., & Nahm, A. C. (2007). *An introduction to Korean culture.* Seoul, South Korea: Holly.

Ladson-Billings, G., & Tate, W. (1995). Toward a critical race theory of education. *Teachers College Record, 97*(1), 47-68.

Lim, S. G. (2006). Forward: Identities Asian, female, scholar: Critiques and celebrations of the North American academy. In G. Li & G. H. Beckett (Eds.), *Strangers of the academy: Asian women scholars in higher education* (pp. xiii-1). Sterling, VA: Stylus.

Li, G., & Beckett, G. (Eds.). (2006). *"Strangers" of the academy: Asian women scholars in higher education.* Sterling, VA: Stylus.

Lin, A., Kubota, R., Motha, S., Wang, W., & Wong, S. (2006).Theorizing experiences of Asian women faculty in second-and foreign-language teacher education. In G. Li & G. H. Beckett (Eds.), *Strangers of the academy: Asian women scholars in higher education* (pp. 56-84). Sterling, VA: Stylus.

Litrell, R. L. (2005). Teaching student from Confucian cultures. In I. Alon & J. R. McIntyre (Eds.), *Business and management education in China: Transition, pedagogy, and training* (pp. 141-164). Hackensack, NJ: World Scientific.

Liu, N. F., & Littlewood, W. (1997). Why do many students appear reluctant to participate in classroom learning discourse? *System, 25*(3), 371-384.

Luthra, R. (2002). Negotiating the minefield: Practicing transformative pedagogy as a teacher of color in a classroom climate of suspicion. In L. Vargas, (Ed.), *Women faculty of color in the White classroom* (pp. 79-92). New York, NY: Peter Lang.

Ma, W. (2008). Participatory dialogue and participatory learning in a discussion-based graduate seminar. *Journal of Literacy Research, 40*(2), 220-249.

McIntosh, P. (1995). White privilege and male privilege: A personal account. In M. Anderson & P. H. Collins (Eds.), *Race, class, and gender: An anthology* (pp. 76-87). Belmont, CA: Wadsworth.

McLean, C. A. (2007). Establishing credibility in the multicultural classroom: When the instructor speaks with an accent. In K. G. Hendrix (Ed.), *Neither White nor male: Female faculty of color* (pp. 15-24). San Francisco, CA: Jossey-Bass.

Muhtaseb, A. (2007). From behind the veil: Students' resistance from different directions. In K. G. Hendrix (Ed.), *Neither White nor male: Female faculty of color* (pp. 25-34). San Francisco, CA: Jossey-Bass.

Nykiel-Herbert, B. (2010). Iraqi refugee students: From a collection of aliens to a community of learners. *Multicultural education: The magazine of the National Association for Multicultural Education, 17*(3), 2-14.

Perry, G., Moore, H., Edwards, C., Acosta, K., & Frey, C. (2009). Maintaining credibilityand authority as an instructor of color in diversity-education classrooms: A qualitative inquiry. *The Journal of Higher Education, 80*(1), 80-105.

Reed-Danahay, D. E. (Ed.). (1997). *Auto/Ethnography: Rewriting the self and the social.* Oxford, England: Berg.

Rist, R. (2000). Student social class and teacher expectations: The self-fulfilling prophecy in ghetto education. *Harvard Educational Review, 70*(3), 257-301. (Original work published 1970)

Roithmayr, D. (1999). Introduction to critical race theory in educational research and praxis. In L. Parker, D. Deyhle, & S. Villenas (Eds.), *Race is … race isn't: Critical theory and qualitative studies in education* (pp. 1-6). Boulder, CO: Westview Press.

Smith, D. G., & Wolf-Wendel, L. E. (2005).*The challenge of diversity: Involvement or alienation in the academy?: ASHE Higher Education Report.* Hoboken, NJ: Wiley.

Stanley, C. A. (2006). Coloring the academic landscape: Faculty of color breaking the silence in predominantly White colleges and universities. *American Educational Research Journal, 43*(4), 701-736.

Tate, W. F. (1999). Separate and still unequal: Legal challenges to school tracking and ability grouping in America's public schools. In L. Parker, D. Deyhle, & S.

Villenas (Eds.), *Race is ... race isn't: Critical theory and qualitative studies in education* (pp. 231-250). Boulder, CO: Westview Press.

Turner, R. (2002). Women of color in academia: Living with multiple marginality. *The Journal of Higher Education, 73*(1), 74-93.

Ture, K. & Hamilton, C. V. (1992). *Black power: The politics of liberation.* New York, NY: Vintage Books. (Original work published 1967)

TuSmith, B., & Reddy, M. T. (Eds.). (2002). Race in the college classroom. Piscataway, NJ: Rutgers University Press.

Vargas, L. (2002). *Women faculty of color in the White classroom.* New York, NY: Peter Lang.

Vargas, L. (1999). When the "Other" is the teacher: Implications of teacher diversity in higher education. *The Urban Review, 31*(4), 359-383.

Villenas, J. S., Deyhle, D., & Parker, L. (1999). Critical race theory and praxis: Chicano(a) and Navajo struggles for dignity, educational equity, and social justice. In L. Parker, D. Deyhle, & S. Villenas (Eds.), *Race is ...race isn't: Critical theory and qualitative studies in education* (pp. 31-52). Boulder, CO: Westview Press.

Wei, F. F. (2007). Cross-cultural teaching apprehension: A coidentity approach toward minority teachers. In K. G. Hendrix (Ed.), *Neither White nor male: Female faculty of color* (pp. 5-15). San Francisco, CA: Jossey-Bass.

Wong, K., & Wen, Q. (2001). The impact of university of education on conceptions of learning: A Chinese study. *International Education Journal, 2*(5), 138-147.

Yoon, B. (2007). Offering or limiting opportunities: Teachers' roles and approaches to English-language learners' participation in literacy activities. *Reading Teacher, 61*(3), 216-227.

CHAPTER 7

WHAT ACCOUNTS FOR TENURE OF ASIAN AMERICAN FACULTY?

Findings From NSOPF: 04

Wenfan Yan and Qiuyun Lin

This study explored several individual and institutional factors related to Asian American faculty tenure in postsecondary institutions. Data came from the National Study of Postsecondary Faculty (NSOPF: 04) by the National Center for Education Statistics (NCES, 2005). Findings revealed a complex picture of Asian American faculty tenure status. On the one hand, Asian Americans had the highest percentage of tenured faculty with a high level of human capital, research productivity, and other advantageous background characteristics; on the other, these advantages and high achievements did not yield equally high returns. After taking into account factors such as gender, marital status, education, publications, time on instruction, and research fields, Asian Americans lost ground gradually. Compared with White faculty, they were less likely to hold tenured positions. The study calls for greater understanding of Asian American faculty and the need to address equity issues facing Asian American faculty in higher education.

Asian American Education—Identities, Racial Issues, and Languages, pp. 159–179
Copyright © 2011 by Information Age Publishing
159

INTRODUCTION

University faculty members create knowledge. The creation of knowledge requires nurturing, patience, and tolerance for experimentation. *Tenure* is the carrot held out to junior professors for an indefinite appointment that provides them with a sense of security, accomplishment, and success while they engage in knowledge creation and experimentation. Tenure protects faculty from dismissal except for reasons of immoral conduct, financial corruption, or very poor performance (Bess, 1998). It helps create favorable conditions inside an institution (Carver, 2005; Trower, 2009). It is considered the keystone for academic freedom and stability in a position for the remainder of one's career. Clearly, receiving tenure signifies success for tenure-track faculty.

However, the process of coming up for tenure was characterized by many faculty of color as "hazing" (Stanley, 2006). Although some would say that higher education has made progress over the years and would not wish to revisit the historical legacy of exclusion, the reality is less rosy (Stanley, 2006). Faculty of color are still persistently underrepresented among the successful group, and subtle discrimination in the academic workplace continues (August, 2006).

Among faculty of color, Asian American faculty can be considered one of the most misunderstood populations in higher education in the United States (Museus, 2008, 2009). Historically, Asian Americans have been viewed as the "model minority"—a community in which everyone is educated, economically successful, and somehow not subject to health problems or social or other barriers in society, even when empirical evidence suggests the contrary (Museus, 2009; Museus & Kiang, 2008).

It is becoming increasingly important that current levels of knowledge about Asian American faculty be deepened. Given the rapid growth of the Asian American population, it is imperative to investigate the factors that relate to one aspect of the success of Asian faculty—tenure status. Examining these factors will allow us to benchmark and monitor higher education diversity and develop programs to enhance success for Asian faculty.

LITERATURE REVIEW

Faculty Characteristics in Postsecondary Education

In postsecondary education, the largest proportion of full-time faculty and instructional staff were White. Of the population, full-time White faculty made up 80% compared to 9% Asian American, 6% African American, 3% Hispanic American, and 2% other racial/ethnic groups. More

Asian American faculty were employed as full-time rather than part-time faculty (NCES, 2005). Among a national sample of faculty and instructional staff in all institution types, 9% of all full-time faculty were Asian/Pacific Islanders, compared with 4% of those employed part time (NCES, 2005).

Regarding gender and marital status, Perna (2005a) stated that a smaller percentage of women than men were married and a higher percentage of women than men were separated, divorced, or widowed regardless of employment status, institutional type, tenure status, or academic rank. The percentage of male and female faculty having doctoral degrees in 2-year institutions during their early, mid-, and late careers was 55% versus 45%, 53% versus 47%, and 72% versus 28%, respectively. In 2-year institutions, the difference between the percentage of male and female faculty having doctoral degrees in early and mid-careers was smaller than that in 4-year institutions (Conley, 2005). Overall, about 74% of male faculty held doctoral or first professional degrees compared to 54% of women faculty. Lee (2002) found that more Asian Americans have dependents (77%) compared to Whites (68%). Additionally, more Asian Americans were married than Whites (70% vs. 58%). Differences in racial and gender composition have important implications for faculty career advancement.

Inequality in Postsecondary Education

According to dual or split labor market theories, women and minorities have been segregated in the dual labor market (Feagin & Feagin, 1986). White women and minorities have been segregated in the peripheral sector of the dual labor market giving White men more power in the core sector. This form of segregation has left women and minorities with jobs in the peripheral sector. Jobs in this sector often have lower pay, less security, and fewer chances for advancement (Lee, 2002).

In her study of Asian American faculty and the glass ceiling directly related to the ideal of education as a meritocracy, Lee (2002) provided data to encourage appropriate policymaking to address issues of increased racial and ethnic diversity and equitable treatment of female and minority faculty. While she found no clear evidence of a glass ceiling for Asian American faculty, she also found some evidence that Asian Americans did not benefit from some of the characteristics that translated into higher salaries for Whites, which could be interpreted as consistent with the glass ceiling hypothesis. As noted by Lee, when the effects of particular independent variables such as academic rank, tenure, years of experience, productivity, and field or area of specialization were further evaluated, a more complex picture emerged: Asian Americans had fewer paths available than White faculty to increased earnings. For instance, Whites derived substantial and statistically significant benefits from being male, being native born, being a professor or associate professor, having at least a low level of publication record, and being located in the West. In contrast, Asian Americans were either negatively affected by the same characteristics or experienced very small and statistically nonsignificant positive effects.

Identifying Factors Related to Career Advancement of Women and Faculty of Color

The conceptual framework for this study integrates aspects of economic and sociological theoretical perspectives (Perna, 2001, 2003). Economic theory of human capital focuses on the individual level factors. The most common human capital variables include education level, working experience, training, motivation, and emotional and physical health (Becker, 1964). On the other hand, sociological perspectives emphasized the roles of structure and institutional factors, such as the type of institution and academic fields.

Research on faculty of color has focused largely on identifying the barriers that may prevent particular groups from equal access and opportunity (e.g., Bain & Cumming, 2000; Brennan & Naidoo, 2008; Stanley, 2006). These include individual factors such as gender, marital status, and educational attainment as well as institutional factors such as faculty research productivity and faculty satisfaction.

Gender, Marital Status, and Career Advancement

Relationships between background factors and the career advancement of faculty are well established. Male faculty earned higher salaries than female faculty, even after controlling for conventional salary predictors (Bellas, 1993). In addition, male faculty who are married occupy higher level positions and earn more than their unmarried counterparts, a relationship that does not appear to hold for women (Bellas, 1993). Whites are more likely to occupy the upper ranks than faculty of color.

The gender differences between married men and women are higher at public doctoral and private 4-year institutions and smaller at public two-year institutions (Perna, 2005a). Gender differences in marital status are also larger among faculty with the highest status positions, such as tenured and full professors (Perna, 2005b). Gender differences in marital status among faculty are smaller for faculty who worked at less prestigious ranks (Perna, 2005b). Perna (2005a) noted that human capital theorists predicted that married women, when compared with men and single women, tended to pursue less demanding jobs because of household responsibilities. This may be the reason why many women choose part-time or lower ranking faculty positions (Conley, 2005; Perna, 2001).

For married women and women with children in higher education, challenges associated with balancing work and family roles may limit access to a faculty career in general as well as the specific types of academic positions that are available. Household responsibilities and child rearing are bigger sources of stress for women faculty than for men faculty (Perna, 2005a). For instance, women faculty members with small children may avoid overnight conferences because of child-care responsibilities (Perna, 2005b). Also, in our society many families prefer to maximize the husband's employment status rather than the wife's (Conley, 2005).

The relationship between family variables and career achievement is mixed, however. Some research (Bellas, 1993; Perna, 2001) demonstrated that marital status and dependents had a negative effect on women faculty members' job performance. Some, however, demonstrated no relationship between marital status and productivity for women (Conley, 2005). Some evidence suggested that married faculty were more productive than other faculty after controlling for other differences (Bellas & Toutkoushian, 1999).

Educational Attainment and Career Advancement

In addition to gender and family-related factors, educational attainment is an important predictor of the career achievement of postsecondary faculty. Education is considered a form of human capital (Becker, 1964). Research found that female faculty had lower educational backgrounds than male faculty (Nettles, Perna, & Bradburn, 2000). Male faculty, on average, held their highest degrees for longer periods of time than women faculty (Bradburn & Sikora, 2003). The percentage of male and female faculty holding advanced degrees depends on the type of institutions in which they are employed. A terminal degree is not a prerequisite for employment in 2-year public institutions where women faculty members are often employed (Conley, 2005).

Research also shows that a higher percentage of White males than female faculty had doctorate degrees, yet Asian Americans had a higher percentage rate of doctorates when compared to White Americans in general. Asian Americans make up less than 3% of the U.S. population, but account for more than 8% of the doctorates awarded in the United States.

Despite these statistics, Asian Americans have a lower percentage of tenured faculty positions compared to White Americans because Asian Americans tend to be younger than their counterparts and have less work experience (Lee, 2002). Furthermore, the current literature details how human capital can affect tenure status for women. These same findings can be applied to Asian American females.

However, despite the popularity of human capital theory for explaining differences in labor market experiences, Perna (2001, 2003) noted the limitations of this theory. Among the limitations is the inability of human capital theory to explain adequately the lower returns to educational investments among women and minorities.

Research Productivity and Career Advancement

In the academic field, there are three criteria by which candidates for tenure and promotion are judged: teaching, service, and research. These three criteria are not equally weighted (Park, 1996). Although all faculty are expected to do some teaching and service, outstanding teaching and service do not guarantee tenure and promotion except in 2-year postsecondary institutions. Research is the decisive factor for promotion or tenure in most higher education institutions (Park, 1996). According to human capital theory, an individual's status and rewards in the academic labor market are determined primarily by his or her research productivity. Productivity is expected to be determined by the investments that individuals make in themselves, particularly the quantity and quality of their education and the amount of their on-the-job training, as well as their geographic mobility and their motivation.

Both time on instruction and research field are closely related to research productivity (Sax, Hagedorn, Arredondo, & Dicrsi, 2002). For instance, differences in the resources required for research may lead to differences among groups in research output (Sax et al., 2002): The more time on instruction, the less time on research (Middaugh, 2001).

Time on instruction. Using data from the 1993 National Survey of Postsecondary Faculty (NSOPF-93), Bellas and Toutkoushian (1999) analyzed a number of significant differences in the time expenditure of faculty by gender, race/ethnicity, and marital status and their subsequent research productivity. On average, men devoted about 6% more work time than women to research, mainly at the expense of teaching. Similar differences are evident by racial/ethnic group, with Asians and Latinos spending greater average proportions of their work time on research than other groups. While married faculty spent more time on research than unmarried (single) faculty, the percentage differences were relatively small. These findings suggest that differences in the time expenditures of faculty across gender, racial/ethnic, and marital groups may affect research productivity. Given the critical role of research productivity in tenure and promotion decisions and salary increases, these differences have obvious consequences for the status of underrepresented groups within the academy (Allen, 1993). For example, women's greater time expenditures in teaching may reflect their disproportionate representation at teaching-oriented institutions within the lower ranks and in the humanities—all factors that increase time spent in teaching activities.

Research/academic field. The career achievement of postsecondary faculty is also related to research or academic field (Harvey, 2002; Xie & Shauman, 2003). Beutel and Nelson (2006) surveyed 150 top research universities in the field of social science. Findings revealed both gender and ethnic differences. The gender gap in faculty representation was greatest in economics and smallest in sociology. In sociology and political science, it appeared that there were critical masses of females in top research departments. In terms of racial/ethnic diversity, there were statistically significant differences in gender composition across ranks for Whites and Asians in economics, but not for Blacks and Hispanics. For Whites, Blacks, and Hispanics, the gender difference in faculty representation was smallest in sociology and largest in economics. Among Asians, the gender difference in faculty representation was smallest in political science and largest in economics. Other research (Kulis, Sicotte, & Collins, 2002) has found that, in the field of science, the underrepresentation of females and native-born Blacks and Hispanics among science and engineering faculty persists when national origin of faculty is considered. A study conducted by August (2006) demonstrated that in the fields of humanities, arts, and the social sciences, women were tenured at a higher rate than women in other areas. In the humanities and arts, nearly four out of five women attained tenure compared to two out of five men. In the social sciences, nearly two-thirds of women attained tenure compared to over half of the men. August's findings suggested that, since the majority of tenured faculty are men, at this rate, it will take more than three decades for women to hold half the tenured faculty positions in the humanities and arts and nearly a century in the social sciences.

Job Satisfaction and Career Advancement

Job satisfaction can be defined as the positive emotional feeling resulting from attaining what one wants or values from a job (Olsen, 1993). Job satisfaction also has a subjective nature because the degree to which each individual positively evaluates his or her job is dependent on individual and personal values (Hagedorn, 1996). All factors (e.g., background, research productivity and related factors) mentioned above are more or less related to an individual faculty member's job satisfaction. Lin, Pearce, and Wang (2009) found that job autonomy was the most satisfied aspect of job satisfaction, while salary was the least satisfied item among faculty members. Olsen, Maple, and Stage's (1995) findings in research-oriented institutions further indicated that satisfaction with teaching and research depended on institutional fit. Satisfaction with research was related to the clarity of promotion or tenure criteria and satisfaction with one's academic department. In contrast, satisfaction with teaching had a negative impact on recognition and support.

The job satisfaction of minority and women faculty members especially deserves attention (Hagedorn, 2000). Hagedorn (1996) found that women faculty members reported receiving significantly less support and recognition. Olsen et al. (1995) found significant gaps between the satisfaction of minority racial and ethnic groups and that of White faculty. For instance, all minority faculty groups except Hispanics were less likely than Whites to feel that they had satisfactory personal interaction with colleagues and a good fit with their departments. Asian faculty reported significantly less satisfaction than their White colleagues with regard to the fairness with which their immediate supervisors evaluate their work, the amount of both personal and professional interaction with tenured colleagues, and their sense of 'fit' in their departments.

NEED FOR THE STUDY

The literature reviewed here provides the background of this paper. Higher education literature found evidence that inequalities remain in various aspects of faculty life, such as salaries, academic rank, and tenure status, yet what accounts for the inequality is less clear.

Although research on Asian Americans in higher education has increased significantly in the past thirty years, important issues facing Asian American faculty have been masked by their treatment in educational research and policy. While Asian Americans have been included in debates about racial and ethnic minority representation in American colleges and universities since the 1980s, they have mostly been used to make legitimate or devalue the experiences of other racial and ethnic groups. Rarely have Asian American experiences and issues been given attention in and of themselves. Furthermore, much of the literature reviewed above has focused on minority and women's experience with career achievement in higher education—few specifically on Asian Americans and their tenure status. Understanding factors related to Asian

American faculty tenure will contribute to the knowledge of equity and diversity in the field of higher education. This study will meet this need by exploring several individual and institutional factors that may relate to the tenure of Asian faculty and examining the racial/ethnic differences.

The purpose of this study is to: (a) describe characteristics of Asian faculty including gender, family status, and educational attainment; (b) identify factors including research productivity, research field, time spent on instruction, and faculty satisfaction that may relate to the tenure of Asian faculty; and (c) compare the research productivity and tenure of Asian faculty with other ethnic groups.

METHODOLOGY

Data Source

This study used the National Study of Postsecondary, NSOPF-04. The NSOPF database is sponsored by the United States Department of Education's National Center for Education Statistics (NCES) and was designed to provide nationally representative data on faculty and staff at 2- and 4-year degree-granting institutions in the United States. The survey included questions on the activities and instructional duties of postsecondary faculty and instructional staff during the 2003 fall term. Faculty and instructional staff participating in the survey were asked a series of questions regarding their teaching, research, life, and job situations, including salary, benefits, workload, job security, decision making, and job satisfaction (Cataldi, Bradburn, Fahimi, & Zimbler, 2005). For several reasons, the NSOPF-04 is well suited for our research. First, the database is the most current and comprehensive source of information relating to Asian faculty. Second, the database provides detailed information about faculty characteristics and productivity and has sufficient numbers of Asian American faculty for reliable analysis. Finally, the NSOPF-04 is a nationally representative survey, thus findings can be generalized.

Variables

In this study the dependent variable is tenure. Since many Asian American faculty members work in science and engineering fields, which usually have higher salaries, we used tenured status for this study instead of salary as a measure of outcome. The independent variables included several individual characteristics that were identified in previous research. Individual characteristics selected for this study include gender, marital status, educational attainment, research productivity, time on instruction, and job satisfaction. Educational attainment was measured by doctorate, the highest degree attained in postsecondary education. Research productivity was measured by the number of published articles in referred and nonreferred journals and the number of book chapters produced in the previous two years. Most recent years' publications were used because they were more reliable than self-reported total numbers of career publications. *Faculty job satisfaction* includes satisfaction with employment and teaching in the last two years. Both variables are composite index variables. *Satisfaction of employment* is an index of satisfaction with aspects related to employment, including: (a) workload, (b) salary, and (c) benefits. *Satisfaction of instruction* is an index of satisfaction with aspects related to instructional activities in these areas: (a) authority to make decisions on content and methods in instructional activities, (b) institutional support for implementing technology-based instructional activities, (c) quality of equipment and facilities available for classroom instruction, and (d) institutional support for teaching improvement.

Analysis Procedures

Binary logistic regression is used to predict tenure success of Asian faculty and to understand the impact of several faculty characteristics such as productivity, doctoral degree, and job satisfaction. Logistic regression is used instead of Ordinary Least Squares (OLS) regression, because the dependent variable (tenured status) is a dichotomous outcome. In this way, logistic regression estimates the odds of tenure. Note that logistic regression has many analogies to OLS regression: logit coefficients correspond to b coefficients in the OLS regression equation, the standardized logit coefficients correspond to beta weights, and a pseudo R^2 statistic is available to summarize the strength of the relationship.

The analysis for this study was conducted in three stages. In the first stage, descriptive statistics were used to describe the characteristics of Asian faculty. In the second stage, comparative analysis (e.g., ANOVA, chi square tests) was used to compare dependent and independent variables for Asian faculty against other ethnic groups. In the third stage, logistic regression analysis was conducted to examine the relationship of individual characteristics with tenure for Asian faculty. In the first step the model contained only one independent variable, measured as dummy variable for race/ethnicity, similar to a base model. In subsequent models, additional independent variables were entered into the equations. In all six steps logistic analysis was performed.

FINDINGS

Characteristics of Asian American Faculty

Table 7.1 summarizes the observed differences in each dependent and independent variable between Asian American faculty and other ethnicities. Compared with other ethnicities, higher percentages of Asian American faculty have tenure. With regards to research productivity, Asian American faculty had a higher publication record but spent less time on instruction. They are more likely to have doctoral degrees and more likely to be represented in the fields of health, science, and engineering. However, they are less likely to be satisfied with employment and instruction.

Results From Logistic Regression Analysis

The relationship between individual characteristics and Asian American faculty were examined by using logistic regression in several steps. The estimated findings based on the six models are presented in Table 7.2. The results of logistic regression analysis are better interpreted by the use of odd-ratios than logistic coefficients. In this study, the odds-ratios represent the change in the odds of holding a tenured position that is associated with a one-unit change in a particular independent variable. An odds-ratio greater than one represents an increase in the likelihood of achieving tenure, where an odds-ratio less than one represents a decrease in the likelihood.

Model 1. Model 1, a base-line model, estimates the effects of dummy variables for race/ethnicity on tenure status. Compared with the excluded category (White non-Hispanic), African Americans and Hispanic Americans were less likely to receive tenure; both odds-ratios were less than one. However, as the model shows, being Asian is a positive factor (odds-ratio was greater than one), indicating Asians were more likely to receive tenure than other ethnic groups. In terms of probability, being an Asian faculty member, compared to being a White faculty member, led to about an 11% increase in the chance of receiving tenure.

Model 2. In Model 2, demographic and family characteristic variables were entered into the equation: dummy variables for gender and marital status. Both additional independent variables had significant effects on tenured status. Being male and married increased the odds of holding a tenured position. After controlling for gender and marital status, the odds of holding a tenured position are higher for Asian Americans than for Whites, but it is not significant.

Table 7.1. Selected Population Characteristics, by Race and Ethnicity (N = 21,529)

Measure	Asian		African		Hispanic		White (non-Hispanic)	
	n (%)	M (SD)	n (%)	M (SD)	n (%)	M (SD)	n (%)	M (SD)
Tenure Status								
Tenured	556 (30.8)		366 (24.0)		213 (23.9)		6,106 (28.4)	
Tenure Track	386 (21.4)		238 (15.6)		152 (17.1)		2,381 (11.1)	
Nontenure Track	760 (42.2)		799 (52.3)		450 (50.6)		11,104 (51.6)	
Marital Status								
Married	1,408 (78.1)		881 (57.7)		591 (66.4)		15,978 (74.2)	
Not Married	394 (21.9)		646 (42.3)		299 (33.6)		5,551 (25.8)	
Gender (%)								
Male	1,187 (65.8)		749 (49.1)		490 (55.1)		12,365 (57.4)	
Female	616 (34.2)		777 (50.9)		400 (44.9)		9,164 (42.6)	
Highest Degree								
Doctoral/ Professional	1,345 (74.6)		695 (45.5)		386 (43.3)		10,260 (47.6)	
Master's	353 (19.6)		619 (40.5)		331 (37.2)		8,281 (38.5)	

Bachelor's or Less	96 (5.3)	193 (12.7)	156 (17.5)	2,679 (12.5)
Recent Total Publications	5.65 (8.86)	2.61 (5.16)	2.83 (5.40)	3.28 (6.05)
Percentage of Time Spent on Instruction	57.56 (32.95)	73.50 (28.50)	71.76 (30.94)	72.14 (30.95)
Principal Research Field				
Business	142 (7.9)	81 (5.3)	32 (3.6)	1,057 (4.9)
Health	188 (10.4)	77 (5.0)	42 (4.7)	1,258 (5.8)
Humanities	108 (6.0)	115 (7.5)	96 (10.8)	1,748 (8.1)
Science/Engineering	587 (32.6)	149 (9.8)	87 (9.8)	2,607 (12.1)
Social Science/Education	129 (7.2)	196 (12.8)	108 (12.1)	2,088 (9.7)
Satisfaction of Employment	7.50 (2.56)	7.95 (2.59)	8.04 (2.72)	8.17 (2.63)
Satisfaction of Instruction	8.63 (2.29)	9.18 (2.41)	9.00 (2.38)	9.21 (2.22)

Table 7.2.   Results of Logistic Regression of Tenure Status

VARIABLES	Model 1	Model 2	Model 3	Model 4	Model 5	Model 6
Race/Ethnicity						
Asian	1.14*	1.07	0.71***	0.61***	0.59***	0.64***
African	0.81***	0.88*	0.88*	0.91	0.90	0.91
Hispanic	0.81**	0.83*	0.88	0.88	0.86	0.86
Gender						
Male		1.89***	1.51***	1.45***	1.40***	1.40***
Marital Status						
Married		1.30***	1.26***	1.25***	1.29***	1.31***
Education						
Doctorate			5.10***	3.84***	3.49***	3.48***
Research Productivity						
Publication				1.03***	1.03***	1.03***
Time on Instruction				0.99***	0.99***	0.99***
Discipline						
Business					1.63***	1.58***
Health					0.57***	0.54***
Humanities					1.70***	1.67***
Science/ Engineering					1.47***	1.53***

Social Sciences/ Education				1.28***	1.26***
Job Satisfaction					
Satisfaction of Employment					1.06***
Satisfaction of Instruction					0.92***
MODEL FIT					
Pseudo R^2 (Cox & Snell)	0.00	0.02	0.14	0.15	0.16	0.17
χ^2	27.53*** ($df = 3$)	635.02*** ($df = 5$)	3949.57*** ($df = 7$)	4106.70*** ($df = 8$)	4432.14*** ($df = 13$)	4618.85*** ($df = 15$)

Note: * $p < 0.05$. ** $p < 0.01$. *** $p < 0.001$.

Model 3. A human capital variable was entered into the equation. Having a doctoral degree significantly increased the odds of holding a tenured position. After controlling for human capital variables, interesting changes occurred in the race/ethnicity variable. The odds-ratio for Asians dropped and became less than one, indicating that odds of holding a tenured position are significantly lower for Asians than for Whites. The odds-ratio for Hispanic Americans was statistically insignificant, indicating that the statistically significant difference in tenure status between Hispanic Americans and Whites can be attributed to their demographic/family factors, and human capital. In terms of probability, being an Asian faculty member compared to being a White faculty member led to about a 25% decrease in the chance of receiving tenure.

Model 4. Two variables measuring productivity were estimated in Model 4. As expected, the effect of publication was positive, the effect of time spent on instruction was negative, and both were statistically significant. After controlling for productivity variables, odds-ratio for Asians decreased, indicating that odds of holding a tenured position are significantly lower for Asians than for Whites. The odds-ratio for African Americans was statistically insignificant. In terms of probability, being an Asian faculty member, compared to being a White faculty member, led to about a 33% decrease in the chance of being tenured.

Model 5. Dummy variables for academic fields were entered into Model 5. The excluded category is "other fields." All fields' odds-ratios were greater than one and significant, except health, which is significantly less than one. Compared with other fields, faculty in business, humanities, science/engineering and social science/education, except for health, were more likely to receive tenure. After controlling for research field variables, the odds-ratio for Asians continued to decrease, indicating that odds of holding a tenured position are significantly lower for Asians than for Whites. The effects of the remaining variables in Model 5 did not substantially change. In terms of probability, being an Asian faculty member, compared to being a White faculty member, led to about a 35% decrease in the chance of being tenured.

Model 6. The final model includes variables measuring job satisfaction. The effect of satisfaction level for employment was positive, while the effect of satisfaction level for instruction was negative. After controlling for these institutional variables, the odds-ratio for Asians remained less than one, indicating that odds of holding a tenured position were significantly lower for Asians than for Whites. The effects of the remaining variables in Model 6 did not substantially change. In summary, the regression model suggests that once these interdependent variables are accounted for, the odds of holding a tenured position are statistically significantly lower for Asian Americans than for Whites. In terms of probability, being an Asian faculty member, compared to being a White faculty member, led to about a 31% decrease in the chance of being tenured.

DISCUSSIONS

The purpose of this study is to describe characteristics of Asian faculty and to identify several individual and institutional factors that may relate to their career advancement and the goal of tenure. Findings revealed a complex image of Asian American faculty. On the one hand, Asian Americans had the highest academic achievement among all racial/ethnic groups: the percentage of them holding tenured ranks and doctoral degrees, and the number of their recent publications were among the highest. As a group, they were more likely to come from backgrounds such as being male and married, more likely to be productive within a research field such as science/engineering. They also spent less time on instruction. All these translated into a higher level of human capital and research productivity, which in turn positively affected their tenure status. On the other hand, their satisfaction levels with employment and instruction were among the lowest, and they were at a disadvantage when differences in their background were accounted for. Compared with Whites, the probability of achieving a tenured rank was 25-35% lower for Asian Americans, when gender, marital status, education, research productivity and its related factors were controlled. Consistent with the literature (Lee, 2002; Perna, 2001, 2003), Asian American's higher human capital and personal achievement do not produce equally higher returns when it comes to career advancement. It would appear that an invisible obstacle has impeded their success to some extent. Based on the research literature introduced earlier in this chapter, the invisible obstacle could be subtle racial discrimination combined with xenophobia against Asian American faculty members. These findings bring into the spotlight the grim reality of inequality facing faculty of color in higher education. The following are some recommendations to address the issue.

Identifying the Character of Job Satisfaction

Among all ethnic/racial groups, Asian American satisfaction with instruction and employment was the lowest. This warrants attention. The characteristic of job satisfaction is necessary to ensure faculty retention and to facilitate matching the right person to the right job. Inherent in identifying job satisfaction is maximizing job satisfaction and ultimately improving organizational effectiveness. For instance, Asian Americans, together with other faculty of color, need more recognition and support so that they have more control over their careers (Pearson, 2005).

Understanding Inequalities in Higher Education

Inequality is a complex, multifaceted issue; however, if U.S. higher education is going to continue to excel by attracting and retaining the best and brightest women and men of all races and ethnicities into the profession, it needs to understand the inequalities facing faculty of color in higher education to maximize the possibility of success for all faculty members.

Preventing Potential Problems Facing Tenure-Track Faculty of Color

Understanding what accounts for tenure has important implications for tenure-track faculty. The tenure-track years constitute a complex institutional socialization process that is very stressful for all races and ethnicities, in particular, for women and faculty members of color. Understanding what accounts for tenure for the Asian faculty will not only reduce their anxieties and maximize their success for tenure but also help prevent potential problems facing all tenure-track faculty of color.

CONCLUSIONS

The rise of America has historically benefited from different minority groups, and higher education has played a crucial role in that rise. Since higher education is one of the core foundations of American economic strength, racial/ethnic diversity at American colleges and universities has system wide importance. Asian Americans have been characterized with high personal achievements and high intellectual talent. They occupy a special niche in basic and applied science research. The belief that Asian Americans do not need attention because they exhibit better outcomes in the aggregate than other groups is disturbingly misleading. Furthermore, using the higher tenure rates alone to dispute the facts that Asian American faculty, like other faculty of color, suffer from racial discrimination hinders the necessity to bring the race issues against Asian American faculty in higher education into the open. Higher education researchers and educators must take greater responsibility for understanding and addressing why Asian Americans, especially in disaggregated categories, are not succeeding sufficiently in the workforce so that colleges and universities can more effectively prepare them to achieve equity in the workplace.

REFERENCES

Allen, H. L. (1993). Faculty workload and productivity: Ethnic and gender disparities. *The NEA 1997 Almanac of Higher Education.* Washington, DC: National Education Association.

August, L. (2006, May). *It isn't over: The continuing under-representation of female faculty.* Paper presented at the Association for Institutional Research, Chicago, IL

Bain, O., & Cumming, W. (2000). Academe's glass ceiling: Societal, professional-organizational, and institutional barriers to the career advancement of academic women. *Comparative Education Review, 44*(4), 493-514.

Becker, G. S. (1964). *Human capital, a theoretical and empirical analysis, with special reference to education.* New York, NY: Columbia University Press.

Bellas, M. L. (1993). Faculty salaries: Still a cost of being female? *Social Science Quarterly, 74,* 62-75.

Bellas, M. L., & Toutkoushian, R. K. (1999). Faculty time allocations and research productivity: Gender, race and family effects. *The Review of Higher Education, 22,* 367-390.

Bess, J. L. (1998). Contract systems, bureaucracies, and faculty motivation: The probable effects of a no-tenure policy. *The Journal of Higher Education, 69,* 1-22.

Beutel, A. M., & Nelson, D. J. (2006). The gender and race-ethnicity of faculty in top social science research departments. *The Social Science Journal, 43,* 111-125.

Bradburn, E. M., & Sikora, A. C. (2003). Gender and racial/ethnic differences in salary and other characteristics of postsecondary faculty: Fall 1998. *Education Statistics Quarterly, 4*(4), 1-7.

Brennan, J., & Naidoo, E. R. (2008). Higher education and the achievement (and/or prevention) of equity and social justice. *Higher Education, 56,* 287-302.

Cataldi, E. F., Bradburn, E. M., Fahimi, M., & Zimbler L. (2005). 2004 *National Study of Postsecondary Faculty (NSOPF: 04): Report on faculty and institutional staff in fall 2003.* Washington, DC: NCES.

Carver, D. A. (2005). No, it can hamper their roles. *Chronicle of Higher Education, 52*(6), B10-B11.

Conley, V. M. (2005). Career paths for women faculty: Evidence from NSOPF: 99. *New Direction for Higher Education, 130,* 25-39.

Feagin, J., & Feagin, C. (1986). *Discrimination American style: Institutional racism and sexism.* Malabar, Florida: R. E. Krieger.

Hagedorn, L. S. (1996). Wage equity, and female faculty job satisfaction: The role of wage differentials in a job satisfaction causal model. *Research in Higher Education, 37,* 569-598.

Hagedorn, L. S. (2000). Conceptualizing faculty job satisfaction: Components, theories, and outcomes. *New Directions for Institutional Research, 105*, 5-20.

Harvey, W. B. (2002). *Minorities in higher education 2001–2002: Nineteenth annual status report.* Washington, DC: American Council on Education.

Kulis, S., Sicotte, D., & Collins, S. (2002). More than a pipeline problem: Labor supply constraints and gender stratification across academic science disciplines. *Research in Higher Education, 43*, 657–691.

Lee, S. (2002). Do Asian American faculty face a glass ceiling in higher education? *American Educational Research Journal, 39*(3), 695-724.

Lin, Z., Pearce, R., & Wang, W. (2009). Imported talents: Demographic characteristics, achievement and job satisfaction of foreign born full time faculty in four-year American colleges. *Higher Education, 57*, 703-721.

Middaugh, M. F. (2001). *Understanding faculty productivity: Standards and benchmarks for colleges and universities.* San Francisco, CA: Jossey-Bass.

Museus, S. D. (2008). The model minority and inferior minority myths: Stereotypes and their implications for student learning. *About Campus, 13*(3), 2-8.

Museus, S. D. (2009). A critical analysis of the exclusion of Asian American from higher education: Research and discourse. In L. Zhan (Ed.), *Asian American Voices: Engaging, Empowering, Enabling* (pp. 59-76). New York, NY: NLN Press.

Museus, S. D., & Kiang, P. N. (2008). Deconstructing the model minority myth and how it contributes to the invisible minority reality in higher education research. *New Directions for Institutional Research, 142*, 5-15.

National Center for Education Statistics. (2005). 2004 *National Study of Postsecondary Faculty (NSOPF: 04): Report on faculty and instructional staff in fall 2003.* (NCES 2005-172). Washington, DC: U.S. Department of Education.

Nettles, M. T., Perna, L. W., & Bradburn, E. M. (2000). Salary, promotion, and tenure status of minority and women faculty in U.S. colleges and universities. *Education Statistics Quarterly, 2*(2), 1-4.

Olsen, D. (1993). Work satisfaction and stress in the first and third year of academic appointment. *Journal of Higher Education, 64*, 453-471.

Olsen, D., Maple, S. A., & Stage, F. K. (1995). Women and minority faculty job satisfaction. *Journal of Higher Education, 66*, 267-293.

Park, S. M. (1996). Research, teaching, and service: Why shouldn't women work count? *Journal of Higher Education, 67*, 46-84.

Pearson, L. C. (2005). The relationship between teacher autonomy and stress, work satisfaction, empowerment, and professionalism. *Educational Research Quarterly, 29*, 37- 53.

Perna, L. W. (2001). The relationship between family and employment outcomes among college and university faculty. *The Journal of Higher Education, 72*, 584-611.

Perna, L. W. (2003). The status of women and minorities among community college faculty. *Research in Higher Education, 44*, 205-240.

Perna, L. W. (2005a). The benefits of higher education: Sex, racial/ethnic and socioeconomic group differences. *The Review of Higher Education, 29*, 23-52.

Perna, L. W. (2005b). Sex differences in faculty tenure and promotion: The contribution of family ties. *Research in Higher Education, 46*, 277-307.

Sax, L. J., Hagedorn, L. S., Arredondo, M. A., & Dicrsi III, F. A. (2002). Faculty research productivity: Exploring the role of gender and family-related factors. *Research in Higher Education, 43,* 423-447.

Stanley, C. (2006). Coloring the academic landscape: Faculty of color breaking the silence in predominantly White colleges and universities. *American Educational Research Journal, 43,* 701-736.

Trower, C. A. (2009, Septermber/October). Toward a greater understanding of the tenure track for minorities. *Change, 41*(5), 38-46.

Xie, Y., & Shauman, K. A. (2003). *Women in science: Career processes and outcomes.* Cambridge, MA: Harvard University Press.

CHAPTER 8

NEGOTIATING LANGUAGES AND PRACTICES

Field Experience of a Preservice High School Teacher of Chinese

Yanan Fan

This paper reports findings of an ethnographic study of field experiences among Chinese preservice teachers as they learn to teach in high school World Language classrooms in Northern California. Drawing on a sociocultural view of learning and documenting one teacher candidate from Mainland China, the study explores how the candidate negotiated languages and teaching throughout her credential program and fieldwork. Through classroom vignettes, interview, student work, and observations, this paper reveals that the candidate's learning experiences were intertwined with negotiations of language competences, classroom interactions, and teacher identities. The study suggests that language teachers should consider how they can be sensitive and responsive to the dynamics of student interactions, and how they can create a flow of interactions that build students' language skills on top of the social practices of sharing and constructing experiences. Implications for teacher education programs are also discussed.

Asian American Education—Identities, Racial Issues, and Languages, pp. 181–200
Copyright © 2011 by Information Age Publishing

Chinese is the national language of more than 1.3 billion people in China and millions more ethnic Chinese around the world. Given China's rapid economic growth and increasing geopolitical power, the United States is witnessing a steadily growing interest in this widely spoken first language. This interest, and China's growing clout in the world, is creating new opportunities and challenges in national defense and in economic and cultural exchange for the younger generations in the United States. However, the dearth of certified teachers in comparison to the demand is "the major roadblock to building efficient pipelines for Chinese language programs in the U.S." (Asia Society, 2005, p. 9). The gap between the need for and the lack of certified Chinese language teachers is related to (and is somewhat caused by) another current deficiency in the U.S. educational system: the small numbers of Asian Americans and Pacific Islanders in teaching. The latter only constitute 1% of all teachers in the United States (e.g., Goodwin, 2005; Rong & Preissle, 1997).

Both shortages could be addressed in part by utilizing Chinese immigrants. However, the paucity of research on Asian American and Pacific Islander teachers, and on Chinese teachers in particular, is troubling (Sheets & Chew, 2002), and little is known about the recruitment, retention, and preparation of teachers of Chinese in U.S. teacher preparation programs (Goodwin, Genishi, Asher, & Woo, 2006).

Still, more and more Chinese-speaking immigrants are considering utilizing their home language and obtaining a teaching credential in order to teach Chinese in public schools, which seem to offer better career benefits and security than private weekend Chinese schools and other professions. Many prospective teacher candidates and teacher educators wonder how Chinese preservice teachers develop the knowledge base necessary to teach Chinese in U.S. public schools. A coherent response to this may help educate Chinese preservice teachers, and support those who are trying to build sound teacher education programs for them.

Drawing on a sociocultural view of learning, this paper reports preliminary findings of an on-going ethnographic study of field experiences among Chinese preservice teachers as they learn to teach in high school World Language classrooms in Northern California. Documenting one teacher candidate, Meiling,[1] who emigrated from Mainland China, I explore how she negotiated languages and teaching throughout her credential program and fieldwork. I will first discuss a theoretical perspective through which Meiling's learning experience was examined, as well as the broader scholarly conversation about Chinese teachers and their learning. I will then explain the nature of the research project and methods used to collect and analyze data. In the findings section, I discuss the challenges and resources Meiling had in (re)learning both her home language and English with her high school students through classroom vignettes, interview excerpts, student work, and observations.

LEARNING TO TEACH AS SOCIAL PRACTICE

Guided by a sociocultural perspective, I view learning to teach as a social practice in which every participant—with participant defined as being either a member of a social group (e.g., a class) or of a community of practice (Lave & Wenger, 1991)—plays an active role in constructing the experience. People participate by using their past experiences to anticipate recurrent actions through the interaction of situations and events and negotiating their social roles vis-à-vis other people. For every person, this participation is informed by his or her understanding of how the world works, and of how language itself works (Hymes, 1974; Rogoff, 2003; Vygotsky, 1978).

In a language classroom, where the target language is both the content and the medium of instruction, the dialogic nature of language use in classroom interactions further illuminates the social, political, and intellectual processes where teachers and students appropriate and connect each other's utterances as they are contextualized in specific settings and under particular ideological circumstances (Bakhtin, 1981). The notions of authority, native speaker, and relevance of discussion topics are thus negotiated and positioned within the local context and in response to larger sociopolitical climates. Learning to teach, therefore, is "socially negotiated and contingent on knowledge of self, students, subject matter, curricula, and setting" (Johnson, 2006, p. 239).

Seminal works by Vygotsky (1978), Bakhtin (1981), Lave and Wenger (1991) and other theorists from various disciplines have supported an epistemological shift in the field of second language teacher education from the positive stance toward a sociocultural stance. To be exact, teachers are seen as social beings that gain, rather than disseminate, knowledge "out of a dialogic and transformative process of reconsidering and reorganizing lived experiences" of themselves and their students (Johnson, 2006, p. 241).

Qualitative research has documented the sociocultural nature of teaching and learning in various sites and communities among language teachers (e.g., Dyson, 1997; Florio-Ruane, 2001; Johnson, 2006). In particular, many studies investigate individual teachers' identity formation and interactions in classroom teaching. Duff and Uchida (1997), for instance, examined identities, teaching practices, and understanding of culture among Japanese teachers of English in college EFL classrooms in Japan. The authors described intercultural situations that impacted teachers' understanding of the interrelationship between language and culture, and between self and teaching. Beynon, Ilieva, & Gichupas (2004) interviewed 28 immigrant teachers (11 were Chinese descendents) in Canada on their negotiation of voice, agency, authorship, and identity in Canadian school contexts. This negotiation, according to the authors, was situated in the clashes between varied teaching philosophies of these immigrant teachers and those from their Canadian master teachers and students. In Australia, Santoro (1999) reports in a case study the struggles Chinese-born and educated non-native English speaking preservice teachers had in their fieldwork in a Melbourne secondary school where they had to overcome such institutional barriers as racism and lack of understanding and support from master teachers. The study that particularly focuses on teachers of Chinese was conducted by Curdt-Christiansen (2006) in a Canadian heritage school between 2000 and 2002. Using discourse analysis, the author asserts that teacher talks (e.g., authoritative discourse) were embedded in culturally specific practices underscoring teaching and learning of the Chinese language; however, the authoritative talks need to be reshaped in order to respond to the contexts of the heritage language school and to the perceptions of young heritage learners. Still, little is known concerning Chinese teachers' learning and teaching experience in secondary schools in the United States.

THE STUDY

The assumption underlying this ethnographic case study is not discovering (nor is it my attempt to discover) the truth and the universal in people's lives; instead, I have decided to focus on one particular human experience. A close investigation of one teacher is beneficial and it entails knowing her entire school and university community to some extent, "because more than one theoretical notion may be guiding an analysis, confirmation, fuller specification, and contradiction all may result from one case study" (Vaughan, as cited in Stake, 2000, p. 448).

Meiling was born in China as one of the 1980s Generation (八零后), a widely used Chinese cultural term that distinguishes young people born after China's massive economic reform spearheaded by the Open Door Policy in the late 1970s. Meiling holds a bachelor's degree in Chinese literature and a master's in comparative literature from a prestigious Chinese university. She became a U.S. citizen in 2003 and started her new life with her husband, a native speaker of English and a fluent speaker of Chinese, in Northern California. During 2003-2007, Meiling took English courses at a local community college while working part time as Chinese Sunday school teacher and copy editor of a local Chinese newspaper. In

Fall 2007, she was admitted into a Single Subject Credential Program at a public university. Meiling was invited to participate in this research project because she was willing and interested to share her experiences as a student teacher throughout the year. She was also chosen as a major participant because she represented a growing number of potential Chinese teachers who shared similar cultural and educational backgrounds; that is, they are native speakers of Mandarin and have considerable experience and/or knowledge in the language and Chinese culture, and yet are new to the American education system and school culture.

Meiling's selection was also situated in the overall sociocultural context of new international collaboration in promoting Chinese language teaching in the United States. California has become a transition point where imported teachers from China are trained and sent out to all parts of the country to teach in new Chinese programs in secondary schools in order to fill the gap between demand and lack of qualified teachers (College Board, 2008). The California Department of Education has recently adopted its own World Languages standards for K-12 public schools; these standards are specifically designed for California's language diversity (California State Board of Education, 2009), whereas most states follow the National Standards of Foreign Language Education.

In terms of Chinese language, California is witnessing a new shift of instructional focus in public school Chinese curricula from Cantonese to Mandarin. For example, a Bay Area School District was awarded a federal multiyear foreign language assistant grant in 2009 to promote biliteracy and bilingual programs in Mandarin Chinese (other languages include Japanese, Korean, and Russian) from kindergarten through 12th Grade, as well as to train teachers for these burgeoning programs. As a result, processes in which new immigrants who are native speakers of Mandarin seek to teach Chinese language in the United States have become a crucial phenomenon to investigate, given that little is known concerning how they learn to teach and how to help them teach effectively in the classroom.

The initial broad question that triggered the study was how Meiling, an educated new immigrant from China, learned to teach Chinese in an American public school. More informed and specific research questions were later derived from reflections, as were new directions of inquiry along the way. Some key questions were: "What knowledge and skills did Meiling believe to be crucial for a Chinese teacher?" "How did she interact with students in class?" "How did she negotiate her role as a teacher of Chinese?"

Data sources included typed field notes, audiotaped interviews and lessons Meiling taught, photocopies of her teaching materials (e.g., lesson/unit plans, reflective memos), credential course assignments, and performance portfolios. Information of the placement school, district, and employment for foreign language teachers was also compiled to provide a broader picture of history, need, and current status of Chinese teachers in K-12.

Data Collection took place during the 2007-2008 academic year in a state university teacher preparation program in the San Francisco Bay Area that has seen a steady increase of Chinese credential applicants. The research project took place during Meiling's 1-year credential program. Data collection occurred in her placement school, Garden High School, which is located in the center of a public school district that serves a diverse city population. At the time of this study, 40% of the Garden's students were Asian. The remainder of the student population was equally divided among White, African American, and Latino students, with nominal numbers of Arabic and African students. The school had a large Chinese language program with four full time faculty members. Chinese courses, along with Japanese, Russian, Spanish, German, and Italian, were offered to students of all grade levels as part of their required foreign language credits. Whereas heritage speakers (including Cantonese speakers) comprised a fair portion of all enrollees, some started with zero Chinese. The two classes Meiling student-taught were predominantly Asian; however, students varied in Chinese proficiency, language backgrounds, and personal interests.

I served as Meiling's field supervisor, observing her teaching, debriefing with her, and discussing field-related issues with her throughout the year. This dual role of supervisor and researcher had a rather positive impact on Meiling's practice because she gained more time than other candidates to sit with a supervisor who would listen to her thoughts and concerns about her teaching. When the project started, I explained the purpose and nature of the study to Meiling several times, which helped ease her anxiety that she was being judged rather than understood.

In Fall 2007, I visited Meiling once a month while she observed the classes she would teach in the spring. The purpose of these visits was to understand how Meiling familiarized herself with the school, student population, master teachers, curriculum demands, and classroom management. In Spring 2008, when Meiling taught her two classes independently, I observed her twice a month for 4 months. The focus was Meiling's planning and execution of the lessons. While at the site, I jotted down fieldnotes during observations, audiotaped Meiling's interactions with students, and debriefed with Meiling afterwards. I also conducted four open-ended interviews with Meiling in Chinese[2] and her two master teachers in both English and Chinese to collect different perspectives on Meiling's learning over time.

The fieldnotes, transcribed materials, and Meiling's written reflections and other related work provided multiple sources for triangulation—matching related data in an inductive data analysis process (Emerson,

Fretz, & Shaw, 1995; Erickson, 1986). This process involved (1) reading the whole data set multiple times; (2) naming preliminary coding categories (e.g., language use, language competence, pedagogy, resources, curriculum, cultural understanding, identity, relationship with the master teacher, expert versus newcomer, and relationship with students); (3) arranging data in chronological order and by setting; (4) selecting key language events as units of analysis (Street, 2000); (5) looking across time, settings, and events to develop thematic data analysis categories that later replaced or merged the preliminary coding categories, or made them sub-categories (e.g., new categories such as language expertise, cultural expectations of teacher and students, appropriation of language use, and interpretation of participation); (6) selecting key language events for close study (these episodes were either representative of the routine practices, or theoretically rich in unraveling the dynamics of the case); and (7) initializing assertions that addressed Meiling's teaching and learning.

I LEARN AS I GO: THE FINDINGS

In this section, I use classroom vignettes and other qualitative data to describe Meiling's challenges and resources in negotiating Chinese and English in the cultural contexts of American public school classroom. I argue that Meiling's learning experiences were intertwined with negotiations of language competences, classroom interactions, and teacher identities.

Negotiating Language Competences

Meiling was passionate about language and excited to become a language teacher. She chose to teach Chinese because she was confident about her competence as a native speaker and as a professional during her graduate studies and early career in China, when she had worked as a textbook editor for an education publisher. In comparison to other Chinese candidates in the program who were second generation Asian/ Chinese Americans mainly educated in the United States, Meiling believed she had solid preparation in the Chinese language as she had survived severe academic competitions for higher education in China. However, during her fieldwork and credential courses, she realized that not everybody who can speak Chinese fluently could teach Chinese language class in a K-12 classroom.

The urge to reexamine language competence came from Meiling's student teaching. The Chinese curriculum at Garden High was rigorous compared to those in the neighboring district schools. Garden's Chinese department followed a strict pacing guide that covered much more content and skills for students who were expected to aim for college. According to Ms. Chien, Meiling's master teacher who also chaired the department, students at Garden would complete twice the amount of content required by the district for regular Chinese programs. Meiling's initial reaction to such a demanding curriculum was self-imposed pressure to polish and relearn Chinese. For instance, in a professional development workshop for local Chinese teachers, Meiling learned about some policy changes towards more rigid listening and speaking assessment in regional and national standardized Chinese tests. "I need to be careful about my pronunciation because sometimes I accidentally use tones that are unique in my hometown dialect in Eastern China," Meiling commented on a few occasions in class when her students questioned her pronunciation. In addition to pronunciation and intonation, she practiced writing traditional Chinese characters, which was also required in the curriculum. "I'm so used to the simplified forms.[3] When I have to look up the traditional forms, it is like re-learning Han Zi [Chinese characters] again." The trickiest part of teaching Chinese for Meiling was to clearly explain and justify usage and grammatical structures that native speakers took for granted.

> For example, I find it difficult to explain the differences between " 两 " and " 俩 " when students suddenly ask me the question. Both can mean 'two of,' but in different situations. I don't know any dictionary or textbook that can offer some systematic and reliable explanations that my American students can easily understand. I need to combine the official reference to everyday examples to help my students. (Meiling, interview transcripts)

The same challenge applied to clarifying culturally specific words and expressions, such as idioms and proverbs. Meiling once shared her opinion on her native language.

> I don't think it is right to take your native language for granted in the case of teaching. When an American [friend] knew in our conversation that I was teaching Chinese, this person said, "You are cheating!" Perhaps they really think that way. As a native speaker, you may not have to spend a lot of time in pronunciation and intonation, but that does not mean you have much advantage as a teacher. Speaking the language and teaching it are two separate concepts. (Meiling, interview transcripts)

While honing her native language, Meiling was catching up with her English. She felt lucky to have passed the California Basic Educational Skills Test (CBEST), an English test that turned many Chinese candidates away in their attempt to enter a credential program. Meiling understood that English was a crucial criterion that her future principal would use to measure her ability to blend into the American school culture. While taking courses in educational foundations, adolescent development, literacy and language development, theories of learning, and foreign language teaching pedagogies, Meiling paid attention to both the content of these courses and the use of English in constructing the content. Speaking as a person new to the social, cultural, and educational system, she regarded these courses as highly necessary and beneficial.

> I think the university courses help me greatly. I am able to understand what is really going on in [the] classroom, why my master teacher chose to deal with issues in [a] certain way, and why it is the best solution. It is all because many classroom issues are covered in credential courses that equipped me with theoretical lenses. Even though theory and practice in reality may not match perfectly, without theory I would not know how to analyze practice and convince myself why it is appropriate to do certain things in [the] classroom. Also, I learn to improve my English so that I can speak the language properly and effectively as a faculty member in school. I think I need to work on my pronunciation because I know I have an accent, and work on written English because I was not an English major at college. (Meiling, interview transcripts)

Whereas Meiling had a strong background in her subject area, Chinese, and she could also express herself fairly clearly in spoken and written English, she frequently reflected on her growth in both languages as she positioned herself in high school classrooms. In terms of Chinese, she challenged the misconception among Chinese speakers that if one could speak Chinese fluently, one could teach Chinese language class in a K-12 classroom. Meiling believed she had to reteach herself the language based on the curricular and demographic demands of the school and its students.

In terms of English, Meiling thought that it was not only a tool for her to survive the credential program, but to understand her teaching environment and better communicate with her students. At the same time, she was well aware of the dynamics in everyday classroom teaching because "that is where [she] made sense of the history [of American schools] and theories [of language teaching]" (Meiling, interview transcripts) with her students.

Negotiating Classroom Interactions

The sociocultural view of language teaching and learning states that a teacher's interaction with students goes beyond the traditional teacher initiation, student response, and teacher evaluation (IRE) model (Cazden, 1988); furthermore, the teacher's interaction with students, as well as the overall pedagogy, should respond to the dynamics of classroom interaction where participants are not merely reproducing the language structures, but engaging in a process in which "meaning is treated as tentative, provisional and open to alternative interpretations and to revision" (Wells, as cited in Boyd & Maloof, 2000, p. 166).

Meiling taught two Chinese classes at different levels—freshmen and juniors. She soon recognized the students' liveliness in class, their curiosity about her as student teacher, and more importantly, their diverse backgrounds.

> Students [in my placement school and classes] were from different races, ethnic groups, and family socioeconomic backgrounds. Moreover, students' language levels were different as well. Some students grew up in Chinese speaking families, but some students did not. Some students had been to Chinese schools or in Chinese immersion programs before they went to middle school, but some students never started learning Chinese until they went to middle school. Some students were new Chinese immigrants, but some had never been to China. As a result, some students already knew most of what the teacher taught, while some students were still struggling to get in the threshold of Chinese language and culture. (Meiling, written reflection)

Throughout her semester-long period of student-teaching, Meiling found the in-class interactions with and among students most fascinating but somehow challenging, which could be best illustrated in the following vignette. During a typical review lesson on using descriptive words to portray people, Meiling invited students to pick their favorite character (from a novel, television show, film, or completely fictitious or drawn from real life) and write about that character. This group activity evolved into a contest in which students competed to have the most detailed and accurate description without giving away the name of their character. Free to choose their favorite character and eager to produce the best description, students came up with a variety of personalities with their group members—real, fictitious, historical, contemporary, male, female, celebrity or common people.

Not every character was as easy to recognize as the Big Bird in Table 8.1. For example, Group B's description in Table 8.2 looked too general (e.g., moustache, middle-aged) and yet too context specific (e.g., black pearl, chocolate) for Meiling. However, instead of being singled out as the only person in the room that did not know the character, Meiling quickly shifted her strategy of monitoring language use to inviting Group B to give more explanations and hints in Chinese about their character. With much enthusiasm, Group B explained in a mixture of English and Chinese that *qiaokeli* (巧克力 , chocolate, line 7, Table 8.2), *zise* (紫色 , purple, line 7, Table 8.2), and heizhu (黑 ［珍］珠 , Black Pearl, line 8, Table 8.2) were key words for two movies this actor (who turned out to be Johnny Depp; the details were from the films *Charlie and the Chocolate Factory* and *Pirates of the Caribbean*) had starred in. After filling the information gap, Meiling was able to suggest adding more details in the Chinese description to help students construct more complicated sentences rather than bulleted lists.

For Meiling, seeing her students' active participation was reassuring; however, when she proceeded to respond to their inaccurate language in the presentation, she found herself surrounded with students' heated discussions. Some classroom interactions went beyond checking facts into debating opinions and language use. For example, debates arose when Group C presented Hillary Clinton, former Senator of New York and current U.S. Secretary of State (the descriptive words are shown in Table Table 8.3). Meiling was caught off-guard by students' rejection of her grammar-related suggestions.

Other than personal information, Group C described Clinton's political life in the 2008 Presidential Campaign. The presentation drew a few giggles and side conversations from the audience. Meiling then began to address what she perceived to be typical errors, such as confusion over singular vs. plural nouns (e.g., *heiren*, 黑人 , a Black man vs. Black men; *yige,* 一个 , a or one, lines 4 & 5, Table 8.3) and multiple meanings of verbs (e.g., *da,* 打 , to beat or to fight; *bu xihuan,* 不喜欢 , dislike or hate, lines 4 & 5, Table 8.3). She suggested that in order to avoid errors, *renhe* (任何, any) be added to 我不喜欢一个黑人 (line 5, Table 8.3) to make the sentence, *wo bu xihuan renhe yige heiren* (我不喜欢任何一个黑人 , I do not like any Black man), because the quantifier, *renhe* (任何 , any), should be used with *bu* (不 , not) in this negative statement. In making the grammar-related change, Meiling was, in fact, creating a more important content error.

Table 8.1.   Group A's Description
[With English Translation by Researcher]

Line 1	他是黄色的。	He is yellow.
Line 2	他是一只很大的鸟。	He is a very big bird.
Line 3	他是男的。	He is a guy.
Line 4	他常常唱歌。	He often sings.
Line 5	他有很多朋友。	He has many friends.
Line 6	他常常有小孙子来一起唱歌。	He often sings with small children.
Line 7	他住在芝麻街。	He lives in Sesame Street.

**Table 8.2.   Group B's Description
[With English Translation by Researcher]**

Line 1	他是男的。	He is a guy.
Line 2	有胡子	Has moustache
Line 3	喜欢戴帽子	Likes wearing hats
Line 4	• 是个演员	• Is an actor
Line 5	• 中年男子	• Middle-aged man
Line 6	• 白人	• White man
Line 7	• 巧克力 （紫色）	• Chocolate (purple)
Line 8	• 黑珠	• Black Pearl

**Table 8.3.   Group C's Description
[With English Translation by Researcher]**

Line 1	我是五十岁。	I am 50 years old.
Line 2	我的爱人对我不忠。	My spouse is not faithful to me.
Line 3	今天我的名字在报纸上出现得比较多。	My name often appears on newspapers.
Line 4	我跟黑人打	I fight against Black man.
Line 5	我不喜欢一个黑人。	I do not like a Black man.
Line 6	我是大学毕业的。	I am a college graduate.
Line 7	我住在美国的东边儿。	I live in the east part of the U.S.
Line 8	我是一个女。	I am a woman.

Meiling's grammar critique prompted immediate defense from Group C that her revision would misinterpret what they meant, which was that if Clinton does not like *one particular* (*yige,* 一个 , as a numerical) Black man —presidential candidate Barack Obama at a particular time period, it doesn't mean she did not like Black people. Before Meiling could elaborate more on the differences that *yige* makes as a determiner, a pronoun, or a numerical, class discussions took a drastic turn on whether Hillary Clinton and former candidate Barack Obama were enemies based on Group C's use of *xihuan* (喜欢 , like). For Group C, Clinton hated that Obama obstructed her path to the White House, while others challenged this statement by questioning the difference between "do not like" and "hate" in both languages. One girl shouted out loud: "Clinton did not necessarily hate Obama. She *fights* against Obama for political reasons. It's just politics!" (class discussion transcripts)

At this point, Meiling had to decide how she would react to her students and how much more she would expand on the new topics her students raised. On one hand, she was pleased to see her students actively using Chinese as a tool to make meaning out of a brief description. Watching her students arguing in both English and Chinese with one another concerning Clinton's and Obama's candidacies and their relationship, Meiling noticed a variety of potential topics she could use to build lessons and activities, including race, gender, and politics. On the other hand, she was reassessing her role as an evaluator, a monitor, and a newcomer with little background knowledge about the political passion and interests of her American students during a heated presidential campaign of Democratic Party's primary.

In our debrief after this lesson, Meiling pointed out her weakness of not being able to channel student discussions into tangible language products (for example, a concrete revision of the character description using at least one key language point that strengthens description, or an oral report in Chinese on the quality of the character descriptions). Meiling reflected on the challenging task of seizing a teachable moment in classroom:

> The room sounded a bit chaotic. The presentations provoked many conversations and second opinions among students. Sometimes we couldn't hear the presenters at all. This has been a frequent problem. I tried not to let students get too hyper, but then they were bored and did not concentrate. If they were too excited, they would never stop talking in class. This was the most difficult and challenging for me. Still, I am interested in the topics students raise and will learn more about how to help them get their ideas across in Chinese, how to correct their errors, and how to react to their discussions in general (Meiling, interview transcripts).

Negotiating Teacher Identities

With the traditional image of a Chinese *jiaoshi* (教师, teacher) as a master of both content knowledge and of pedagogy, Meiling explored new meanings of *jiaoshi* at Garden High where her confidence in Chinese and commitment to students were reshaped by her students and by the many unpredictable events in everyday classroom life. As Meiling explained afterwards, she was experimenting with a change of role from an authority on Chinese to a learner new to the teen culture. "My students have their own expertise and interests from which I need to learn. Otherwise, I would not understand what they are talking about and how to respond other than nodding or smiling at them." She further explained, "Learning to teach is, for a great part, learning to be responsive and sensitive to my students" (Meiling interview transcripts).

Ms. Chien, Meiling's master teacher, explained another layer in the delicate relationship between a teacher candidate and students in a meeting with Meiling. According to Ms. Chien, the presence of a teacher candidate invited curiosity and excitement among students. Meiling was a less-threatening power figure to students than their regular classroom teacher because of her apprentice status. It might become all the more stimulating for students to test Meiling's limits in all aspects—from her skills to connect to their underground curriculum (Dyson, 1985) to her skills to conduct class. Much of the testing occurred in class time and during classroom interactions.

In her school environment, which strongly pushed for academic excellence, Meiling experienced what Ms. Chien had described. Her initial plan to teach the language clearly and correctly soon fell apart because the plan only addressed the language structures rather than her students who were appropriating and experimenting with the language. Meiling realized that she was learning as much or more from her students than they were learning from her, and that learning to teach was a process of negotiating her identity vis-à-vis her students, with each different student perhaps requiring a different approach. In a position paper on teaching, Meiling explained explicitly the co-construction of meaning-mediated language learning and how she thought it would benefit students.

> In my Chinese classroom, we will talk about world events like the Iraq War, global warming or international trade. In these topics, students will not only develop their reading, speaking, and listening literacy in the objective language but also they will develop their critical thinking when they try to see world events from the perspective of diverse ethnic and cultural groups. In addition, students will see how people's lives interconnect. What Chinese people do in their economy, environment, and social reforms influences American people's lives, and what Americans do influences Chinese lives as well. As a result, students will broaden their horizon in seeing the world, feeling a connection to Chinese society, and understanding their own values and identities better. (Meiling, position paper on teaching)

This coconstruction, in turn, benefited Meiling as a teacher as she actively learned to communicate with her students and make connection with their lives. She and Ms. Wong, her second master teacher both put forward in a debrief meeting the many identities of a Chinese teacher. These identities included the teacher as a learner of both languages, a facilitator in the classroom, a resource person for students, a negotiator of curriculum, and more. As Meiling rightly put it, "There is so much more a teacher should do than being a native speaker of a target language" (Meiling, interview transcripts)

DISCUSSION

Meiling's (and her students') experiences lead us to fundamental questions concerning what language teachers need to know, and how they develop this knowledge base in practice. Freeman and Johnson (1998) repudiate the widely accepted assumption that if you speak the language, you can teach it. Along a similar research line, traditional language teacher education focuses primarily on target language competency, teaching methods, and development of pedagogy through observation and practice in the classroom (Johnson, 2006); however, it overlooks the dialogic nature of classroom teaching and learning and its impact on teacher learning. In Meiling's case, learning to teach takes place in cross-cultural negotiations of meaning facilitated through an intensely interactive (collegial, but possibly adversarial in other circumstances) relationship with students. Furthermore, these cross-cultural negotiations take place both in English and in Chinese. That is, she learns how to teach as she negotiates her identities in relation to her students, and her use of Chinese and English in particular circumstances may be dictated not just by language competence of a particular student or pedagogy, but rather, by a certain sociocultural context.

Although the cultural tradition of teaching Chinese assumes teachers as the absolute model and authority (Leung, 2003), the language expert vs. novice relationship between teacher and student in Meiling's Chinese classroom had turned into a fluid, collegial relationship where "novices do not merely copy experts' capabilities; rather they transform what the experts offer them as they appropriate it" (Lantolf, 2000, p. 17). As shown in the character guessing activity described above, students went beyond simply describing the physical appearance of their characters. They further situated their characters in their social and cultural environment, making unique references to popular culture and current affairs. For instance, students' choice of Hilary Clinton (and Barack Obama) reflected the impact of the historical 2008 presidential election in the United States that inspired an unprecedented number of young people to participate and vote.

Johnson and Golombek (2003) characterize teacher learning as emerging "out of and constructed by teachers within the settings and circumstances of their work" (p. 735). In the case of Meiling, I would add another dimension: teacher learning takes place through a collegial relationship with students who co-construct the classroom dynamics with the teacher. This ever-shifting collegial relationship requires teachers to build their knowledge of themselves and of their students during everyday classroom interactions that make space for students to negotiate and sometimes create the use of language.

Several facets of this experience can now be recapitulated. First, knowledge of self and students requires ongoing examination of the social role played by each class member. Meiling sees herself as an expert in the Chinese language, a novice of American teenagers' cultural worlds, and an able yet still-learning facilitator in conversations between cultures and languages. Although her students are classified as intermediate learners of Chinese, Meiling sees them as active participants in social interactions, and critical reviewers of class content. In Meiling's Chinese classroom, the notions of authority, native speaker, and relevance of topic are constantly negotiated through a dialogic process, in which the teacher and the students appreciated and appropriated each other's unique contributions to each classroom activity and language event. Through her experience, Meiling learned to listen to her students, respond to their questions, and adjust the content of the course based on the interests of her students. Second, language teachers should consider how they can be sensitive and responsive to the dynamics of student interactions, and how they can create a flow of interactions that build students' language skills on top of the social practices of sharing and constructing experiences (Lave & Wenger, 1991). As Florio-Ruane (2002) points out:

> Because a teacher works with many students within emergent, normative, and negotiated settings, his or her knowledge is not simply instantiated in patterns of observed behavior, nor is it simply invisibly scripted and in the head.... Teachers retain sufficient agency to act in new, creative ways. As such, teaching is both ordered and responsive to norms and standards and also improvisational and responsive to other participants. (pp. 209-210)

Therefore, it is through participation with students and reflection on teaching that language teachers learn to create supportive social conditions for students to actively construct their understanding of the world and era they are in, experiment with language as a symbolic meaning-making tool, and critique appropriate forms of language that convey their thoughts accurately (Halliday, 1980). It would be inadequate, and impractical, to ask new teachers like Meiling to cram for a few names in popular culture just to make it to the end of a school day, because the premise of this "crash course" would be contrary to the fundamental understanding that learning to teach is "socially negotiated and contingent on knowledge of self, students, subject matter, curricula, and setting" (Johnson, 2006, p. 239). In addition to Larsen-Freeman and Freeman's (2008) suggestion that teachers understand the interests and needs of students, I would argue further that teachers' taking advantage of the information gap regarding language uses and cultural connotations is also key to making the target language both an effective "means to an end" and a fruitful "end in itself" (Larsen-Freeman & Freeman, 2008, p. 162).

It is critical for language teachers to listen, observe, and ask their students about what potential uses of the target language are (in this case, Chinese), and how these potential uses can be employed to create meaning-making opportunities. In other words, language teachers should consider how they can create flow of interactions and build students' language skills on top of the social practices of sharing and constructing experiences (Lave & Wenger, 1991; Vygotsky, 1978). In the meantime, language teachers develop their knowledge and perspectives through this process as they participate with students in the classroom and reflect on teaching.

Language teachers should be encouraged to embrace what their students bring to the classroom and to link it to various topics and registers – various styles of using language that is appropriate for particular settings. Without an interest in and knowledge of what students care about, language teachers are less likely to create space for students to participate in learning. Meiling's master teacher shared her insights into what potential teachers should be aware of as they learn to teach.

> We see more and more young Chinese [men and women] coming to the United States pursuing a teaching career. Most of them are like Meiling who are well-educated recent immigrants. Because of the overwhelming pressure brought about by immigration, many tend to be less flexible when adjusting to the new cultural environment [in the United States], with youth culture in particular. In order to succeed in teaching American students, new Chinese teachers need to understand what interests them and how to communicate with them, because this is not China where education is dominated by teacher-centered instruction and test-driven curriculum. (Ms. Wong, interview transcripts)

IMPLICATIONS

This article examines how teacher learning is contingent upon and embedded in literacy practices (Street, 2000) in the classroom by looking at Meiling's experience of blending content and pedagogy (Shulman, 1987) into everyday interaction with her students. Through this individual case, an understanding is developed concerning how languages, topics, and sociocultural issues are negotiated and presented in the classroom in a dynamic process between students and teacher. It aims to extend the conversation on foreign/second language teacher education with a focus particularly on Chinese teachers—an overwhelmingly underrepresented teacher population.

In practice, teacher educators and teacher preparation programs should strongly support language teachers from different sociocultural backgrounds by providing a theoretical framework for observation of language events in the classroom as well as various forums for reflecting teacher's roles and strategies. Implementation of this concept would empower teachers as they gain an understanding of cultural meanings, norms, and goals of communication in environments that are not a direct reflection of the sociocultural contexts they know best. At the same time, teacher educators and teacher preparation programs should devote more time to investigation of how teachers learn, and what role language plays in the process. Instead of prescribing top-down instructional models and imposing innovations on teachers, teacher education should attend more to how to integrate theoretical innovations to practice in the real-life setting—the classroom.

In Meiling's case, it would not make sense to tell Meiling what she should say to students, because interactions happen in varied social situations and are affected by site, participants, mood, and goal of communication (Hymes, 1974). Therefore, "L2 [second language] teacher education must accept the multiple forms that teachers' ways of knowing and their ways of coming to know may take" (Johnson, 2006, p. 242). To support teachers in this process of perpetual learning, teacher educators encourage student teachers to ask more questions about their beliefs in learning, the philosophy that guides their teaching, and strategies to create a class community based on the various demographic composition of the student population.

Teacher's action research of their own interaction with students, and their ethnography of communication (Watson-Gegeo, 1988) can be effective vehicles to examine the language dynamics in a classroom. Projects that push teachers to relate to their students can also help teachers better understand what students bring to the classroom, and what the interests of these students are. Teacher education programs should offer a variety of language-focused courses to broaden student teachers' view of the nature of language teaching and learning.

NOTES

1.   All names are pseudonyms.
2.   The researcher is a native speaker of Mandarin Chinese.
3.   The simplified form of Chinese characters has been widely used and taught in schools in mainland China since the People's Republic of China was founded in 1949, whereas the traditional form is used in Taiwan, Hong Kong, and overseas Chinese communities. For example, the simplified form for *teacher* is 师; the traditional form is 師 . *To study* is 学习 (simplified) or 學習 (traditional). In Meiling's placement school, both forms were introduced to students, but only the simplified form would be tested for.

REFERENCES

Asia Society. (2005). *Expanding Chinese language capacity in the United States: What would it take to have 5 percent of high school students learning Chinese by 2015?* New York, NY: Asian Society.

Bakhtin, M. M. (1981). Discourse in the novel. In C. Emerson & M. Holquist (Eds.), *The dialogic imagination: Four essays by M. M. Bakhtin* (pp. 259-422). Austin, TX: University of Texas Press.

Beynon, J., Ilieva, R., & Dichupas, M. (2004). Re-credentialing experiences of immigrant teachers: Negotiating institutional structures, professional identities and pedagogy. *Teachers and Teaching, 10*, 429-444.

Boyd, M., & Maloof, V. M. (2000). How teachers can build on student-proposed intertextual links to facilitate student talk in the ESL classroom. In J. K. Hall & L. S. Verplaetse (Eds.), *Second and foreign language learning through classroom interaction* (pp. 163-182). Mahwah, NJ: Erlbaum.

California State Board of Education. (2009). *World language content standards for California public schools, kindergarten through grade twelve.* Sacramento, CA: California State Board of Education, Executive Office.

Cazden, C. B. (1988). *Classroom discourse.* Exeter, NJ: Heinemann.

College Board. (2008). *136 New Chinese guest teachers arrive for assignments in schools across the United States.* Retrieved from http://www.collegeboard.com/press/releases/197820.html

Curdt-Christiansen, X. L. (2006). Teaching and learning Chinese: Heritage language classroom discourse in Montréal. *Language, Culture and Curriculum, 19,* 189-207.

Duff, P. A., & Uchida, Y. (1997). The negotiation of teachers' sociocultural identities and practices in postsecondary EFL classrooms. *TESOL Quarterly, 31,* 451-486.

Dyson, A. H. (1985). Writing and the social lives of children. *Language Arts, 62,* 632-639.

Dyson, A. H. (1997). *What difference does difference make? Teacher reflections on diversity, literacy, and the urban primary school.* Urbana, IL: National Council of Teachers of English.

Erickson, F. (1986). Qualitative methods in research on teaching. In M. Wittrock (Ed.), *Handbook of research on teaching* (3rd ed., pp. 119-161). Washington, DC: American Educational Research Association.

Emerson, R. M., Fretz, R. I., & Shaw, L. L. (1995). *Writing ethnographic fieldnotes.* Chicago, IL: University of Chicago Press.

Florio-Ruane, S. (2001). *Teacher education and the cultural imagination: Autobiography, conversation, and narrative.* Mahwah, NJ: Erlbaum.

Florio-Ruane, S. (2002). More light: An argument for complexity in studies of teaching and teacher education. *Journal of Teacher Education, 53,* 205-215.

Freeman, D., & Johnson, K. E. (1998). Reconceptualizing the knowledge-base of language teacher education. *TESOL Quarterly, 32,* 397-417.

Goodwin, A. L. (2005). *Asian Americans and Pacific Islanders in teaching. Eric Digest.* New York, NY: ERIC Clearinghouse on Urban Education.

Goodwin, A. L., Genishi, C., Asher, N., & Woo, K. (2006). Voices from the margins: Asian American teachers' experiences in the profession. In C. Park, R. Endo, & A. Goodwin (Eds.), *Asian and Pacific American education: Learning, socialization, and identity* (pp. 99-117). Greenwish, CT: Information Age.

Halliday, M. A. K. (1980). Three aspects of children's language development: Learning language, learning through language, learning about language. In Y. M. Goodman & D. S. Strickland (Eds.), *Oral and written language development research: Impact on schools* (pp. 9-19). Urbana, IL: International Reading Association.

Hymes, D. (1974). *Foundations in sociolinguistics: An ethnographic approach.* Philadelphia, PA: University of Pennsylvania Press.

Johnson, K. E. (2006). The sociocultural turn and its challenges for second language teacher education. *TESOL Quarterly, 40,* 235-257.

Johnson, K. E., & Golombek, P. R. (2003). "Seeing" teacher learning. *TESOL Quarterly, 37,* 729-738.

Lantolf, J. P. (2000). Introducing sociocultural theory. In J. P. Lantolf (Ed.), *Sociocultural theory and second language learning* (pp. 1-26). New York, NY: Oxford University Press.

Larsen-Freeman, D., & Freeman, D. (2008). Language moves: The place of "foreign" languages in classroom teaching and learning. *Review of Research in Education, 32,* 147-186.

Lave, J., & Wenger, E. (1991). *Situated learning: Legitimate peripheral participation.* Cambridge, England: Cambridge University Press.

Leung, P. P. (2003). *On becoming a Chinese language teacher: Pre-service teachers' perceptions of Chinese learning and teaching, and their classroom practices in Hong Kong.* Unpublished doctoral dissertation, Griffith University, Australia.

Rogoff, B. (2003). *The cultural nature of human development.* New York, NY: Oxford University Press.

Rong, X. L., & Preissle, J. (1997). The continuing decline in Asian American teachers. *American Educational Research Journal, 34,* 267-293.

Santoro, N. (1999). Relationships of power: An analysis of school practicum discourse. *Journal of Intercultural Studies, 20,* 31-42.

Sheets, R. H., & Chew, L. (2002). Absent from the research, present in our classrooms: Preparing culturally responsive Chinese American teachers. *Journal of Teacher Education, 53,* 127-141.

Shulman, L. S. (1987). Knowledge and teaching: Foundations of the new reform. *Harvard Educational Review, 57,* 1-22.

Stake, R. E. (2000). Case studies. In N. Denzin & Y. S. Lincoln (Eds.), *Handbook of qualitative research* (2nd ed., pp. 435-454). Thousand Oaks, CA: SAGE.

Street, B. (2000). Literacy events and literacy practices: Theory and practice in the new literacy studies. In M. Martin-Jones & K. Jones (Eds.), *Multilingual literacies: Reading and writing different worlds* (pp. 17-29). Philadelphia, PA: John Benjamins.

Vygotsky, L. S. (1978). *Mind in society.* Cambridge, MA: Harvard University Press.

Watson-Gegeo, K. A. (1988). Ethnography in ESL: Defining the essentials. *TESOL Quarterly, 22,* 575-592.

CHAPTER 9

HIDDEN JEWELS

San Francisco Chinese Language Immersion Programs

María E. Torres-Guzmán, Christy Lao, and Yi Han

This paper is a multicase comparative description of Chinese immersion programs (CIPs) in the San Francisco Unified School District. The paper examines elementary school CIPs in the context of Thomas and Collier's (1997) theory about which factors are necessary for successful strong bilingual education programs. All but one of the factors were found to be in place in the elementary school CIPs and thus prompted the researchers to examine the need for balanced linguistic groups in light of the students' learning of the Chinese language and the dynamic nature of the theory itself.

INTRODUCTION

Chinese immersion programs (CIPs) in the San Francisco Unified School District (SFUSD) are the focus of this study. Immersion is a strong form of bilingual education or what is also called an enrichment program (Baker

Asian American Education—Identities, Racial Issues, and Languages, pp. 201–222

& Jones, 1988). Initially, 80 to 90% of the instructional time is in the minoritized[1] language, Chinese, and by the end of the elementary school years the time allocated to Chinese is 50%. This is similar to what the literature refers to as dual language education or two-way immersion. Like Canadian immersion programs (Genesee, 1987), the enrolled students are not necessarily proficient in the minoritized language. Chinese is the second and, in some cases, the third language of many of the students. The CIPs are different from the Canadian programs in that the majority of the student population is not from the mainstream. The majority of the student population is of Asian background. The additive nature of the CIPs (Landry, Allard, & Thebrge, 1991), however, also attracts English-dominant students from diverse backgrounds including Euro-Americans, African Americans, and Latinos. Non-Asians comprise up to one-quarter of the CIP enrollments.

Within the U.S., bilingual education has primarily focused on Spanish and Spanish-speaking students. Yet, educational programs for Asian language-speaking students have been around for decades. The importance of the CIPs and the role of the Chinese community in struggles for bilingualism are like hidden, buried jewels that need to be unearthed.

The first documented two-way immersion program was established in 1962 at Coral Way Elementary School in Dade County, Florida (Feinberg, 1999). The 1965 Saint-Lambert experiment in Montreal, Canada promoted the minoritized language, in this case French. It was transformed into what has come to be known as a maintenance bilingual education program where the goal was to keep the minoritized language in use amongst the students and in the communities from which they came in order to prevent a shift to the total use of the dominant language. The first Canadian-style immersion program in the United States was established in 1971 in Culver City, California (Leslow-Hurley, 2000). It was similar to the Canadian model in that speakers of the dominant language, English, were immersed in a minoritized language, Spanish. However, the minoritized population also participated in the immersion program. The first program to name and define itself as a two-way 90:10 immersion model, which implied that both language minoritized and language majority students were enrolled and receiving instruction in both languages, was implemented in San Diego, California in 1975 (Christian, 1996; Leslow-Hurley, 2000). During this same period, in 1974, the San Francisco Chinese community established Wah Mei Preschool as the first pre-school CIP, yet, very little has been written about the San Francisco CIPs.

We are currently witnessing the growing importance of Chinese within the U.S. and in the world. It is imperative that as Chinese bilingual education programs grow, we look towards the programs that have been in existence in order to expand knowledge of the implementation of strong bilingual education models. We need to acknowledge their significance and learn from their strengths as well as from the obstacles they have encountered. The growing international demand for Mandarin language development and the lack of attention paid to Chinese language programs in public schools (Chang, 2003; Chang, Huang, Mao, Ma, & Montgomery, 2003; Kwong & Miscevic, 2005) are part of the context that frames the purpose of our study.

We will describe in detail the existing San Francisco elementary school CIPs and examine them within the context of Thomas and Collier's (1997) theory of successful factors associated with strong forms of bilingual education. According to Thomas and Collier, the major factors associated with successful two-way dual language education/immersion programs are that: (a) students participate for at least 6 years, (b) that there is a balanced ratio of speakers of each language, (c) that the instruction is carefully separated according to language, (d) that the instruction in the early grades is strong, and (e) that the parent population is supportive and highly involved in school matters.

Thomas and Collier (1997) further propose that the presence of these factors generates academically strong educational programs and bilingualism (Lindholm-Leary, 2001; Torres-Guzman, 2002, Torres-Guzman, Kleyn, Morales-Rodriguez, & Han, 2005). When the focus is on creating academically rigorous environments in which multiple languages are used, August and Hakuta (1997) and Brisk (1998) propose other important factors, such as the quality of teachers and school leadership. While we agree that there may be other factors associated with bilingual education program success, our purpose is primarily to describe the CIPs and use the Thomas and Collier lens heuristically and as an occasion for critical reflection on the framework itself and/or on its implementation within the context of CIPs.

HISTORY OF CHINESE IMMERSION PROGRAMS IN THE SFUSD

The Chinese population (Cantonese and Mandarin-speaking) today constitutes more than 12% of the population of San Francisco, and the city's long history of Chinese community struggles in education are exemplified by Lau vs. Nichols, an important landmark case in the field of bilingual education (Wang, 1980).

The history of the CIPs in San Francisco and their importance are tied to the history of the Chinese in the U.S. During the California gold rush of the 1800s, many Chinese came to the U.S. to pursue the American Dream, full of hopes of getting rich and returning home with great wealth. Instead, the majority eventually entered low-paying jobs as laborers. Initially, most of the migrants were men. The 1882 Chinese Exclusion Act suspended the immigration of Chinese laborers, imposed a certification and registration system, and forbade the nationalization of Chinese. This act was abolished in 1943, but it was not until the 1965 Immigration Act and the elimination of national origin quotas that the number of Chinese immigrants began to increase significantly. Since then, more than 3.4 million have immigrated. The early Chinese immigrants to San Francisco were primarily Cantonese-speakers while more recent immigrants have been primarily Mandarin-speakers.

Prior to the 1960s, education was an isolated, segregated experience for many Chinese. In San Francisco, the majority of the Chinese children went to English-only schools, and many second and third generation children no longer lived in Chinese enclaves but were dispersed throughout the city. Feelings of physical, linguistic, and cultural loss emerged when these generations found it difficult to communicate in Chinese and connect to their ancestral past.

In the early 1970s, a group of Chinese professionals realized that their hopes of recuperating their Cantonese heritage language needed more than after-school and Saturday school classes. They noticed that the new primarily Mandarin-speaking Chinese immigrants were receiving language services in the form of English as a second language, transitional bilingual programs, and other language-based alternative schooling, whereas the children of the second and third generation went to private after-schools and Saturday schools to maintain Cantonese as a heritage language. The American-born Chinese children needed to attend schools that had a strong model of bilingual education. This realization lead in 1974 to the establishment of the Wah Mei Cantonese preschool program, a precursor to the public school CIPs.

A community group of Chinese parents and professionals sought to learn more about bilingual education by studying the Canadian model. It was a model that was well-documented as being successful in teaching a second language from early childhood through secondary school. It was also a model that did not focus on teaching the dominant language but instead immersing students in a minoritized language. With this information, the community group moved to negotiate with the San Francisco school district administration.

The school district approved an experimental Cantonese program at West Portal Elementary School. At the time, West Portal was not very popular and had relatively few students. It was located in an affluent area that had experienced a decline in birth rates and therefore in school enrollment. When Chinese community leaders began to explore the school as a site for a CIP, the school building was three-fourths empty and housed a neighborhood day care center. Many of the Chinese children had to be bussed to the school.

The CIP started in 1984 as a small program within the school. Ling-chi Wang, a professor at the University of California, Berkeley, an early advocate of minoritized linguistic group rights, and a key person in the Lau vs. Nichols case, was a central figure in the initiation and establishment of the CIP. Robert Alioto, the school district superintendent, set the following conditions for the experiment: (1) that there be a sufficient number of parents interested in enrolling their children to form a class, and (2) that the class be racially integrated. Mei Lam, special assistant to Alioto, was given the responsibility of overseeing the CIP's implementation. Gordon Lew from San Francisco City College and the publisher of the *East-West Chinese American Weekly* was recruited as a volunteer curriculum consultant.[2] The community group worked to include day care as part of the program to attract working class Chinese who saw support of the heritage language as necessary for the academic development of their children in English. Ms. Forte, the principal of West Portal who had a background in a Spanish-based bilingual education program in another district, facilitated the implementation of the CIP. Her vision of native languages as mediums of instruction for English language learners anchored the CIP intellectually. The CIP started as a kindergarten and first grade program and later expanded through the elementary grades.

The program soon attracted the attention of Chinese and non-Chinese parents alike as its academic outcomes were very good. Its growth also accentuated some tensions among the staff and between the staff and the administration. A group of teachers felt the need for more independence in establishing the vision of the program. They rallied around a request for a Chinese immersion school and the result was Alice Fong Yu Elementary School, a school in which all students participated in a Chinese/English immersion education.

With the opening of Alice Fong Yu, the West Portal teaching staff decreased significantly as many went to work at the new school, but West Portal was able to recruit new quality teachers, primarily from Golden Gate Elementary School. The distinction that emerged between the two schools was in the kinds of students who enrolled. We will examine this issue later.

The school district decided to expand the two-way immersion programs at the middle school level with initial support from Elementary and Secondary Education Act Title VII grants. The first program began at Marina Middle School followed by one at Hoover Middle School, which is near West Portal. In 1999, Alice Fong Yu added a middle school and became the Alice Fong Yu Alternative School.

Around the year 2000, a group of community activist parents and professionals began discussing the idea of a CIP at the high school level as children in the existing CIPs were about to graduate and needed a place to continue their Chinese language development. The first attempt to establish a CIP at the high school level failed. A second attempt was successful. Under the leadership of its principal, Margaret Chew, Galileo High School opened a CIP with two teachers and 13 students in 2003, the same year we began our study.

The community dream of teaching Chinese as a second language from elementary through high school has slowly become a reality in the SFUSD. In 2006 the San Francisco board of education passed a resolution to offer bilingual education for all students by 2023 and on March 23, 2010, the school district approved a seal of biliteracy to be stamped on the certificates of graduates who achieved such proficiency. The evolution of the CIPs[3] reflected the dynamics of educational institutions as they encountered the challenges presented by the Chinese community.

METHODOLOGY

This research is a multicase comparative descriptive study of the CIPs in the SFUSD from the perspective of the teachers, administrators, and community members involved. Over a 3 year period (2003-2006), we visited, observed, and interviewed administrators, teachers, and parents in five schools—Alice Fong Yu Alternative School, West Portal Elementary School, Hoover Middle School, Marina Middle School, and Galileo High School. We excluded the Wah Mei Preschool as it did not receive its financing from the school district.

During the first year, we interviewed school administrators, community members, parents, and students, conducted a teacher survey in all the

Table 9.1. Student Enrollments at Schools With Chinese Immersion Programs, 2003-2004 Academic Year*

School	Number o Students	Number of English Language Learners	Number of CIP Students
West Portal Elementary	538	168	178
Alice Fong Yu Alternative	547	50	547
Hoover Middle	1,400	160	81
Marina Middle	961	285	65
Galileo High	2,400	484	13+

*Enrollments have remained relatively stable since 2003-2004.

schools, and visited classrooms. The focus was on the history of each of the programs and to lay the groundwork for future research. The teacher survey identified the students' dominant language, grade level, ethnicity, length of time in the United States, and prior schooling. It also requested information about teachers' perspectives of their program and the professional development they received. We collected 43 teacher surveys. We visited 20 classrooms (4 in West Portal, 10 in Alice Fong Yu, 5 in Marina, and 1 in Hoover) and informally spoke with over 29 classroom teachers, focusing on curriculum or interactions that we observed. Program-based issues were identified in data generated by teacher group meetings at each school. We interviewed seven administrators (including the coordinators and principals) and five key community members (one historian, one university professor, three central school district personnel) with respect to the history of each program, its school context, and issues that they felt were strengths and obstacles. Finally, five parents and two high school students were interviewed during the school visits about their satisfaction with the programs.

During the second year, we focused more closely on instruction. We videotaped four hours of classroom instruction. We conducted group interviews of teachers dealing with the strengths they perceived, their salient instructional struggles, the support and leadership of the school, and their professional development. Three teachers were interviewed after classroom visits to explore the issues observed and to talk about particular curriculum and instructional language and culture-based issues. The teachers for the post-visit interviews were carefully selected based on their senior status within the programs, the quality of the teaching observed, and their openness and willingness to dialogue. The purpose of the post-visit interviews was to triangulate the data and to clarify some issues that remained ambiguous. We gathered documents including one teacher-generated CD on the program, school portal information on the English language learner population, and the schools' academic achievement data. We also interviewed four administrators, four parents, and one community member.

In the third year, we revisited the schools and talked with the teachers as well as community members. The third year was mostly focused on providing the schools with our narratives for review and asking questions about issues that remained unresolved or unclear in our minds.

Our analytical method was a qualitative global analysis (Flick, 2002) of each case and across cases aimed at identifying themes emerging in the CIPs with regard to characteristics identified by Thomas and Collier (1997) as keys to the success of two-way dual language education programs. We decided in this paper to highlight West Portal and Alice Fong

Yu and to exclude the other schools because of the lack of disaggregated test data and distinctions about the nature of the CIPs.

Our research group was composed of one Latina and two Chinese; of the latter, one is based in New York and the other in San Francisco. The San Francisco-based researcher privileged the group in relation to the data collection; the mix of researchers provided a range of insider and outsider vantage points that served to pose questions and dialogue about our analysis and interpretations.

FINDINGS

The findings are first organized at the case level. Profiles of each school will be presented. A comparative analysis will then be done in the discussion section and within the context of the theory framing the study.

West Portal Elementary School

Very far southwest of Grant Street in Chinatown on the M streetcar, one arrives at a quaint shopping area in a neighborhood with a suburban atmosphere. West Portal Elementary School (WPE) is physically composed of a main building and various trailers parked on the backside.

WPE had 538 students enrolled in 2004-5, mostly Asians (69%) and Whites (11%), with some Latinos (4.8%), African Americans (3%) and Filipinos (3.2). A third were from socioeconomically disadvantaged families. The proportion of English language learner students was small (30%). The majority of the students in the CIP were English-dominant American-born Chinese students who were learning Chinese as a second language. Admissions to the eight classes that made up the CIP was limited and guided primarily by the school district's diversity index.[4] At WPE, Chinese-speaking recent immigrant children were admitted.

In the beginning in the lower grades, English was taught only one period per day but was later extended to include two weekly 20 minute sessions for story time in English at the kindergarten and first grade levels. The English language arts program for kindergarten and first grade was offered for 1 hour and 20 minutes daily. The school's approach to language allocation (see Table 9.2) was guided by the belief that English should not be neglected and that Chinese, as the minoritized language, needed protection since the linguistic environment external to the school did not favor the learning and maintenance of the Chinese language and culture. During the early grades in particular, students were provided guidance in linguistic choice. While children were free to use the language with which they were most comfortable, particularly in their initial years of enrollment, when one teacher heard students reverting to English too often during Chinese time, she told us that she reminded them gently that "there are too many English words in the air." This type of reminder, in her view, helped create linguistic consciousness. Thus, teachers could direct the children to return to the language of instruction. Special efforts to develop libraries of supplementary literature in Chinese also served as symbolic visual reminders of the need to protect and privilege the Chinese language.

WPE had a highly qualified group of teachers who were credentialed and experienced. Most had been with the program for more than a decade. One third of the teachers in the school were of Asian background and strong Chinese speakers. They brought their linguistic strengths into the social and linguistic organization of classroom environments, outside educational activities, ongoing materials development, and their teaching. Although most had graduated as English as a second language teachers and felt they did not have the proper education and training, they were nonetheless willing to take on the challenges that the two-way immersion program presented. Many of them were pioneers and self-taught.

The teachers at WPE collaborated with those at other schools. The teachers mentioned their collaborations with a Cupertino immersion program and their assistance to a North Carolina school district setting up a new immersion program. They mentioned these collaborations as sources of reflection and professional development. In addition, four teachers had taken up a credentialing program that included travel to South and

Table 9.2. Percent Allocation of Chinese/English Instructional Time at West Portal Elementary School and Alice Fong Yu Alternative School

Grade Level	West Portal	Alice Fong Yu
Kindergarten	80/20	85/15
First	80/20	80/20
Second	70/30	80/20
Third	70/30	80/20
Fourth	50/50	50/50
Fifth	50/50	50/50
Sixth		4 periods/3 periods
Seventh		2 periods/5 periods
Eighth		2 periods/5 periods

Central America; these experiences inspired their work in culturally-relevant curriculum.

While working with the school district curriculum and state standards, the teachers talked about looking for areas to "Chinesize." In particular, they searched for spaces to help the children in oral language as they perceived this to be the biggest challenge. The curriculum was constantly evolving with their new understandings and with continual changes in the student population. The teachers emphasized the scaffolding of the language in both literacy and content areas.

WPE ranked ninth statewide on the Academic Performance Index, which is a composite of standardized scores. There is also some evidence that the school did well with respect to the performance of its English language learners. Table 9.3 shows the performance of the whole school and the English language learners on the 2006 California Standardized Test.

The students' parents served as coteachers, sources of community knowledge, and fundraisers. In an interview, one parent spoke about the privilege of being a part of the school:

> My dream was to get my children to at least speak it, so the selection of the pre-school was a no-brainer. Then I got the children into West Portal. It is beyond what I dreamt could happen. My dad comes here every winter and volunteers. We both volunteer but I don't know how to read or write. He does. The teachers here are encouraging and nurturing and they focus on the children's needs. It's like a family.

Non-Chinese-speaking families supported the program for different reasons. One of the active Latina parents said she wanted her "child to know the Chinese culture and felt that learning a third language was a privilege" she did not want her children to miss.

During the 2005-2006 academic year, the parents raised $100,000. A parent from a Chinese/Japanese household told us the following:

> We are very driven to do a melting pot, but to know the cultures as well. The teachers know each child's abilities and they work with each child; they

Table 9.3. Percentage of West Portal Elementary School Students at or Above Grade Level on the California Standardized Test, 2006

	English Language Arts	Math
All WPE Students	73	82
WPE English Language Learners	64	82
Students Statewide	42	40

focus on improving each child's abilities. It is a very cohesive group. We do fund raisers for things like reconstruction of the auditorium where the children and teachers perform. We do fundraising for teacher development and the like.

The teachers made connections with the parents and the community to motivate children to learn the language and to live the culture through participation in community events. Their annual participation in the Chinese parade and other such community activities and the school's oral language competitions, theatrical activities and other extracurricular events offered students extended social spaces for using Chinese.

Alice Fong Yu Alternative School

Ms. Szeto, the founding principal of Alice Fong Yu (AFY), was part of the original experiment at West Portal Elementary School. The idea of having a Cantonese immersion school rather than a program, however, was a community dream toward which she worked. When asked to boast about AFY, she centered her comments on those that surrounded her. She described a very coordinated and active program, bragged about the well-trained staff and great leadership amongst the teachers, and was emphatic that without parent and community support the school would not exist.

AFY enrolled 547 students in 2006-07. A majority of the students, 67.5%, were of Asian background with the remainder being White (13.7%), Latino (6.0%), African American (3.5%), and other backgrounds. The daily attendance rate was high at 97.4%. A minority of students (24%) were eligible for free or reduced lunch; AFY was primarily a middle class school. The English language learner population was 9.1%, and about one third (38.3%) of the students came from Chinese-speaking homes. A distinct characteristic of this school was that all the students knew some English when they started; this was a requirement for admission. The immersion program mirrored the Canadian immersion design with three exceptions. First, there were Cantonese-dominant speakers; second, all of the latter had a minimal proficiency in English, which in very few cases was the second language; and language arts and literacy instruction began in English in kindergarten. Only 7 of 370 students on which we gathered information through surveys were very dominant in Chinese. The majority (71%) were English- dominant, and one fourth were proficient in both languages. When we asked teachers which language the students spoke the most, they indicated that 48% of the students spoke in both languages, 35% spoke mostly in English, and 17% spoke mostly in Chinese. Most of the students had been in the school since kindergarten.

The language allocation policy at AFY can be seen in Table 9.2. The school curriculum (math, science, social studies, etc.) was taught primarily in Chinese from kindergarten through third grade, and English instructional time increased during fourth and fifth grades. By the fifth grade, children could communicate effectively in Chinese and English and had fulfilled all the requirements for promotion to middle school. In middle school, a 50:50 language allocation (by time and teacher), begun in the fourth grade, continued, but a course in Mandarin was introduced.

When we visited AFY, 20 teachers were permanently certified and 11 had emergency credentials; 72% were Chinese-speaking and 88% were female. Most of the teachers were originally from West Portal Elementary. According to the principal, all personnel, whether monolingual or bilingual, had been hired because they demonstrated a willingness and ability to support the Chinese language development of children.

Great care was taken to plan and coordinate across and within grade levels. Teachers were continuously communicating around curriculum and instructional issues. Every 2 weeks, the Chinese component teachers met to plan and work on issues related to the teaching of, and the teaching in, Chinese. The teachers met to talk about, among other things, strategies for teaching character writing and to assess student work, the kind of homework the children were being assigned, the teachers' understanding and implementation of the school district's standards on oral language, and afterschool offerings. There were also kindergarten-third grade, fourth-fifth grade, and middle school team meetings every week.

The coordination of the curriculum showed up when we observed kindergarten classes. In the three kindergarten classrooms, students were involved in similar group activities. One group was writing Chinese characters, another was completing a drawing, a third was reading independently, another group was listening to the teacher assistant read a book, and the last group was with the teacher. The teacher was discussing future careers. The children had brought in their baby pictures. They talked about growing up and being big boys and girls, and the teacher began to help them project into the future by asking them what they thought they might want to be when they grew up. There was a connection between the teacher's work with this group of students and the group that worked on Chinese characters. For example, there were characters next to pictures illustrating careers such as nursing. The classrooms were not physically identical, but they were organized similarly for different types of activity. The first through third grades similarly reflected joint planning.

The cognitive level of the curriculum significantly increased in fourth grade; this was also the grade where the 50:50 language allocation policy came into effect. There was a difference between the materials available to the English teacher in literacy and those available to the Chinese component teacher. As the teachers commented, there were instructional issues associated with language and content; at this stage, instructional questions were more complex because the vocabulary and conceptual loads in the subject matter required more work for teachers. The problem was that most of the students were learners of Chinese as a second language and their literacy levels were not at grade level from the perspective of the reading levels assumed in the content area materials. The teachers spent greater time and effort in the teaching and learning of Chinese characters. When we observed one classroom, the teacher used a projector to demonstrate how to write the characters and the students practiced the characters through composition writing. We observed the students and the teacher do Venn diagrams to establish what they would attempt to say in their writing, and the teacher walked around the classroom assisting individual students. Every now and then, she would return to the projector to teach a character.

At the middle school level, many different kinds of issues emerged. Science, for example, posed significant usefulness questions, as scientific terminology was exclusively academic. There was little, if any, social use for scientific language outside the classroom. Furthermore, the available material was at a reading level far more difficult than the developed linguistic capabilities of the students. As one of the teachers put it, "getting students to apply what they know and getting students interested in reading in Chinese are issues." The school had many after-school activities that stressed Chinese culture and, in the eighth grade, all the students participated in a U.S.-China exchange program where they had the opportunity to visit pen pals, go to school with them, and stay with a host family in Beijing, China. Despite all of these efforts, one of the teachers told us, "English is a dominant and overpowering force. It eats you up." Even though the elementary school privileges Chinese, the students' writing in Chinese, at the middle school, according to the teachers, was only fair. One of the teachers stated, "In Chinese the focus is almost exclusively on the oral language beyond a certain point." She believed that one of the ways they could deal with the issues around Chinese writing was to introduce Mandarin in the earlier grades. She felt that while it would be a challenge—inguistically, educationally, and politically—but it would make the program more attractive to parents because it would address the reality that Mandarin is the national dialect in China.

The opinion of this teacher touched on a controversy centered on linguistic varieties and the mediums of instruction. The question posed was whether to respond to the needs of the community's spoken language, primarily Cantonese, or to the literacy needs of the students' future outside the community, which might be in Mandarin. Embedded in this was the felt need to unify different Chinese language groups.

While Chinese was a constant issue in relation to learning content areas in the upper grades, the students of AFY performed above their peers within the school district in all areas. Table 9.4 shows the performance of the whole school and the English language learners on the 2006 California Standardized Test. In this school, the scores of the school reflected the benefits of the program as the entire school participated in bilingual learning.

At AFY, parental involvement was strong. The principal referred to parents as the "backbone" of the school. Parents participated through the San Francisco volunteer program. They read to students in the library, went on field trips with classes, and did projects for individual teachers. The parents also volunteered their expertise in printing, carpentry, and technology. They participated in the School Site Council and the Parent Association, which was composed of school board members and parents elected by the parent community. While the parents had many different subcommittees focused on activities such as the Chinese parade, cultural exchange, and so forth, their strength was fundraising. They raised of over $100,000 through direct appeals, sales, a walk-a-thon, a spring gala/ auction, and grant writing. All the money went into school enrichment programs and funded the Chinese teachers work on Chinese language development issues.

DISCUSSION

In this section we will look at the two schools comparatively and within the context of the Thomas and Collier (1997) theory. We will conclude with a discussion of the one factor within this framework that was not present in the CIPs, a balanced ratio of linguistic groups, and a discussion of the dynamic nature of the theory.

Table 9.4.   Percentage of Alice Fong Yu Alternative School Students at or Above Grade Level on the California Standardized Test, 2006

	English Language Arts	Math
All AFY Students	84	92
AFY English Language Learners	66	85
Students Statewide	42	40

The first two factors associated with program success within the Thomas and Collier framework are related to students and programming issues: length of enrollment of students in the program for at least 6 years and a balanced ratio of speakers of each language. Each school was set up to have students enrolled for 6 years, assuming that they began with kindergarten. In both schools, students were very unlikely to be admitted after the kindergarten year; less than 5% of the students enrolled after kindergarten.

Although both schools used the school district's diversity index, they had different admissions strategies. West Portal Elementary permitted students who were non-English-speaking newcomers to enter after kindergarten, whereas Alice Fong Yu did not. At Alice Fong Yu, all students were required to have some knowledge of English upon admission. The percentage of non-English-dominant students was 30% at WPE and 10% in AFY. The reason for the low numbers of Chinese-dominant students stemmed from the programs' focus on American-born Chinese. Thus in terms of the second Thomas and Collier factor, there wasn't a balanced ratio of speakers of each language.

The third factor in Thomas and Collier's framework is that instruction be carefully separated by language. As was revealed in each of the school profiles, there was careful planning for the separation of languages and the minoritized language was protected. For example, at Alice Fung Yu, kindergarten and first grade students did not experience their Chinese language teachers ever speaking in English. For English, the teachers switched classrooms.

The language allocations for the two schools differed slightly but not significantly. In both schools, the language allocations strongly favored Chinese. Despite the privileging of Chinese, it is important to point out that the emphasis on Chinese as a medium of instruction did not seem to harm students' overall academic development as some opponents of bilingual education have argued. At both schools, English and math test scores were significantly better than scores at the district and state levels.

The fourth factor in Thomas and Collier's framework is that instruction in the early years be strong. However, despite the strength of Chinese instruction at the elementary school level, we were unable to locate any consistent school district measures of student language proficiency in Chinese. Thus, we used qualitative data generated by the teacher interviews, both in groups and individually, to identify issues related to the teaching in and of Chinese and to the students' Chinese language development. We found two types of conversations that helped us decipher what might have been going on with respect to Chinese language teaching and learning: (1) the identification of issues about the teaching of and in Chinese across programs, and (2) the perceptions of high school teachers as to how far along the CIP students were in Chinese language learning when they arrived in their classrooms and what the teachers had to do about language programming.

Regarding point #1 above, we identified two sets of themes. Teachers spoke about the confluence of curricular demands, the lack of appropriate material, and the decline of student interest as significantly influencing their programmatic decisions. And they identified broader societal-level issues that affected their teaching decisions as to language varieties, Chinese writing pedagogy, and social spaces for Chinese language use. All of these seemed to impact the quality of Chinese teaching. What seemed to be occurring was that while the language allocation for Chinese and English was equal by the time students reached the fourth grade, the structures supporting the students' learning of Chinese had begun to weaken.

By this time in regard to first set of themes, the curriculum became increasingly loaded conceptually beyond the Chinese language levels of the students and reliant on the use and production of literate texts, which added pressure on the teachers to take the time to introduce Chinese characters more frequently. In addition, the students' motivation and desire to continue learning Chinese began to decline, taking on more prominence in relation the students' attitudes towards learning in the language and/or learning the language itself. The confluence of these factors had implications for material selection as finding appropriate instructional material to support both Chinese language learning and the content of subject areas seemed to be exponentially more difficult for the teachers in comparison to the earlier elementary grades.

In addition, teachers felt that broader societal-level issues posed difficulties regarding language varieties, Chinese writing pedagogy, and the need to expand the social uses of Chinese in everyday life. In San Francisco, many members of the Chinese community were Cantonese-speakers, but the number of Mandarin-speakers has been growing. In addition, there was the issue of the importance of Mandarin and its status as a world language. Issues of language status, language variation, social mobility, and literacy converged in this discussion. The questions the teachers asked were: What language varieties ought to be taught? And, to what end? For example, although the main communicative medium in the Chinese community was Cantonese, meaning that discussions of everyday life events occurred in Cantonese, why would the CIPs use Cantonese to teach chemistry if the literature and scientific discussions were likely to be in Mandarin?

Concomitantly, there was the broader issue involving Chinese writing pedagogy. Different schools of thought exist about whether to initially introduce complex or simplified Chinese characters. There are various thought processes associated with this controversy. One of the arguments is constructed around what a typically literate person does. Usually, while most people are comfortable writing with one system over the other, an individual must be simultaneously proficient in both forms in order to read. This suggests that pedagogically-speaking, there may be no need to balance complex and simplified characters in precise ways. The argument is that the introduction of complex characters brings an ease to the learning of the simplified characters, whereas the reverse process is more tedious. On the other hand, for the English-speaking children in the CIPs who were learning Chinese as a second language, the teachers observed that they tended to initially rely heavily on the Romanization of Chinese, and this seemed to curtail their efforts to learn Chinese characters. Thus, the pedagogical question raised was how to differentiate the different student needs within the Chinese classroom, where both language and content have to be taught in ways that accommodate different learner needs.

Another broader societal-level issue raised by the teachers was the limited social space for the use of the minoritized language and even more so for Chinese academic language. Methodologically, the desire for expanded social spaces for students to practice Chinese posed interesting pedagogical questions such as how to bring together traditional Chinese texts with Western ways of learning. The teachers wanted their classrooms to be more student-centered and for students to be more active participants. They realized that neither literal translations of their materials nor the full-fledged adoption of Hong Kong or mainland China curricula would respond to student's needs or U.S. academic standards. Furthermore, they realized that juxtaposing traditional texts with the school district curriculum required alternative ways of teaching and assessing students' Chinese language development.

The second type of conversation that helped us decipher what might have been going on with respect to Chinese language teaching and learning had to do with the perceptions of high school teachers as to how far along CIP students were in their language learning when they arrived in high school and what the teachers had to do about language programming. During our three years of data collection, the number of students enrolled the in the high school CIP was low, and teachers told us that the majority of students were non-Asian. The high school teachers felt that the lack of curriculum alignment, the lack of uniform understanding of methodological foci at different developmental levels, and the controversies about language varieties to be taught and for what purposes had resulted in uneven Chinese language development among the CIP students that enrolled at the high school level. One of the teachers told us that she could immediately identify the schools the students came from by how expressive they were in Chinese and by the strategies they used for language learning. Her preference was to teach students who were brand new to the language rather than those that came from the CIPs with deeply ingrained habits of language learning that she felt were acting as obstacles rather than enhancing their Chinese language development.

Thus, from high school teachers we found a somber assessment of the Chinese language development of CIP students. And from the cross section of teachers in all the CIPs we came to understand that the time of exposure in itself was insufficient to sustain the language development of the students. It was important to attend to other factors impinging on instruction.

The last of the five factors within the Thomas and Collier framework is the strength of parental support. In both schools, parental support in generating funding and participating in community events was very strong. Our own experience was that parents were more than willing to attend events associated with the CIPs and to communicate to others their experiences with these programs. Due to our encounters with many parents, who were professionals, we realized that despite the school district lottery system, the majority, (more so at Alice Fung Yu than at West Portal) were of middle class background.

In summary only four of Thomas and Collier's five factors seemed to characterize the CIPs. The factor that was missing was a balanced ratio of linguistic groups. One of the main goals of the CIPs was to attract American-born Chinese so that they could improve their Cantonese heritage language. To varying degrees, the majority of the children in both schools were American-born Chinese and Chinese was their second language. In neither school was there anywhere near a balanced ratio of language groups or a balanced ratio of Asian/non-Asian students. Yet it was by thinking about this factor that we could see the importance of the language balance as a resource and support for language learning.

Both AFY and WPE were well-known for their overall academic success. They ranked among the top schools in the San Francisco district, and parents expressed a strong desire to have their children enrolled. The schools had long waiting lists. Nonetheless, there were no specific measures of how well the schools were doing from the standpoint of the minoritized language. When we looked at Chinese language development, we could identify some weaknesses—the support structures—that ultimately affected the language learning of the students.

The weakening of support structures also revealed the lack of broader school district and even national education leadership in ensuring standards that might guide Chinese language teaching. Not only was there a lack of conscious alignment of the curriculum across schools, there was also no external trigger, such as standardized tests in Chinese, to motivate the collective development of a Chinese etymologically-based pedagogy of language teaching that might guide teaching in the CIPs. Furthermore, conversations with middle and high school teachers led us to understand the implications of these problems on students' language development and programming. As we were able to observe, by middle school the CIPs went from having a strong bilingual education design to a second language enrichment design (Genesee, 1991) and the teachers found the teaching in Chinese much more difficult.

When we began the study, the high school program was in its first year and had only 13 students. There was a big drop in CIP enrollments beyond the elementary school level. Of course, enrollments at the middle and high school levels were dependent on many factors. Nonetheless, we found that high school students enrolled in CIPs were primarily from non-Chinese backgrounds; most American-born Chinese students did not continue to pursue Chinese language development academically. Chinese language instruction was unable to keep up a strong academic presence beyond the elementary school level. In fact, the middle and high school programs were called CIPs more to indicate of who was being served—students coming from the elementary school CIPs—than because these programs followed a strong bilingual education model. The conclusion one could reach is that the development of Chinese was truncated programmatically and such curtailment directly or indirectly affected the students' Chinese language development. Any future development requires strengthening the systems supporting the teaching and learning of Chinese.

The preceding discussion provides the basis for our argument that CIPS need to push for more balanced linguistic ratios to ensure that students have sufficient Chinese language models that will support their development and will inspire them to continue their Chinese language learning scholastically.

CONCLUSIONS

The CIPs were examined using Thomas and Collier's framework on factors that need to be present for the successful implementation of strong bilingual education programs. All but one of the factors, a balanced ratio of speakers of each language, was present within the elementary school CIPs.

We can tentatively conclude that the CIPs were successful from the standpoint of students' academic performance in English. The data seems to confirm that the introduction of the second language did not harm students' academic development in the dominant language. It also suggests a need for more appropriate, extensive and alternative forms of Chinese language assessments.

We do feel that the balanced language group factor may be significant for the level and quality of Chinese language development, especially beyond the elementary school level. While we think that the privileging of the enrollment of English-speakers is reasonable from the perspective of the desire to attract American-born Chinese, we also feel that having a significant proportion of students with strong Chinese language abilities may be critical for the enterprise of teaching Chinese as a second language as it provides authentic language modeling and becomes a resource for the Chinese language development of non-Chinese-speakers.

Furthermore, we see the need for additional work on the teaching of minoritized languages. It is evident that teacher creativity is necessary for CIP teaching. Faced with the need to create curriculum and materials appropriate for the students, teachers must be creative, and they need time, support, and technical assistance that might collectively facilitate an environment for such creativity. For future work in this area, we recommend that efforts be organized collectively to support teachers individually.

We believe that district-wide conversations need to be held about a variety of programmatic and societal issues in order to strengthen the delivery of the Chinese components of bilingual programs. In particular, we believe that the San Francisco school district should take a leadership role in pushing the development of a Chinese etymologically-based pedagogy that could guide teachers in the San Francisco CIPs and in other Chinese language education programs.

We conclude by stating again that the San Francisco CIPs are hidden jewels programmatically and instructionally, particularly at the elementary school level. The Chinese community has made their dream a reality. Our critiques stem from a desire to contribute toward improving what already exists. The CIPs are unique because, unlike other strong bilingual programs, their focus is on Chinese Americans and on non-Chinese English-speaking students rather than on immigrants. We want to acknowledge the significance of the CIPS and learn from their experiences in order to expand knowledge of the implementation of strong Asian language bilingual education models.

NOTES

1.   We refer to minoritized languages because while languages like Chinese are world languages, in the context of the United States, the Chinese population is not considered mainstream but economically, socially and culturally different. Chinese is a less-valued language in comparison to the dominant language, English, and thus minoritized.

2.   This historical information is based on interviews with community members and school administrators and teachers.

3.   In this chapter, CIP refers to both Chinese immersion programs within schools as well as the Alice Fong Yu Alternative School, which is a Chinese immersion school.

4.   The diversity index is a formula, made up of five race-neutral factors (extreme poverty, socioeconomic status, home language, academic performance rank of sending school, and academic achievement status), that calculates the probability that, in a given grade, randomly chosen students will be different from each other based on the five race-neutral factors.

REFERENCES

August, D., & Hakuta, K. (1997). *Improving schooling for language-minority children: A research agenda.* Washington, DC: National Academy Press.

Baker, C., & Jones, S. P. (1988). *Encyclopedia of bilingualism and bilingual education.* Clevedon, England: Multilingual Matters.

Brisk, M.E. (1998). *Bilingual education: From compensatory to quality schooling.* Mahwah, NJ: Erlbaum.

Chang. J. (2003, July/August). Strategies for effective two-way immersion (twi) programs: A Chinese American perspective. *Asian/Pacific-American Education Concerns, 28,* 28-30.

Chang, J. M. Huang, C., Mao, S. Ma, V. H., & Montgomery, M. S. (2003). Developing a successful Chinese two-way immersion program. *New Wave: Educational Research & Development, 8,* 45-50.

Christian, D. (1996) Two-way immersion education: Students learning through two Languages. *Modern Language Journal, 80,* 66-76.

Feinberg, R. C. (1999). Administration of two-way bilingual elementary schools: Building on Strengths. *Bilingual Research Journal, 23*(1), 34-47.

Flick, U. (2002). *An introduction to qualitative research.* Thousand Oaks, CA: SAGE.

Genesee, F. (1987). *Learning through two languages: Studies of immersion and bilingual education.* New York, NY: HarperCollins.

Kwong, P., & Miscevic, D. (2005). *Chinese America: The untold story of America's oldest new community.* New York, NY: The New Press.

Landry, R., Allard, R., & Thebrge, R. (1991). School and family French ambience and development of Francophone Western Canada. *Canadian Modern Language Review, 47,* 878-915.

Leslow-Hurley, J. (2000). *The foundations of dual language instruction* (3rd ed.). White Plains, NY: Longman.

Lindholm-Leary, K. (2001). *Dual language education.* Clevedon, England: Multilingual Matters.

Thomas, W. P., & Collier, V. (1997). *School effectiveness for language minority students.* Washington, DC: National Clearinghouse for Bilingual Education.

Torres-Guzmán, M. E. (2002). *Dual language programs.* Washington, DC: National Clearinghouse for Bilingual Education.

Torres-Guzmán, M. E., Kleyn, T., Morales-Rodríguez, S., & Han, A. (2005) Self designated dual-language programs: Is there a gap between labeling and implementation? *Bilingual Research Journal, 29* (2), 453-474.

Wang, L. L. (1980). Lau v. Nichols: History of a struggle for equal and quality education. In R. Endo, S. Sue, & N. N. Wagner (Eds.), *Asian Americans: Social and psychological perspectives* (pp. 181-222). Palo Alto, CA: Science and Behavior Books.

ABOUT THE AUTHORS

Liv Thorstensson Dávila is assistant professor of second language education in the Department of Middle, Secondary and K-12 Education at the University of North Carolina, Charlotte. Her research interests include immigrant identities and language learning and the experiences of students with interrupted formal education.

Russell Endo has retired from teaching in sociology and ethnic studies at the University of Colorado, but he continues to be coordinator of research in education and urban sociology. His current work focuses on Asian Americans in higher education and urban ethnic communities. He has authored or coauthored many studies and has coedited numerous books including *The Social Reality of Ethnic America; Asian Americans: Social and Psychological Perspectives; Frontiers of Asian American Studies;* and several Asian American education anthologies.

Yanan Fan is currently an assistant professor at San Francisco State University. She studies literacy learning of immigrant adolescents and second/foreign language teacher education. Her recent publications appear in *Journal of Southeast Asian American Education & Advancement, Journal of Early Childhood Literacy,* and *TESOL Essential Teacher.*

Keonghee Tao Han is an assistant professor at the University of Wyoming. After having relocated to the U.S. as a graduate student, she has since worked as a classroom ESL teacher/coordinator and a university professor for 2 decades. Her research interests include multicultural education ESL education, and racial/cultural issues in education.

Yi Han is professor and chairperson of the Mathematics Department at The City University of New York, Borough of Manhattan Community College. She is the author of many national/international journal articles. Her research interests include bilingual mathematics education, teacher education, history of mathematics education, and differential geometry and its applications.

Claudia Galindo is an assistant professor at University of Maryland, Baltimore County. She received her doctorate in educational policy from Pennsylvania State University. Galindo was a postdoctoral fellow at the Center for Social Organization of Schools, Johns Hopkins University. Her research focuses on educational inequality and minority students' educational experiences. Her work integrates the fields of sociology, educational policy, and immigration.

Christy Lao is associate professor of education at San Francisco State University. Her scholarly specializations are in second language acquisition, Chinese pedagogy, and literacy. She has published widely with a focus on Chinese learners and has worked with Chinese bilingual teachers in San Francisco, New York City, Hong Kong, and China.

Qiuyun Lin is associate professor in the Department of Childhood Education at Plattsburgh State University of New York. Her research interests include equity issues for people of color, technology integration in teacher education and student achievement in early/elementary years.

Suet-ling Pong is professor of education and sociology at Pennsylvania State University. Pong's research centers on educational inequalities related to students' immigrant status, family structure, and parental involvement. Pong has conducted international research in European and East Asian countries. She is currently visiting professor at the Faculty of Education, Chinese University of Hong Kong.

Oiyan Poon is a research associate at the University of Massachusetts at Boston Institute for Asian American Studies. She earned her PhD in education and certificate in Asian American Studies at the University of California at Los Angeles. Her research focuses on Asian American communities, civic engagement, public policy and racial inequalities, social demography and GIS spatial analysis.

Xue Lan Rong is professor of social science education and sociology of education at the University of North Carolina, Chapel Hill. Her research focuses on culture, race/ethnicity and education, and the effects of immigrant generation on young adolescents schooling. An author of five books, three edited journal volumes, and 40-plus journal articles and book chapters, Rong's publications include book *Educating Immigrant Students in the 21st Century* (Sage-Corwin, 2009), and articles published in professional journals, such as *American Sociological Review, American Educational Research Journal*, and *Harvard Educational Review*.

Michelle Samura is interested in U.S. racial politics, racial and ethnic identity formations, race-space connections, and visual methodology. Currently, she is the academic coordinator for the University of California Center for New Racial Studies, research fellow with the Interdisciplinary Humanities Center, and lecturer in the Department of Asian American Studies at the University of California, Santa Barbara.

María E. Torres-Guzmán is professor of bilingual/bicultural education in the Department of International and Transcultural Studies at Teachers College, Columbia University and the author of numerous publications—5 books, 3 edited journal volumes, and 50-plus journal articles. Her latest book is *Freedom at Work* by Paradigm Press.

Yang S. Xiong is a doctoral candidate in the Department of Sociology at the University of California at Los Angeles. His research interests include racial and ethnic relations, English learners in K-12, and Asian American communities. His dissertation research examines the sources and claims-making activities of intraethnic conflicts, specifically linguistic conflicts within Hmong American communities.

Wenfan Yan is professor and chair of the Department of Leadership in Education at the University of Massachusetts, Boston. His research interests have been focused in the area of policy analysis around national and international educational issues in equity, access, effectiveness, and assessment of P-16 education.

Min Zhou, is professor of sociology and Asian American studies at the University of California at Los Angeles and Walter & Shirley Wang Endowed Chair in U.S.-China relations and communications. She has done work on Asian immigration, Asian American education, immigrant transnational organizations, and ethnic entrepreneurship. Currently, she is writing a book on the ethnic system of supplementary education in Chinese and Korean immigrant communities in Los Angeles.

CPSIA information can be obtained
at www.ICGtesting.com
Printed in the USA
FSOW03n0047190517
34330FS